Scottish Local Government

Allan McConnell

Edinburgh University Press

© Allan McConnell, 2004

Edinburgh University Press Ltd
22 George Square, Edinburgh

Typeset in Ireland by Compuscript, and
printed and bound in Great Britain by Antony Rowe Ltd, Chippenham,
Wilts

A CIP record for this book is available from the British Library

ISBN 0 7486 2004 4 (hardback)
ISBN 0 7486 2005 2 (paperback)

The right of Allan McConnell to be identified as author of this work
has been asserted in accordance with the Copyright, Designs and
Patents Act 1988.

Published with the support of the Edinburgh University Scholarly
Publishing Initiatives Fund.

Contents

Expanded Contents List   v

List of Figures and Tables   viii

Abbreviations   xi

Preface and Acknowledgements   xiv

Introduction   1

1. Thinking Politically: The Nature of Local Government
   in Scotland   5

2. Mapping the Networks and Relationships of Scottish
   Local Authorities   27

3. Scottish Local Authority Structures: From Feudal Burghs
   to Single Tier Authorities   43

4. Council Decision-Making Structures: From Traditional
   Administration to Post-Devolution Modernisation   69

5. Councillors, Elections and the Electoral System:
   A Healthy Democratic Foundation?   93

6. Beyond Elections: Non-Electoral Forms of Public
   Participation and Non-Elected Local Governance   121

7. Political Parties in Scottish Local Government   137

8. Reconstructing Accountability: Value for Money and the
   Rise of the Performance Culture in Scottish Councils   155

Contents

9. Financing Scottish Local Government   179
10. The Bigger Picture: Central–Local Relations, Multi-
    Level Governance and Globalisation   211
Conclusion: Has Devolution Made a Difference to Local
    Government in Scotland?   233

Bibliography   239
Index   261

Expanded Contents List

List of Figures and Tables   viii
Abbreviations   xi
Preface and Acknowledgements   xiv

Introduction   1

**1. Thinking Politically: The Nature of Local Government
   in Scotland**   5
   Defining Characteristics of Scottish Local Government   5
   The Legal Basis of Scottish Local Authorities   7
   The Purpose of Local Government in Scotland:
      A Quasi-Constitutional View   15
   The Purpose of Local Government in Scotland:
      A Political Science View   17
   Conclusion   23

**2. Mapping the Networks and Relationships of Scottish
   Local Authorities**   27
   Relations with the Scottish Executive   27
   Relations with Boards/Quangos/Agencies/NDPBs   30
   Relations with Local Communities   32
   Relations with the Scottish Parliament and Party
      Political Interests   33
   Relations with Bodies Representing Local Authority
      Interests   35

    Relations with the Legal System and Associated Bodies   38
    Conclusion   38

3. **Scottish Local Authority Structures: From Feudal Burghs to Single Tier Authorities**   43
    From Feudalism to Capitalism: Early Local Authority Structures in Scotland   44
    1966–75: Wheatley Reforms and the Advent of the Two Tier System   47
    1991–6: The Creation of a Single Tier System   50
    A Flawed Case for Change?   52
    Single Tier Authorities, Conservative Style: A Critique   57
    Scottish Structures: Distinctiveness in the UK?   62
    Conclusion   66

4. **Council Decision-Making Structures: From Traditional Administration to Post-Devolution Modernisation**   69
    1950s–60s: The 'Traditional' Approach to Council Decision-Making   71
    1970s: The Corporate Approach in Scotland   75
    1979–97: The Impact of the Conservatives: Fragmentation and 'Depoliticisation'   79
    Post-1996: Unitary Authorities and the Modernisation of Political Management Arrangements   83
    Conclusion – Continuity rather than Discontinuity   89

5. **Councillors, Elections and the Electoral System: A Healthy Democratic Foundation?**   93
    The Multiple Roles of Councillors: Representative, Politician and Manager   93
    Elections and the Electoral System: Turnout, Voting Behaviour and FPTP v. PR   106
    Conclusion – A Healthy Democratic Foundation?   116

6. **Beyond Elections: Non-Electoral Forms of Public Participation and Non-Elected Local Governance**   121
    Non-Electoral Forms of Public Participation   121
    The Growth of Non-Elected Local Governance   128
    Conclusion – Beyond Elections: Contributing to a Healthy Local Democracy?   133

7. Political Parties in Scottish Local Government   137
Scottish Labour Party   138
Scottish National Party   141
Scottish Conservative and Unionist Party   142
Scottish Liberal Democrats   144
Scottish Green Party and Scottish Socialist Party   146
Independents   147
Conclusion – A Scottish Distinctiveness in Party Trends?   148

8. Reconstructing Accountability: Value for Money and the Rise of the Performance Culture in Scottish Councils   155
Background: The Old Regime of CCT   156
Best Value   161
The Rise of the Performance Culture in Scottish Local Government   166
Conclusion – VFM as the 'New' Accountability   174

9. Financing Scottish Local Government   179
Local Government Finance in Scotland: An Overview   180
Revenue Finance: Sources, Restrictions and Issues   181
Capital Finance: Sources, Restrictions and Issues   197
Scotland's 32 Local Authorities: Free to Spend?   205
Conclusion   207

10. The Bigger Picture: Central–Local Relations, Multi-Level Governance and Globalisation   211
Central–Local Relations   211
Scottish Local Government and Multi-Level Governance   223
Globalisation and Scottish Local Government   227
Conclusion   230

Conclusion: Has Devolution Made a Difference to Local Government in Scotland?   233

Bibliography   239
Index   261

Figures and Tables

Figures

1.1 Main Scottish Parliamentary legislation affecting local government in the first term of the Scottish Parliament, 1999–2003. 9

1.2 Standards Commission for Scotland – range of sanctions available against councillors for breach of the Councillors' Code of Conduct. 13

2.1 The main relationships of local authorities in Scotland. 29

2.2 Main functions of the Convention of Scottish Local Authorities (COSLA). 36

2.3 A sample of the work undertaken by the Legal Division of Dundee City Council. 39

3.1 Advantages of a single tier system as proposed by Scottish Office ministers, June 1991. 51

3.2 Community councils in Scotland – the basics. 52

4.1 The 'traditional' approach to council decision-making processes. 72

4.2 A summary of the main recommendations of the 1973 Paterson Report into the organisation and management of councils in Scotland. 77

4.3 An example of executive decision-making structures – City of Edinburgh Council. 88

5.1 The competing priorities of councillors in Scotland. 97

5.2 System of councillor remuneration in Scotland, 1995 onwards. 103

5.3 Approximate annual salary/remuneration for posts in Scotland, 2003. 105

5.4 A model of local election voting choice in Scotland. 111

6.1 A summary of 'modern' participation methods in local government. 125

6.2 The potential inhibitors and drawbacks of public participation exercises in local government. 127

8.1 CCT legislation applying in Scotland, 1980–97. 158

8.2 Core principles of Best Value in Scotland. 162

8.3 Aspects of Glasgow City Council's Best Value review of museums, heritage and visual arts, 1998–2001. 163

8.4 Examples of Statutory Performance Indicators for Scottish councils, 2001–2. 169

8.5 The auditing of Scottish public bodies (including local authorities). 173

9.1 Sources of revenue funding for Scottish local authorities, 2001–2. 181

9.2 A general guide to non-domestic rates in Scotland. 187

9.3 A general guide to the Council Tax in Scotland. 192

9.4 Factors which affect local authority charges. 196

9.5 Services areas in Scottish local authorities typically subject to charging. 197

9.6 Objectives for EU Structural Funds, 2000–6, the Scottish dimension. 201

9.7 Examples of major local authority PFI projects in Scotland. 203

10.1 Central and local resources in the power-dependence model. 220

10.2 Scottish local authorities and their means of information exchange and influence in the context of multi-level governance. 226

Tables

1.1 Main legislative foundations of local government in Scotland. 8

3.1 Scotland's 32 unitary authorities post-1996. 54

3.2 Touche Ross Report (1992) on the predicted costs and savings of local government reorganisation. 61

5.1   Average turnout at local elections in Scotland,
      1974–2003.   107
5.2   Examples of the mismatch between voting patterns
      and council composition as a result of the 2003
      local elections.   112
5.3   Voting patterns and seats won as a result of the
      2003 local elections in Scotland.   113
7.1   Performance of the main Scottish political parties in
      local government elections, 1974–2003.   139
7.2   Political control of Scotland's 32 local authorities
      based on election results, 1999–2003.   140
7.3   Independent councillors in Scottish local government,
      1974–2003.   147
9.1   Projected ring-fenced funding of local government in
      Scotland, 2001–2 to 2003–4.   185
9.2   Non-domestic rate poundages in Scotland and
      England, 1999–2000 to 2004–5.   188
9.3   Glasgow City Council non-domestic rate income,
      1996–7 to 2001–2.   190
9.4   Council Tax increases in Scotland, 1993–4 to 2003–4. 193
9.5   COSLA 2001 estimate of future capital expenditure
      needs.   200
9.6   Net current expenditure by service, general fund,
      1996–7 to 2001–2.   206
10.1 Local government subordinate legislation considered
      by the Local Government Committee of the Scottish
      Parliament, 1999–2003.   213

Abbreviations

ADES	Association of Directors of Education in Scotland
AEF	Aggregate External Finance
ALACHO	Association of Local Authority Chief Housing Officers
BV	Best Value
CBI	Confederation of British Industry
CCT	Compulsory Competitive Tendering
CCTV	Closed Circuit Television
CEMR	Council of European Municipalities and Regions
CIPFA	Chartered Institute of Public Finance and Accountancy
COSLA	Convention of Scottish Local Authorities
DCMS	Department for Culture, Media and Sport
DERL	Dundee Energy Recycling Ltd
DLO	Direct Labour Organisation
DSO	Direct Service Organisation
ECHR	European Convention of Human Rights
ELAN	European Local Authority Network
ELLD	(Scottish Executive) Enterprise and Lifelong Learning Department
EO	Employers' Organisation
ERDF	European Regional Development Fund
ESF	European Social Fund
ESRC	Economic and Social Research Council
EU	European Union

FCSD	Finance and Central Services Department
FE	Further Education
FPTP	First Past the Post
GAE	Grant Aided Expenditure
GLA	Greater London Authority
GLC	Greater London Council
GLLAM	Group for Large Local Authority Museums
HM(I)	Her Majesty's (Inspectorate)
HRA	Housing Revenue Account
ICT	Information and Communications Technology
IDeA	Improvement and Development Agency
IMF	International Monetary Fund
LAMSAC	Local Authorities' Management Services Advisory Committee
LAP	Leadership Advisory Panel
LEC	Local Enterprise Company
LIT	Local Income Tax
LOA	Local Outcome Agreement
LST	Local Sales Tax
MbO	Management by Objectives
MEP	Member of the European Parliament
MP	Member of Parliament
MSP	Member of the Scottish Parliament
NDPB	Non-Departmental Public Body
NDRI	Non-Domestic Rate Income
NEC	National Executive Committee
NHS	National Health Service
NOC	No Overall Control
NPM	New Public Management
ODPM	Office of the Deputy Prime Minister
OECD	Organisation for Economic Co-operation and Development
PAYE	Pay as You Earn
PESC	Public Expenditure Survey Committee
PFI	Private Finance Initiative
PI	Performance Indicator
PMP	Performance Management and Planning
PPB	Planning, Programming, Budgeting
PPP	Public Private Partnership
PR	Proportional Representation
P&R	Policy and Resources (Committee)

PWLB	Public Works Loan Board
QUANGO	Quasi Autonomous Non-Governmental Organisation
RSG	Revenue Support Grant
SCRA	Scottish Children's Reporter Administration
SEDD	Scottish Executive Development Department
SEED	Scottish Executive Education Department
SEERAD	Scottish Executive Environment and Rural Affairs Department
SEHD	Scottish Executive Health Department
SEPA	Scottish Environment Protection Agency
SLAED	Scottish Local Authority Economic Development Group
SLGIU	Scottish Local Government Information Unit
SNP	Scottish National Party
SOLACE	Society of Local Authority Chief Executives and Senior Managers
SPTA	Strathclyde Passenger Transport Authority
SPTE	Strathclyde Passenger Transport Executive
SQA	Scottish Qualifications Authority
SRA	Special Responsibility Allowance
SSP	Scottish Socialist Party
STUC	Scottish Trades Union Congress
STV	Single Transferable Vote
UBR	Uniform Business Rate
UK	United Kingdom
US(A)	United States (of America)
VFM	Value for Money

Preface and Acknowledgements

I have taught various aspects of Scottish local government for roughly 15 years and have always been well aware of the shortage of books in this area. During this period and more, Professor Arthur Midwinter of the University of Strathclyde has been the main driving force behind keeping academic writings alive in the field of local government in Scotland. Others have ventured and continue to do so, but still the subject area lacks a fairly comprehensive book-length treatment which is based on critical analysis rather than simply 'the facts'. This gap is made all the more significant by the advent of the Scottish Parliament in 1999 and its right under the devolution settlement to legislate for Scotland's 32 local authorities. As a result, the Labour–Liberal coalition in the Scottish Executive is transforming and raising the profile of Scottish local government through electoral reform, modernisation of council decision-making, Best Value, Community Planning, encouraging new methods of citizen participation and reforming the system of local government finance.

This book is an attempt to fill an important gap in the literature. It provides academics, students, practitioners, journalists and others with a broad-ranging yet detailed account, not just of how local government actually works, but also the main political issues and debates surrounding its multifaceted roles in contemporary Scotland. However, it is not a textbook intended to explore virtually every angle of Scottish local government in a completely impartial way. For example, there are areas which it does not deal with:

particularly local government policies in education, housing and social work. Also, the book is not free from my own political judgements. Throughout, however, I have tried to be as balanced as possible in weighing up arguments and evidence. I have used concepts and ideas from political science, public policy and public administration to aid the analysis, but not in an intrusive or overwhelming way. To assist the reader further, the end of each of the main chapters provides key questions to think about, guides to further reading and useful websites.

This book was completed in the first week of January 2004, some seven months after the 2003 elections to the Scottish Parliament and the 32 local authorities. As a consequence, I have been able to incorporate not just the results themselves, but also the beginnings of further reforms such as the introduction of Single Transferable Vote to replace the First Past the Post system and a review of councillors' remuneration. I also completed the book just before taking up a new and life-changing post in the Discipline of Government and International Relations at the University of Sydney. I intend to keep up my interest in Scottish local government from Down Under by the wonders of modern technology!

Finally, I have a number of people I wish to thank. Two anonymous referees of my original book proposal made immensely useful suggestions and the book is much better for their input. I also received encouragement and practical help from (in no particular order) David Denver, Neil McGarvey, Mike Danson, Arthur Midwinter, Roger Mennie, Stephen Fitzpatrick, Bobby Pyper, James Mitchell, David Judge, Peter Lynch, Lucy Davey, Roger Levy, Paul Wallace, Elaine McFarland, Sharon Blair, Jim Smith, Peter Falconer, David Wilson, Chris Game, John Moxen, Maureen Conner and Duncan McTavish. I am also indebted to the staff of Edinburgh University Press: particularly Nicola Carr who has been encouraging, positive and professional from the start. Finally, I would like to thank my wife Iris Kirkpatrick. She has provided invaluable practical guidance and advice throughout. I also thank her for her love, support and patience with me while I have struggled to balance writing and family commitments over the past 18 months. I hope that the prospect of life in Sydney is some compensation!

Allan McConnell
Glasgow, January 2004

For the late May and Jack McConnell

Introduction

Local government in Scotland is big business. The most recent figures provided by the Scottish Executive (2003g: 10) show that its gross expenditure for 2001–2 was roughly £13.9b. This equates to approximately 40 per cent of the Scottish Budget (Scottish Executive 2003d: 149). Scotland's 32 local authorities employ 242,192 full-time equivalent staff: far greater than the NHS which employs 115,500 (Scottish Executive 2003d: 155; Scottish Executive 2003i: table 1). Roughly 45 per cent of all public sector jobs in Scotland are based in local government and roughly 1 in 10 of all jobs in Scotland are in local government (Scottish Executive 2003d: 155). Local authorities themselves are huge enterprises. The budgets of Glasgow City Council and the City of Edinburgh are roughly £1.3b and £1.1b respectively. In 2002, Glasgow City Council had 30,965 full-time equivalent employees, making it the largest employer operating in Scotland (Scottish Executive 2003i: table 5). Comparative figures are Safeway 18,500, Tesco 17,500, Lloyds TSB 7,000, and HBOS 3,100. Other councils are smaller than Glasgow but highly significant in their own ways. Edinburgh City Council employs 15,513 staff, Fife 15,748, Dumfries and Galloway 5,654, and Argyll and Bute 4,225 (Scottish Executive 2003i: table 5). Many local authorities, especially smaller ones, are the largest employers in their areas. Orkney Islands Council, for example, has an annual budget of roughly £81m, employs almost 1,400 people, and is easily the largest organisation in a community of only 20,000 (Scottish Executive 2003i: table 5).

Scotland's 32 councils are vital in delivering several hundred services to local communities. These range from education and social work, through to crematoriums and the provision of licences for taxis. We should not think, however, that local government is concerned simply with the delivery of local services in a fairly uncomplicated way. Three words come to mind when studying local government in Scotland: politics, politics and politics. A quick identification of some issues reveals that major conflicts exist over the proper role, structure, functions, personnel and processes of Scottish councils:

- How much freedom from the Scottish Executive should councils have to raise and spend money, since both are democratically elected to represent the people of Scotland?
- Should councillors be paid full-time salaries, given that they work the equivalent of a full-time post but their remuneration is less than the minimum wage?
- Do local authorities have democratic legitimacy, due to the fact that less than half the electorate don't vote in local elections?
- Given the complexities and bureaucracy surrounding the work of councils, are full-time officials the real power behind the running of councils?
- Does bureaucracy and performance-reporting actually hinder service provision and responsiveness to local communities?

This book explores these issues and more, adopting an approach which combines aspects of public administration, public policy, political science and governance. Chapter 1 examines the broad nature of local government in Scotland. It looks at its key roles from a legal-constitutional perspective, before adopting a political science approach and examining competing pluralist, elitist and marxist models of how local government fits into perceptions of power in Scottish society. Chapter 2 maps out the networks of relationships in which local government is involved, ranging from the Scottish Parliament and the Scottish Executive to quangos and local communities. In doing so it provides the basis for more detailed discussion in subsequent chapters. Chapter 3 concentrates on the development of local government structures, taking us from the early burghs of the Middle Ages through to the current 32 unitary authorities. A particular focus is on the rationale for, and a critique of, the present system as initiated by the Conservative Government in the mid 1990s. Chapter 4 turns its attention to the internal decision-making structures of Scotland's councils. It examines the traditional system of the 1950s and 1960s, the rise of corporate management in the 1970s, the fragmentation and attempted 'depoliticisation' of internal management during the Conservative era, and the post-devolution modernisation of political management structures.

Chapter 5 focuses on the foundations of democracy in Scottish local government: councillors, elections and the electoral system. It outlines and examines competing arguments in relation to matters such as the multiple roles of councillors, the power of party groups, councillor remuneration, electoral turnout and the introduction of proportional representation. Chapter 6 complements the analysis by looking at aspects of democracy 'beyond elections'. In particular it focuses on various forms of non-electoral participation, including contemporary experiments such as citizens' juries, people's panels and innovative consultation methods. It also examines the growth of systems of non-elected local governance (including further education colleges, Scottish Water, police and fire boards) which are wholly or partly removed from local authority control, asking if such systems contribute to a healthy democracy in Scotland. Chapter 7 assesses the roles of political parties in Scottish local government, dealing with the Scottish Labour Party, Scottish National Party, Scottish Conservative and Unionist Party, Scottish Liberal Democrats, Scottish Greens and the Scottish Socialist Party. It also explores the tradition of independent councillors in Scotland.

Chapter 8 examines value for money and the rise of the performance culture in Scottish local authorities. It deals with the shift from Compulsory Competitive Tendering (CCT) to Best Value (BV), as well as various systems of performance measurement and management which are 'policed' by the Accounts Commission and Audit Scotland. Chapter 9 outlines and analyses the financing of local government, with a particular emphasis on the fact that local government finance is an inherently political issue. It covers the basic workings of revenue and capital expenditure systems, as well as controversial issues such Council Tax reform, the financial autonomy of councils, and the role of the Private Finance Initiative (PFI) and Public Private Partnerships (PPPs). Chapter 10 takes a view of the 'bigger picture' and breaks this down into three components. It explores the relationship between the Scottish Executive and local authorities, applying models of central–local relations to the analysis. It also considers issues of multi-level governance, exploring ways in which local governance in Scotland is a product of politics and policies at the local, Scottish, Westminster and EU levels. Finally, it situates Scottish local government within the context and constraints of globalisation. The Conclusion asks and deals with the question – has devolution made a difference to local government in Scotland?

Two points of clarification are needed before proceeding. First, at appropriate points throughout, comparisons are made with local government in England, Wales and Northern Ireland. Sometimes these comparisons are made in the course of outlining and examining the Scottish situation. At other times they are contained in separate sections which examine the distinctiveness or otherwise of Scotland. Second, certain themes recur throughout the book: these include the limits of local democracy, the dominance of the Scottish Executive, the inevitability of central–local tensions, commonalities with local government elsewhere in Britain, the importance of multi-level governance, and the limited autonomy afforded to Scottish local government in an increasingly globalised world.

CHAPTER ONE

Thinking Politically: The Nature of Local Government in Scotland

Any understanding of local government in Scotland needs to recognise the defining characteristics of local government and the roles it performs. In dealing with such issues, one angle of approach is to examine the 'facts' in terms of statutory duties, powers and so on. Another angle involves 'thinking politically'. This means moving beyond a relatively descriptive understanding and adopting a political science perspective which considers the role of local government in upholding the distribution of power within Scottish society. This chapter works progressively through both sets of issues. First, it examines the defining characteristics of local government in Scotland. Second, it outlines and discusses the legal basis of Scottish local authorities, with particular emphasis on their lack of constitutional protection. Third, it identifies the broad functions of Scottish local government, ranging from service provider to implementer of national legislation. Fourth and finally, it attempts to 'think politically' by applying pluralist, elitist and marxist models of power distribution to Scottish local government.

Defining Characteristics of Scottish Local Government

Local government comes in a multitude of forms. It varies from small communes such as those in France with a population of only several hundred, to exceptionally large areas such as the state of Uttar Pradesh in India with over 166m inhabitants. A sensible starting point in our analysis is to identify the defining characteristics of municipal government. Various texts produce a number of different features (Hampton 1991: 3; Byrne 2000: 2–4) although they share many common themes. Midwinter (1995: 13) is particularly useful in identifying the essential characteristics of local government as applied to the UK context:

- It is directly elected by popular franchise.
- It is multi-purpose.
- It has responsibility for service provision within a defined geographical area.
- It may act within the specific powers set by Parliament.
- It has the power to levy local taxes.
- It is corporate, in the sense that each individual council has powers vested in the full council.

Even a brief analysis leads us to conclude that Scotland's 32 local authorities match all these features. There are 1,222 councillors, subject to direct elections on a rolling four-yearly basis with a registered electorate of approximately 3.9m. Councils are responsible for several hundred different types of service as diverse as education, planning, environmental health, libraries, community care, social work and leisure facilities. There is neither uniformity in terms of area covered (ranging from 26 square miles in Dundee to 12,347 square miles in the Highlands) nor population (ranging from under 20,000 in the Orkney Islands to almost 607,000 in Glasgow). Nevertheless, authorities have responsibility for services only within their own geographical boundaries. In terms of their powers, local authorities may only act *intra vires*: within the powers bestowed on them by the Scottish Parliament. They also have the power to levy a local tax: the Council Tax. Finally, each local authority must take corporate decisions and this collective power is reflected in committee structures. There is no legal provision for policies to be made by individual councillors. Indeed, even the few councils which have adopted Executive structures in recent years (see Chapter 4) have been sanctioned to do so by the full council. In a classic sense, therefore, Scotland has 'local' government.

The Legal Basis of Scottish Local Authorities

Fundamentals

In the first instance, the legal basis of local government in Scotland should be viewed within the wider context of local government in the UK system of governance. Laws affecting local government in England are the responsibility of the Westminster Parliament. This may change (in part) if regional assemblies are established. Current plans are for regional assemblies to have strategic responsibilities for matters such as economic development, housing and spatial planning, as well as some decentralised executive functions to promote the delivery of these strategies (Cm 5511 2002). Below this regional level will be a single tier of local government responsible for policy areas such as education and social services. Legislative power will remain at Westminster. For local government in Wales, Westminster remains the primary law-making body. The National Assembly for Wales is able to produce secondary or subordinate legislation in areas such as the implementation of the Council Tax, Best Value and councillors' allowances. It also has complete control of the distribution of Revenue Support Grant (Laffin et al. 2002). Local government in Northern Ireland is different again. Since the suspension of the Northern Ireland Assembly in October 2002, there has been a reversion to 'default' rule from Westminster and a comparatively minor role for local authorities (Carmichael and Knox 1999).

With regard to Scotland, all legislation affecting local government in the pre-1999 period emerged from the Westminster Parliament. The Scottish Office as a territorial department had a role in both shaping and implementing Westminster legislation, but it had no legislative power in its own right (Smith 2001; Mitchell 2003). This lack of Scottish legislative autonomy altered with the Scotland Act 1998 and the arrival of a Scottish Parliament on 1 July 1999. The Scottish Parliament has legislative competence over local government and is able to enact primary and secondary legislation for Scottish local authorities. However, as table 1.1 indicates, most of the core legislation establishing the structures, functions and finances of Scottish local authorities has been inherited from Westminster. This is not to belittle the importance of the Scottish Parliament: far from it. Figure 1.1 details over 20 pieces of

Table 1.1   Main legislative foundations of local government in Scotland.

Act of Parliament/ Scottish Parliament	Purpose
Local Government (Scotland) Act 1973	Abolished the old system of county, district and burgh councils, replacing it with a two tier system of regions and districts. Although the Act has been subject to substantial amendment (particularly with the introduction in 1996 of single tier councils) it remains a vital piece of legislation for conferring powers and duties on Scottish councils.
Local Government Finance Act 1992	Provides for an annual Revenue Support Grant to be paid to councils. It also replaced the Poll Tax (Community Charge) with the Council Tax (a tax on domestic property occupation).
Local Government etc. (Scotland) Act 1994	Replaced the two tier system of councils with 32 unitary authorities, as well as establishing key 'quangos' such as the Scottish Environment Protection Agency and three regional water authorities (replaced in 2002 with a single body, Scottish Water).
Local Government in Scotland Act 2003	Places a statutory duty on councils to secure Best Value, replacing the regime of Compulsory Competitive Tendering which began in 1980. It also requires councils to engage in Community Planning, as well as giving them some freedom to spend on activities which promote the 'well-being' of their area.

legislation enacted by the Scottish Parliament over the period 1999–2003 which have had an impact on local government. The list is wide-ranging and covers areas such as housing, education, community care and local government finance.

Whilst local government is the devolved responsibility of the Scottish Parliament and has not been 'reserved' at Westminster, there are three qualifications to be made. First, section 28 of the Scotland Act 1998 states that 'This section does not affect the power of the Parliament of the United Kingdom to make laws for Scotland'. There is a constitutional logic to this catch-all power remaining at Westminster because it means that the Scottish Parliament's power (over local government and all other areas of competence) is devolved rather than entrenched, as it would be under a federal system. Interestingly, a limitation on section 28 is the 'Sewel convention' (named after Lord Sewel, the former Parliamentary Under-Secretary of State in the Scottish Office), whereby the Westminster Parliament cannot legislate on devolved matters without the Scottish Parliament giving approval to a 'Sewel

Figure 1.1   Main Scottish Parliamentary legislation affecting local government in the first term of the Scottish Parliament, 1999–2003.

Ethical Standards in Public Life etc. (Scotland) Act 2000: Introduces a variety of measures to promote ethical behaviour in local authorities and other public bodies. These include a new code of conduct for councillors, policed by the Standards Commission for Scotland.

Public Finance and Accountability Act 2000: Introduces a series of reforms in the sphere of public sector financial accountability, including the creation of Audit Scotland. The purpose is to assist the Auditor General for Scotland and the Accounts Commission for Scotland in their statutory duty to audit Scottish local authorities and conduct value for money studies as appropriate.

Standards in Scotland's Schools etc. Act 2000: Places new duties on local education authorities in respect of educational standards and improvement.

Abolition of Poindings and Warrant Sales Act 2001: Changes the basis of councils' recovery for unpaid Council Tax debt.

Housing (Scotland) Act 2001: Introduces a variety of reforms and new obligations on councils, in areas such as homelessness, the operation of housing lists, repairs and tenants' right to buy.

Police and Fire Services (Finance) (Scotland) Act 2001: Alters the funding arrangements for police and fire boards.

Transport (Scotland) Act 2001: Reforms various aspects of transport policy and strategy, including empowering local authorities to set up quality partnership schemes for bus services.

Regulation of Care (Scotland) Act 2001: Establishes a new system of care regulation – particularly the Scottish Commission for the Regulation of Care and the Scottish Social Services Council – to regulate social workers and others involved in the delivery of social services.

Education (Disability Strategies And Pupils' Educational Records) (Scotland) Act 2002: Requires local authorities to improve educational access for pupils with disabilities, and gives Scottish ministers various powers over pupils' educational records.

Marriage (Scotland) Act 2002: Allows local authorities to make provision for civil marriages outwith registration offices.

School Education (Amendment) (Scotland) Act 2002: Reforms the right of parents to make placing-requests for their children and abolishes the post of Assistant Head Teacher.

Scottish Local Government (Elections) Act 2002: Introduces a variety of reforms in connection with local government elections, including the right of local authorities to run pilot schemes for innovative electoral procedures.

Scottish Public Services Ombudsman Act 2002: Establishes a new Scottish Public Services Ombudsman to deal with allegations of maladministration against local authorities and other public bodies.

Community Care and Health (Scotland) Act 2002: Introduces new provisions for care of the elderly.

Abolition of Feudal Tenure etc. (Scotland) Act 2002: Abolishes the system of feudal land tenure, affecting local authorities because of their holding of many superiority rights and feudal vassals.

Figure 1.1 *continued overleaf*

Figure 1.1 *continued*

Freedom of Information (Scotland) Act 2002: Establishes a Scottish Information Commissioner and gives the public legal right of access to information from a wide range of public bodies, including local authorities.

Debt Arrangement and Attachment (Scotland) Act 2002: Creates a national statutory debt arrangement scheme, providing local authorities with a new framework for recovering debt and providing an alternative to poindings and warrant sales.

Local Government in Scotland Act 2003: Places statutory duties of Best Value and Community Planning on local authorities and gives them the power (within limits) to incur expenditures which promote the well-being of their area.

Land Reform (Scotland) Act 2003: Introduces numerous land reform measures and places on local authorities a statutory duty to uphold access rights.

Protection of Children (Scotland) Act 2003: Introduces a national list of those considered unsuitable for work with children. Local authorities (as employers of teachers and child care workers) are required to operate their employment policies in this context.

Criminal Justice (Scotland) Act 2003: Introduces a number of reforms in the criminal justice system and places a duty on local authorities to prepare risk-management plans.

Building (Scotland) Act 2003: Reforms the Scottish building control system, altering the context in which local authorities conduct their planning functions and ensure compliance with building regulations.

Title Conditions (Scotland) Act 2003: Supplements the Abolition of Feudal Tenure etc. (Scotland) Act 2002, clarifying and extending a range of landholding rights – including land held by local authorities.

Dog Fouling (Scotland) Act 2003: Creates a new offence of owners failing to clear and dispose of dog excrement in public places. Local authority officers and police constables also have the power to issue fixed penalty notices.

motion' (see Himsworth and Munro 2000: 37). In April 2001, for example, the Scottish Parliament debated and approved a Sewel motion on the UK Government's Adoption and Children Bill in order to ensure a UK-wide tightening up and uniformity in adoption procedures.

A second restraint on the Scottish Parliament is section 29 of the Scotland Act 1998 which states that the Scottish Parliament is not competent to legislate on any matters that are incompatible with the European Convention of Human Rights (ECHR). The ECHR was subsequently incorporated into UK law on 2 October 2000 via the Human Rights Act 1998. In effect, the ECHR has become a 'reserved' matter. What it means for local government is that the Scottish Parliament cannot introduce legislation which conflicts with ECHR rights such as the right to family life, education and freedom of assembly and association. Legislative initiatives in areas such as social work, childcare and special needs education must be particularly cogniscent of ECHR rights.

Third, since 1964 and the landmark case of *COSTA* v. *ENEL*, a well-established principle of EU law is its supremacy over national law. In other words, when there is a conflict between EU and national law, the latter must give way (Dehousse 1998: 41–6). The Scottish Parliament has a variety of informal means of representing Scotland's interests in EU policy-making, but only the UK has the formal right of membership in the Council of Ministers – the EU's principal legislative body. As enshrined in the Concordat on EU Policy, the Scottish Executive and the Scottish Parliament are required to ensure compliance with EU law in areas under their devolved competence, and must also liaise with Whitehall departments to ensure the implementation of reserved matters (Lynch 2001: 148–63; Scottish Executive EU Office 2002). In practical terms, this means that much of the law affecting local government is EU law. In recent years, the EU has been particularly proactive in environmental matters, placing a series of legal obligations on Scottish local authorities in areas such as bathing water, waste disposal and recycling of waste (see Chapter 10 for further discussion).

Restricted Autonomy and Lack of Constitutional Protection

An important factor in the legal context is the lack of autonomy afforded to local government. Councils have the freedom to make local bye-laws in narrow areas specified by ministers. Generally, these are for non-controversial matters, although in some cases (such as Glasgow City Council's ban on the outdoor drinking of alcohol) they are contentious. More controversial are the debates surrounding the freedom which local authorities should have from central legislative direction. Since the advent of modern local authorities in Scotland (see Chapter 3), the centre regularly refused to give councils a 'power of general competence'. This refers to the freedom to undertake initiatives for the benefit of local areas, without the need to point to a piece of legislation as the authority to act. The Wheatley Report (Cmnd. 4150 1969) recommended such a power, although the fiscal crisis of the mid 1970s and the financial and political squeezing of councils by subsequent Conservative administrations was hardly the climate in which to give councils additional powers (McConnell 1995, 1999). Conservative governments in the latter half of the 1980s and into the 1990s persistently refused to sign the 1985 European Charter of Local Self-Government, giving councils in the UK similar rights to many other municipal authorities in Europe – particularly in Sweden, Norway, Denmark and France. Whilst in Opposition, Labour argued regularly for an enhancement of local autonomy and was sympathetic to calls for such a move. The Report of the Commission on Local Democracy (1995) and the Select Committee of the House of Lords chaired by Lord Hunt (1996) were both important in providing the intellectual impetus for a policy change, and one of the first acts of Labour on coming to office in 1997 was to sign the European Charter of Local Self-Government.

In Scotland, the McIntosh Commission (Scottish Office 1999a) pressed for a power of general competence, and a diluted version of this was conceded in the Local Government in Scotland Act 2003. It contains a 'power to advance well-being', allowing local authorities to undertake an activity and/or incur expenditure which they consider of benefit to their area and some or all of the individuals within it. This might include providing goods and services, issuing loans, forming companies, engaging in joint ventures and seconding staff. There are of course limitations to these powers. The power of well-being should not interfere with statutory obligations, duplicate the work of other bodies, or involve the levying of taxes or charges. Ultimately, the test of this power will be what happens in practice. Had it operated in Scotland under the Conservative Governments 1979–97, it is likely that many councils would have used it as a means of circumventing central restrictions and promoting alternative, Labour-led priorities. In the future, a radical Conservative Government at Westminster (or even a Labour Government shifting further to the right) might baulk at Scottish councils (and others south of the border which have been given a very similar power since 2000) incurring expenditures and engaging in political activities in opposition to what it sees as the priorities of the UK political and economic agendas.

Despite this recent loosening of the legal 'leash' which local authorities are attached to, they must still operate within a statutory framework. Activities unsupported by legislation may be deemed *ultra vires*: acting beyond the legal powers bestowed by the Scottish Parliament. The Local Government in Scotland Act 2003 has built-in safeguards in this respect. It allows Scottish ministers to

---

Figure 1.2   Standards Commission for Scotland – range of sanctions available against councillors for breach of the Councillors' Code of Conduct.

1. Censuring the councillor.

2. Suspending, for a period not exceeding one year, the councillor's entitlement to attend one or more but not all of the following:

    – All meetings of the council.
    – All meetings of one or more committees or sub-committees of the council.
    – All meetings of any other body on which that councillor is a representative or nominee of the council.

3. Suspension, for a period not exceeding one year, of the councillor's entitlement to attend all meetings of the council, and of any committee or sub-committee of the council; and of any other body on which the councillor is a representative or nominee of the council.

4. Disqualifying the councillor, for a period not exceeding five years, from being nominated for election or being elected as a councillor.

Note: A period of suspension under points 2 or 3 above, which would continue until or beyond an ordinary election, comes to an end at the beginning of the day on which that election is held. Disqualification of a councillor has the effect of vacating that councillor's office and extending to the councillor's membership of any committee or sub-committee of the council, any joint committee, joint board or other body on which the councillor is a representative or nominee of the council. Where a councillor is a also a member of a devolved public body (as defined in the Ethical Standards in Public Life etc. [Scotland] Act 2000), other than as a representative or nominee of the council, or is the Water Industry Commissioner, the Commission may also remove or disqualify that person in respect of that membership.

Source: Adapted from Scottish Executive 2002d: annex A.

---

serve a preliminary notice on a local authority if they believe it has exceeded its powers. Ministers are also empowered to issue an enforcement notice, requiring councils to take remedial action. Potentially, the Standards Commission for Scotland also comes into play. It is responsible for the enforcement of the Code of Conduct for Councillors which is a product of the Ethical Standards in Public Life, etc. (Scotland) Act 2000. The code places on each councillor 'a duty to uphold the law and act in accordance with the law and the public trust placed in you'. Figure 1.2 indicates the range of sanctions available to Scottish Executive ministers. However, these sanctions may not be enough if ministers feel that a council is in serious breach of the law and intent on posing a major challenge to the political authority of the centre. A war of attrition between the Scottish Executive and local authorities is by no means an unrealistic scenario, given suitable political circumstances. The nearest Scotland got to such a situation was in the early 1980s when a number of councils, particularly in Stirling, Dundee and Lothian, were engaged in a stand-off with the Scottish Office. The issue was selective intervention by ministers to reduce Rate Support Grant when it felt that a council's planned expenditure was 'excessive and unreasonable' (Midwinter 1984; Midwinter et al. 1984). In the event of a major dispute in the future over a council's use of its power of 'well-being', ministers could resort to the long-held reserve power of removing a local authority service (or part of that service) from local authority control.

Issues regarding central–local relations will be dealt with in more detail in Chapter 10. What we can say for the moment is that a recurrent tension between the two levels of government often leaves local government feeling that it does not have sufficient legal status in order to perform its multiple roles effectively. The Convention of Scottish Local Authorities (COSLA), which represents 31 of the 32 Scottish councils, states in its 2003 manifesto:

> Local government now needs to have a strengthened status within the constitutional settlement which has been created by the establishment of the Scottish Parliament . . . [The] new improved relationship should have a statutory underpinning in order for there to be true parity of esteem . . . [A Covenant] between the Scottish Parliament and local government should be concluded as quickly as possible . . . By statute the Scottish Parliament should be required to issue an annual statement of how it has fulfilled its obligations under the Covenant, and in particular, how it has ensured that local government has been properly consulted and involved on [sic] all relevant aspects of the work of the Parliament . . . A Standing Conference, including representatives of all 32 local authorities along with members of the Scottish Parliament and the Executive should be established by statute. The primary role for the conference would be to monitor the Covenant. (COSLA 2003: 2)

COSLA and the Scottish Executive often use the language of 'partnership' to describe their relationship. Arguably, however, COSLA's usage is more aspirational and the Scottish Executive's more of a public relations exercise to mask its dominant role (see Chapter 10 for further discussion). Legislative initiatives are dominated by the

Scottish Executive while councils have to fight to get their views taken on board. It is little wonder that COSLA wants the constitutional status of local government put on a more secure legal footing.

The Purpose of Local Government in Scotland: A Quasi-Constitutional View

What is the purpose of local government in Scotland? As indicated previously, the answer is much less straightforward than we might think. The most basic approach is to view the purpose of local government in a quasi-constitutional sense: outlining the powers conferred on it and the types of function it performs. In this regard, local government in Scotland has two main types of power. First, it has mandatory powers. In other words, there are certain services and other duties which are obligatory. These include:

- Provision of schooling for all 5- to 16-year-olds.
- Provision of fire cover.
- Promotion of social welfare (for example, social work services).
- Provision of housing for the homeless.
- Making arrangements to secure Best Value.
- Initiating, maintaining and facilitating a Community Planning process.

Although difficult to quantify, a reasonable estimate is that between 70 and 80 per cent of local expenditure is incurred because of directed legal requirements. Second, and following on directly, local government in Scotland has permissive powers. These are powers which local authorities are legally permitted to exercise, but there is no requirement to do so. Examples include:

- Permitting civil marriages to take place outwith local registrars' offices.
- Promoting economic development.
- Promoting arts and tourism.
- Producing local bye-laws in areas specified by ministers.
- Cutting service provision, provided this does not interfere with statutory obligations.

Rose (1990) argues convincingly that governments 'inherit' before they choose, and the same applies to local government in Scotland. It does not have free reign in terms of local services. Rather, it inherits a multitude of legal obligations which it must fulfil, leaving the exercise of permissive powers as a marginal rather that a dominant activity.

We can develop this approach further and explore the broad functions performed by local government in Scotland. The list given below is not exhaustive but covers the main range of activities (Scottish Parliament Information Centre 1999, 2003; Leach and Stewart 1992: 10–19):

1. *Provider of services*: Local authorities provide a wide range of services, such as education, housing, social services, leisure and community services, street lighting, refuse collection and crematoria. Local government is typically the direct provider of such services and is legally responsible for them, although some services such as police and fire are delivered by police forces and fire boards.
2. *Regulator*: Councils issue licences and regulate a wide range of activities. These include pubs, taxis, shops, amusement arcades, street collections, cinemas and street traders.
3. *Representative of local communities*: Councillors are elected by the people and held accountable through the ballot box and regular surgeries. Councils as a whole may also consult local communities by a variety of means, such as citizens' juries, people's panels, community forums and residents' surveys.
4. *Planner*: The Local Government in Scotland Act 2003 gives statutory underpinning to a process of Community Planning whereby local authorities are required (in conjunction with public sector partners) to collectively identify the needs and views of local communities, agree a strategic vision for each area, and improve services through more co-ordinated working.
5. *Promoter and advocate*: Councils can persuade other bodies such as private companies and voluntary groups to undertake projects which may benefit the local community. They may give loans to businesses, or grants to charities and voluntary organisations.
6. *Innovator*: The role of councils to innovate is enhanced by the Local Government in Scotland Act 2003 which gives local authorities the capacity to promote the 'well-being' of their area and individuals within it. Some councils have been particularly innovative in community energy, recycling and general community consultation.
7. *Implementer of national legislation*: Councils must operate within the law and be able to point to a specific piece of

legislation to justify their actions. Even the power to promote 'well-being' is derived from an act of the Scottish Parliament.

That local authorities have multifaceted roles is complicated further by the fact that the importance of each is very much a matter of judgement. Councillors hold different views, depending to a substantial degree on factors such as desire for advancement within the party and willingness to represent their constituents at all costs (see Chapter 5). In a major survey of Scotland's councillors in 1999, 35 per cent felt that dealing with the concerns of individuals was their main role. The priority of 9 per cent was setting strategic policy objectives, whilst implementing the manifesto was the priority of a further 4 per cent (Vestri and Fitzpatrick 2000: 72). The issue is even more complex because the roles often conflict. The roles performed by local authorities are an amalgamation of central direction and local autonomy. The balance between the two is often uneasy (see Chapter 10) so we should not expect the roles of local government to be neatly packaged, clearly demarcated, with an unambiguous synergy running through them.

The Purpose of Local Government in Scotland: A Political Science View

The focus here is not on the specific powers or functions of local government, it is on the wider roles which local government performs in terms of the distribution of power within Scottish society. A useful basis for considering these issues is to be found by applying the traditional frameworks of pluralism, elitism and marxism.

Pluralism

Pluralism is a loose collection of perspectives which share many differences (Judge 1995). Despite such variations: 'The key feature of pluralism is difference or diversity. The complexity of the modern liberal state means that no single group, class or organisation can dominate society' (Smith 1995: 209).

The idea that local government contributes to a 'pluralist' society has a long history. Writing originally in 1861, John Stuart Mill (1972) argued that the inability of central authorities to cope with all public business created a need for local authorities based on the elective principle. Doing so would contribute to social and political education as well as the stability of the state as a whole. Arguably influenced by Mill's views were the Fabians, Guild Socialists and others who extolled the virtues of local self-government (Stoker 1994). In the 1950s and 1960s, studies of community power in the United States by individuals such as Polsby, Wolfinger, Dahl, Bachrach and Baratz brought local politics to the forefront of political science. Subsequently in the UK, a series of reports was keen to portray the role of local government as contributing to the spread of power. For example, in the context of a growing recognition of the highly centralist nature of local government in the UK, the 1969 Wheatley Report into the structure of local government in Scotland was permeated by the desire to see a more genuinely localist system, bringing the reality of government closer to the people (Cmnd. 4150 1969). The Widdecombe Report in 1986 provided another classic defence of local government as a vehicle for pluralism. It argued that 'power should not be concentrated in one organ of the state but should be dispersed. Thereby providing political checks and balances and a restraint on arbitrary government and absolutism' (Cmnd. 9797 1986: 48). In the 1990s, the Commission for Local Democracy and work emerging from the ESRC Local Governance Research Programme 1992–7 echoed many of these views. Gerry Stoker, the Programme Director, argued that:

> Democracy matters as a safety net against tyranny or corruption. Opportunities for political participation also matter because they help reduce inequalities in the distribution of power and encourage responsiveness to individual and collective needs. Local government and democracy is especially attractive because it involves a decentralisation of power and the opportunity to use local knowledge to meet local needs. (Stoker 1994: 5)

In modern Scotland, a strong tradition exists which sees a major purpose of local government as its 'pluralist' contribution to the dispersal of power. The 1999 McIntosh Commission on Local Government and the Scottish Parliament suggested that:

> The principle of subsidiarity, which underlies the legislation which has created the Parliament, is equally applicable to the relationship between the Parliament and local government . . . [I]n view of the common

democratic basis of Parliament and local government, relations between local government and the Parliament ought to be conducted on the basis of mutual respect and parity of esteem. The local government and parliamentary representatives of the electorate must earn that respect and esteem from each other, but most importantly from the electorate itself. (Scottish Office 1999a, para. 20)

Many other bodies and groups adopted a similar stance in their submissions to the 2000–2 inquiry into local government finance by the Local Government Committee of the Scottish Parliament. For example, COSLA argued that:

Too many decisions which have direct consequences for local spending are made at national level and the central government gives too many directions about how things should be done . . . everyone needs to recognise that local government needs to be an equal partner. (COSLA 2001b: part 2, para. 6)

Overall, therefore, one perspective on local government in Scotland (and the closest we come to a constitutional position based on the roles and functions performed) is that the purpose of local government is to contribute to the democratic dispersal of power – rather than such power being concentrated in the Scottish Executive and the Scottish Parliament.

Elitism

Elitist theory has a long and varied history, stretching initially from the classical elitism of Pareto, Mosca and Michels, through to the democratic elitism of Weber and Schumpeter (see Dunleavy and O'Leary 1987; Evans 1995). More contemporary elitist theory comes in a variety of configurations such as:

- Studies of national elite power networks (Wright Mills, Burnham).
- Corporate power elitism (Lindblom, Middlemass).
- Corporatist and neo-corporatist elitism (Schmitter, Lehmbruch).
- Public choice studies of bureaucratic and political elitism (Buchanan, Niskanen, Olson).
- Policy community studies (Richardson, Jordan).

The common denominator in all these perspectives is the view that society is typically governed by an elite group or groupings (varying between politicians, bureaucrats and interest groups), who will tend to act in their own interests, rather than the interests of society as a whole.

Writings on local government elitism in the UK come from across the political spectrum. Some views are rooted in the classic free market and arguably right-wing 'public choice' arguments which see elected representatives as driven by the desire to spend money and effectively 'buy' votes, and bureaucrats whose prime interest is to protect and expand their empires (see Dunleavy 1991; Midwinter 1995). Other views can be categorised as neo-Weberian. For example, Rex and Moore (1967) in their study of housing and race relations in an inner-city area of Birmingham provided a groundbreaking examination of the way in which the rules and actions of local officials effectively ghettoised immigrants. Pahl (1970) developed these ideas into an examination of officials as 'urban gatekeepers' who hold ultimate power because they act as a filter for local demands in accordance with their own values. Other views are centrist and left-leaning, seeing the problem as informal relations between local parties, councillors and external interests. The outcome is councils being run by a closed alliance, giving preferential status to certain interests and at times veering into corruption and 'favours' (see Dunleavy 1980). From across the political spectrum, therefore, there is a remarkable convergence of views on the inordinate power of local elites.

Writings on elitism in Scottish local government are virtually non-existent. The Scottish Office and now the Scottish Executive occasionally publish research works which might infer that the 'urban gatekeeper' approach is alive and well. For example, one study found that the single most important reason for members of the public not contacting their council was that nothing would be done (Scottish Office Central Research Unit 1995). A subsequent report found a strong perception that officials often had a poor attitude – including rudeness, complacency and a proneness to passing the buck (Scottish Executive Central Research Unit 1999). More generally, views of local government in Scotland as 'elitist' tend to come from journalists and politicians rather than academics. A view which perhaps exemplifies a common perception is that of George Kerevan, Associate Editor of *The Scotsman*, who argues that:

> Fully a quarter of Labour councillors with a job were employed in local government itself – much higher than for the other parties – and well over 50 per cent in the public sector as a whole. Another

10 per cent of councillors, mostly Labour, work in the voluntary sector, which is heavily dependent on local authority funding. Taking into account full-time councillors, this constitutes an incestuous elite whose governing have [sic] a direct personal interest in how they govern. (Kerevan 2002: 38)

Arguments such as this have been given momentum by numerous allegations of corruption in Scottish local government, receiving ample coverage in *The Scotsman* and *Glasgow Herald/The Herald*. Particularly high profile cases include:

- 1994–5: The ruling group of 15 councillors on Monklands District Council was suspended by the Labour Party after allegations of nepotism and corruption. An independent inquiry did not find any evidence of corruption but Labour's NEC banned councillors from holding political office for two years.
- 1998–9: Bob Gould, Labour Leader of Glasgow City Council, was caught up in 'votes-for-trips' allegations. Investigations widened and the Labour Party suspended six councillors including the Lord Provost.

From an elitist perspective, therefore, the purpose of local government in Scotland tends less towards serving the people of Scotland, and more towards perpetuating the self-interest of political and bureaucratic elites.

Marxism

Marxist and neo-marxist perspectives on local government are enormously varied. A particular area of dispute is whether local government can be used by the working class as an instrument of change, or whether it is simply an arm of the capitalist state and hence cannot be used to transform society from the grassroots upwards. A common denominator in all marxist and neo-marxist writings is the assumption that local government is part of a local state (Castells 1978, 1983; Cockburn 1977; Duncan and Goodwin 1988). From this common base, different points of emphasis emerge. For example, Cockburn (1977: 51) argues that the 'state's primary role is continually to reproduce the conditions within which capitalist accumulation takes place'. The local state is one aspect of this and has a particular focus on capitalist reproduction. In other words, it reproduces the labour force as fit to work and reproduces relations of production through a combination of ideas and repression. Putting this more simply and relating it to Scotland, it can be argued that local government assists the perpetuation of a capitalist system and private property relations in three main ways.

First, it helps maintain 'fitness to work' through the provision of education, housing, social services and so on. Second, a system of democratic four-yearly local elections and systems of accountability such as the Scottish Public Services Ombudsman and the Standards Commission for Scotland contains struggles within the parameters of the state. Thus, when the people of Scotland have grievances about local services, they complain or react (if at all) by using their vote at the next election, contacting their councillor or complaining through official channels, rather than advocating revolution. As Cockburn (1977: 49) argues: 'The process of parliament and local councils serves to institutionalise class contest and . . . project a colourless version of the fundamental struggle that takes place elsewhere'. Third, local government acts in a repressive way, containing the Scottish working class through a combination of formalised policing in the form of the eight police forces, and the 'soft policing' of families via the ranks of approximately 50,000 social work staff employed by Scotland's 32 councils.

A slightly different but not incompatible view comes from Duncan and Goodwin. They argue that:

> State institutions are invaluable in the organization and management of the increasingly large-scale, differentiated and changing societies typical of capitalism. But this very differentiation complicates such management, and one response is to use typically local state institutions to deal with specifically local situations. In other words, without the uneven development of societies there would be no need for local government . . . institutions in the first place. (Duncan and Goodwin 1988: 45)

The corollary of this argument is that local government in Scotland (and indeed the Scottish Parliament) is a product of the British state, with the purpose of managing and containing the different social, economic, legal and political relations which have developed historically in Scotland.

Conclusion

This chapter has sought to make initial sense of local government in Scotland. From the outset, its sheer complexity is evident. Scotland's 32 councils have a combination of mandatory and discretionary powers, covering broad functions ranging from service provision and regulation through to planning and representing local communities. Our analysis takes on an additional dimension when we realise that understanding the role of local government in Scotland is not just about knowing the 'facts'. It is also about thinking politically and trying to comprehend the role that local government plays in upholding the system of power in Scottish society. By the very nature of politics, comprehending these issues involves engaging with very different political perceptions. As indicated, simple pluralist, elitist and marxist models lead us to different conclusions. Applying broad pluralist thinking to local government in Scotland suggests that it plays a vital role in dispersing power within Scottish society, rather than leaving us with a 'top-heavy' system dominated by the Scottish Parliament and the Scottish Executive. An elitist model focuses much more on the failings of local government, seeing it as democratic in theory, but not in practice. It is at heart a self-serving system, which is geared towards perpetuating the interests of political elites and bureaucratic interests (councillors and officers) rather than local communities. More sceptical still is the marxist model, which sees local government as performing functions and containing local relations within defined local structures in order to manage the different social, economic, legal and political relations prevailing in Scotland. In essence, local government in Scotland is part of the British state system, upholding capitalist relations of production.

We will return to these issues and others in Chapter 10 when we engage in wider reflections about local government in Scotland. In the meantime, Chapter 2 will map out the multiple networks in which Scottish local authorities are involved.

Key Questions

1. Do Scottish local authorities have adequate constitutional protection?

2. To what extent do the statutory powers and responsibilities of Scottish local government fully explain what it actually does?
3. Pluralism? Elitism? Marxism? Which of these perspectives, if any, helps us understand the role of local government in Scottish society?

Further Reading

The best starting point for an introduction to the roles and purpose of local government throughout the UK is Wilson and Game (2002) *Local Government in the United Kingdom*. The focus on Scotland is limited but worthwhile and it contains an excellent balance of facts and analysis. Tony Byrne's (2000) *Local Government in Britain*, now in its seventh edition, is unrivalled in providing facts galore and the treatment of Scotland is again limited but well done. Modern texts with a specifically Scottish focus are few and far between. To date, none have been published in the post-devolution era. This said, readers are encouraged to seek out *Local Government in Scotland: Reform or Decline?* by Arthur Midwinter (1995). Its focus is largely on the structural reorganisation of Scottish local authorities in the mid 1990s, but it does cover the key roles of Scottish local government and the distinctiveness of 'Scotland' is evident throughout.

Useful Websites

http://www.scottish.parliament.uk
The Scottish Parliament site. An exceptionally useful aspect of this is the research papers on various aspects of local government in Scotland.

http://www.scotland.gov.uk/library/documents-w10/clg-00.htm
The Report of the Commission on Local Government and the Scottish Parliament (McIntosh Report). This report set the standard for debates about modern Scottish local government.

http://www.scotland.gov.uk
The Scottish Executive with links to publications and news releases.

http://www.cosla.gov.uk
The Convention of Scottish Local Authorities, the body representing 31 of the 32 Scottish local authorities. Particularly useful is the new *COSLA Connections* newsletter for keeping up to date with contemporary developments. In its reports and publications you will regularly find a classic defence of local government in Scotland.

http://www.odpm.gov.uk
The Office of the Deputy Prime Minister which has responsibility for local government in England and to a large extent Wales. This gives a sense of local government beyond Scotland but still within the UK.

CHAPTER TWO

Mapping the Networks and Relationships of Scottish Local Authorities

Local government in Scotland does not exist in a vacuum. It is connected to a variety of organisations, groupings and individuals via a multiplicity of networks. Some connections are formal whilst others are informal, and often there are specific forums where the interests interact. Figure 2.1 gives us some sense of the main connections. The purpose of this chapter is to outline and provide an initial examination of these networks and relationships. In doing so it provides the building blocks for more detailed discussion in later chapters of local authority interactions with the Scottish Executive, Scottish Parliament, local communities, political parties and systems of non-elected local governance.

Relations with the Scottish Executive

Relations between the Scottish Executive and Scotland's 32 local authorities are pivotal to the workings of local government. The Scottish Executive is in effect the 'government' of Scotland, although in the early stages of devolution, the Blair Government baulked at this term, concerned about its separatist implications. As far as Scottish local authorities are concerned, however, the Scottish Executive is 'their' government because of its role in initiating, leading and overseeing the implementation of all new laws affecting local authorities. Unlike England and Wales where principal responsibility for local government is vested in one department (since May 2002 it has been the Office of the Deputy Prime Minister, and previously the Department of Transport, Local Government and the Regions), there is no local government department as such. SEDD takes the lead but local government responsibilities are spread in an arguably haphazard fashion across many departments. The main responsibilities in relation to local government are:

- Scottish Executive Development Department (SEDD): Local government and finance, housing and area regeneration, land use planning, the management of EU structural funds, roads and transport, planning and building control.
- Scottish Executive Enterprise and Lifelong Learning Department (ELLD): Economic and industrial development, tourism.
- Scottish Executive Environment and Rural Affairs Department (SEERAD): Environment, rural issues, economic and industrial development, tourism.
- Scottish Executive Education Department (SEED): Pre-school and school education, children and young people, tourism, culture and sport.
- Scottish Executive Health Department (SEHD): Social work policy, community care and voluntary issues.
- Finance and Central Services Department (FCSD): Local government relations with particular emphasis on financial guidance to councils.

Local authorities and the Scottish Executive need each other. On the one hand, the Scottish Executive needs councils to implement Executive policy. It regularly issues Circulars which vary from the directive to the advisory on how local authorities should interpret and apply legislation. When the Scottish Executive plans to introduce new legislation, it will typically consult with a range of interests. Local authorities and COSLA are voices that it is particularly keen to hear. This does not mean, however, that local authority interests are embodied in Scottish Executive policy. Indeed, a major priority of Scottish Executive ministers is to produce workable policy, and often the role of local authorities amounts to assisting with this function rather than blocking or fundamentally altering the intent of the Scottish Executive. On the other hand, given the legal constraints which local authorities must work within, local authorities need the Scottish Executive to give direction and guidance. Local authorities also need the Scottish

Executive to give them a substantial proportion of their funding through Revenue Support Grant, business rates and ring-fenced grants (see Chapter 9).

Relations between councils and the Scottish Executive are generally as good as they reasonably can be for two sets of bodies

Figure 2.1 The main relationships of local authorities in Scotland.

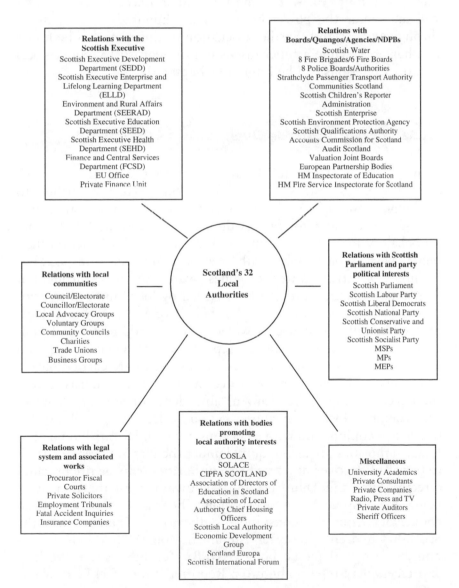

Relations with the Scottish Executive
Scottish Executive Development Department (SEDD)
Scottish Executive Enterprise and Lifelong Learning Department (ELLD)
Environment and Rural Affairs Department (SEERAD)
Scottish Executive Education Department (SEED)
Scottish Executive Health Department (SEHD)
Finance and Central Services Department (FCSD)
EU Office
Private Finance Unit

Relations with Boards/Quangos/Agencies/NDPBs
Scottish Water
8 Fire Brigades/6 Fire Boards
8 Police Boards/Authorities
Strathclyde Passenger Transport Authority
Communities Scotland
Scottish Children's Reporter Administration
Scottish Enterprise
Scottish Environment Protection Agency
Scottish Qualifications Authority
Accounts Commission for Scotland
Audit Scotland
Valuation Joint Boards
European Partnership Bodies
HM Inspectorate of Education
HM Fire Service Inspectorate for Scotland

Relations with local communities
Council/Electorate
Councillor/Electorate
Local Advocacy Groups
Voluntary Groups
Community Councils
Charities
Trade Unions
Business Groups

Scotland's 32 Local Authorities

Relations with Scottish Parliament and party political interests
Scottish Parliament
Scottish Labour Party
Scottish Liberal Democrats
Scottish National Party
Scottish Conservative and Unionist Party
Scottish Socialist Party
MSPs
MPs
MEPs

Relations with legal system and associated works
Procurator Fiscal
Courts
Private Solicitors
Employment Tribunals
Fatal Accident Inquiries
Insurance Companies

Relations with bodies promoting local authority interests
COSLA
SOLACE
CIPFA SCOTLAND
Association of Directors of Education in Scotland
Association of Local Authority Chief Housing Officers
Scottish Local Authority Economic Development Group
Scotland Europa
Scottish International Forum

Miscellaneous
University Academics
Private Consultants
Private Companies
Radio, Press and TV
Private Auditors
Sheriff Officers

with often competing interests. There has never been a complete breakdown in relations and both sides are usually willing to engage in dialogue. Normally, the only real stress period occurs each December when ministers announce councils' budgetary settlements for the forthcoming year. The prospect of Proportional Representation (PR) in 2007 is one issue, however, that has the potential to upturn this relative harmony. Some councillors have talked of a 'four-year war' against a Scottish Executive reform that will undermine the power base of many hundreds of councillors throughout Scotland. Further discussion of this issue can be found in Chapter 5, while a fuller discussion of Scottish Executive–local authority relations can be found in Chapter 10.

Relations with Boards/Quangos/Agencies/NDPBs

Somewhere 'in between' local government and the Scottish Executive *per se* resides a multitude of bodies which contribute to a complex and often obscure system of local governance (see Chapters 3, 6 and 8 for further discussion). These bodies may act on behalf of local government, ask local authorities to act on their behalf, work in partnership with, oversee, regulate, and inspect. For example, Scottish Water provides water services throughout Scotland, a function previously provided by local authorities prior to the 1995–6 reorganisation. On behalf of Scottish Water, local authorities bill and collect a water charge on domestic and non-domestic consumers, contained separately with Council Tax and non-domestic rates bills. Police and fire services are carried out by eight police boards/authorities/forces and eight fire boards. Under the Police (Scotland) Act 1967 as amended, police boards/authorities comprise local councillors and share legal responsibility for policing in conjunction with chief constables and Scottish ministers. Local authorities are also required under the Fire Services Act 1947 to provide fire cover, and two local authorities manage fire brigades directly (Fife, and Dumfries and Galloway), with the remainder being the responsibility of six joint boards (comprising local councillors from the constituent authorities). There is also the Scottish Children's Reporter Administration (SCRA) which is a non-departmental public body (NDPB). Teachers, social workers and others may refer a child to a Reporter if they feel he or she is in need of compulsory-care measures, and the SCRA exists to administer the Reporters system on a national level. Other bodies, such as the Accounts Commission, Audit Scotland, HM Inspectorate of Education and HM Fire Inspectorate for Scotland, exist in effect to 'police' councils on value-for-money matters and performance (see Chapter 8).

In a general sense, we can divide these bodies into two main types. Those such as Scottish Water, Communities Scotland, the Scottish Qualifications Authority, fire brigades/boards and police boards/authorities are involved directly or indirectly in the management and delivery of local services. At least in theory, there is no reason why their responsibilities could not be exercised by local authorities. In practice, however, a modern, complex, developed industrial and post-industrial society such as Scotland needs specialist units to carry out a multitude of functions. Rather than the Scottish Executive increasing the scale and power base of local councils by entrusting them with all these specialist powers, it is more practical and politically expedient to rely on a multitude of extra-local governmental bodies which it can create, disband, reform and direct on an *ad hoc* basis. Furthermore, as Midwinter and McGarvey (2001) point out, devolution was not written on a clean slate. The Scottish Executive inherited the legacy of the Conservative's anti 'big' government philosophy, and a pre-dilection for a disaggregated public sector with an emphasis on separate cost centres, performance targets and so on. Thus, there has been a Scottish drift towards a more fragmented system of local governance (and indeed a European drift as well [John 2001]). The negative impact of this trend is the creation of a system which is complex, lacks transparency and does little for local accountability. Indeed, the fragmented nature of the systems makes it exceptionally difficulty to produce 'joined-up' responses to local issues, but this is the direction in which Scottish Executive policy is heading. As the Scottish Executive stated in its 2002–3 review of Scotland's cities:

> The patchwork of formal and informal arrangements since Local Government re-organisation in 1996 confirms the need for city-region governance arrangements. Nevertheless, the re-introduction of an additional tier of government is not the only response, nor is it the most effective. Effective joint working between local authorities, key stakeholders and the Executive is the basis for improved city-region governance. (Scottish Executive 2003a: 23)

The second type of organisation encapsulates those such as HM Inspectorate of Education and HM Fire Service Inspectorate for Scotland, which are involved in the 'hard' regulation of councils, or those such as the Accounts Commission and Audit Scotland which perform a 'softer' form of performance management (see Midwinter and McGarvey 2001). Local authorities do of course self-regulate and manage their own performance, but there is a broad democratic logic in having a degree of external check on councils.

Relations with Local Communities

Later chapters (Chapter 5 in particular) deal in more detail with most of these relationships. Suffice to say that an important function of councils is to represent local communities. Relationships, however, are neither one-way nor straightforward. The main ways in which councils in Scotland can interact with local communities are as follows:

1. *Councils can be guided by the electorate*: Councillors owe their existence to being elected after conducting a campaign based on matters such as their beliefs, priorities and stance on particular issues. They are not delegates in the sense that they are instructed how to vote by the electorate. Rather, they are 'trustees' in the Burkean tradition who exercise initiative and discretion. As Judge (1999) rightly recognises, however, the importance of constituent representation should not be overstated. It exists alongside competing forms of individualistic, party, and interest representation.
2. *Councils can be lobbied by local communities*: Each local authority area contains a host of individuals, business groups, professional associations, trade unions, community groups, cause groups and voluntary groups who may engage in lobbying. This in turn raises a series of questions concerning unequal access and reasons why some groups are more powerful than others.
3. *Councils deliver services to local communities*: Local people can be classified as consumers or customers. This may involve administrative contacts, exchange of monies and so on. This in turn raises question about 'customer' satisfaction and the pursuit of complaints via officials or councillors. A key feature of service delivery in Scotland is the Best Value regime (see Chapter 8) which sets the agenda for the management, monitoring and improvement of services.

4. *Councils can consult local communities*: Community consultation used to be at the discretion of councils but now it is compulsory. The Local Government in Scotland Act 2003 requires that in the service review programme aspect of Best Value, local authorities consult with stakeholders to identity areas of concern and help shape the future direction of policies. The new Community Planning regime requires similar consultation. Notwithstanding this compulsion, discretionary consultation remains. Particularly as part of a modernisation agenda (but also prompted by Best Value), many councils have introduced citizens' juries, people's forums and other forms of community consultation. Again, however, the real impact of consultation is a matter for debate: possibilities ranging from a genuine willingness to consider community views to a 'cosmetic' consultation in order to confer legitimacy on a particular policy (see Chapter 6).

5. *Councils can fund groups within local communities*: For many years, councils have had legal discretion to fund many activities (particularly in the areas of the arts and disadvantaged minorities) and this discretion has increased via the Local Government in Scotland Act 2003 which allows local authorities to incur expenditures which advance the 'well-being' of their area and/or persons within it.

6. *Councils can raise income from local communities*: Roughly 20 per cent of councils' revenue expenditure in Scotland is raised though charging for services such as sports, leisure, parking, licences and school meals, whilst roughly 12 per cent is raised through domestic property taxation: the Council Tax. On a general level, all forms of revenue raising generate intense debate about who pays and how much they should pay (see Chapter 9).

Relations with the Scottish Parliament and Party Political Interests

The Scottish Parliament is the body which legislates for local government in Scotland, and so local authority relations with the Holyrood body are vital. Scotland's councils now find themselves dealing with an institution which has executive law-making powers, rather than under the pre-1999 Scottish Office regime where ministers had some policy autonomy but were heavily constrained by legislative power residing at Westminster (Midwinter et al. 1991; Mitchell 2003). Later chapters (particularly Chapter 10 and the Conclusion) will explore this relationship in more depth, focusing particularly on the question – does a devolved Scottish Parliament make a difference to local government in Scotland?

For the moment, it is important to note that local authorities come into contact and forge links with MSPs in their area. This is particularly true for constituency MSPs as opposed to 'list' MSPs, which one survey of councillors found to be largely a 'nuisance and an irritant' for councils on account of a tendency to be headline-grabbing (see Bennett et al. 2002). The lobbying or advocacy role of COSLA is the main way most councils seek to influence MSPs and the Scottish Executive in particular, but local authority–MSP links remain at times an important relationship. Local authorities will typically maintain contacts with the MSPs for their area in order to try and exert influence on their committee work, voting behaviour and general views. City councils are particularly active. Indeed, when MSPs were elected to office in May 1999, one of the first documents to cross their desks was a licensing manifesto from Glasgow City Council aimed directly at all MSPs, encouraging them to push for a co-ordinated strategy on liquor licensing and underage drinking. Councils are also active in lobbying and giving evidence to the Committees of the Scottish Parliament – particularly the Local Government Committee. For example, the investigation into Local Government Finance took evidence from local authorities in Angus, Aberdeenshire, Argyll and Bute, Glasgow, and West Lothian.

Individual councillors and party groups also have informal and formal contact with their national parties via some involvement in national policy-making forums (see Chapter 7). Conversely, national parties are keen to ensure councillors conduct their activities in accordance with party rules (see Copus 1999). Scottish Labour Party councillors are bound by the UK Labour Party's Model Standing Orders and regular Advice/Action Notes. The Scottish National Party has similar strong guidelines to ensure discipline. The Liberal Democrats have more flexible Model Standing Orders, emanating from the Association of Liberal Democrat Councillors rather than the Party itself. A reasonable degree of flexibility is also offered by the model rules for Conservative councillors, although the Party's traditional distaste for national interference in local affairs has been watered down somewhat in recent years. Varying degrees of tension run through these national–local relations. In essence, each tries to shape the other. This is not so problematic for the Scottish Liberal Democrats or even the Scottish Conservative and Unionist Party where there is a strong tradition of party decentralisation and a high degree of mutual tolerance. It is more of an issue, at times, in the relatively centralist Scottish Labour Party and indeed the Labour Party generally, particularly in the context of 'New Labour' trying to show the electorate that it is fit to govern. The NEC took action against the Labour Group on Glasgow City Council in 1997 over the 'votes-for-trips' affair, resulting in expulsions, withdrawal of the whip and a protracted legal battle (Copus 1999: 22). More generally, councillors and their relations with their parties are simply one of many forms of representation. Councillors represent the broad electorate, individuals within it, groups and parties. Thus, as Judge (1999) argues, it is unsurprising that representation is neither straightforward nor free from contradictions.

Relations with Bodies Representing Local Authority Interests

As figure 2.1 indicates, Councils have relations with a number of bodies promoting local authority interests on the Scottish, UK and EU stages. The main one is COSLA, which was established in 1975. It is funded by councils themselves and was traditionally the link between Scotland's councils and the legislator for local government (previously the Westminster Parliament and now the Scottish Parliament). Its main functions are contained in figure 2.2. For many years after its inception, the role of COSLA was largely uncomplicated and trouble free as far as local authorities were concerned. Legislative power for local government resided at Westminster, dominated by a government unsympathetic to local authorities (particularly Labour-controlled ones). With the role of the Scottish Office being viewed by many as something of a colonial outpost rather than a government department in tune with the wishes of the Scottish people, the role of COSLA was to speak in defence of local authorities and local democracy.

Figure 2.2   Main functions of the Convention of Scottish Local Authorities (COSLA).

Promote the local government agenda

Engage with the Scottish Executive by:
- Contacts with ministers
- Liaison and joint working with civil servants
- New partnership agreement

Engage with and influence the Parliamentary agenda and initiate policy via:
- The COSLA Parliamentary Unit contacts with committee chairs
- Briefing MSPs, MPs and MEPs
- Evidence to committees
- Development of the Concordat

Engage with partner organisations to develop:
- Common agendas
- Visits to every council
- Receptions at party conferences
- MSP receptions
- Scottish Six

Strategy and development

Develop the political structures through:
- Support for the spokespersons and networks of all councillors
- Review of Advisorate arrangements
- Induction for officer advisers
- Training and development for spokespersons and other members

Provide support, guidance and information to councils through:
- Improving the provision of information
- Producing guidance notes
- Developing the conference and seminar programme
- Developing the website

Improvement function

Establish improvement functions:
- Develop the improvement website(s)
- Set up the improvement consultancy
- Run quality awards
- Run showcase events

Source: COSLA.

Skills development

- Local Government National Training Organisation
- Member development programme
- Scottish Leadership Foundation

Communications strategy

External:
- E-mail to Chief Executives
- Run monthly newsletter
- Develop Who's Who
- Examine possibilities for new logo
- Develop a marketing strategy
- Develop the website

Internal:
- Weekly e-mail to staff
- Show vision/core business in office environment
- Develop media training programme for members

Develop the organisation

Using new technology:
- Review information technology services
- Develop touchdown centre
- Develop electronic COSLA Directory

Organisational development:
- Achieve Investors in People status
- Develop secondment strategy
- Develop and run an organisation 'health check' or review annually
- Achieve Scotland's Health at Work Award

Resources (internal):
- Develop devolved team budgets
- Monitor budgets on a monthly basis
- Undertake a programme of Best Value reviews
- Develop ways of demonstrating value for money across the organisation

Unexpectedly for many in local government, the advent of devolution led to a tension between COSLA's long-held independent stance, and the opportunity to forge 'insider' links within the Scottish Executive. In essence, it shifted towards the latter, leading to animosity on the part of several councils who felt that COSLA was too close to the Scottish Executive, yet failing to get any substantial benefit. A survey of Scottish councillors by Bennett et al. (2002) found 40 per cent agreeing with the statement that COSLA was too close to the Scottish Executive in policy-making terms. Only 28 per cent felt that COSLA was equal and fair in representing the interests of all councils. In 2001, COSLA was hit by the withdrawal from its membership of Glasgow City Council (Labour-controlled), Falkirk Council (no overall control) and Clackmannanshire Council (SNP). Glasgow's withdrawal and the loss of a £220,000 annual membership fee was a particular blow and a major factor in plunging COSLA into financial crisis. This prompted a wide-ranging review, but one which concentrated on finances rather than vision and strategy. There were some initial discussions of alternatives such as smaller territorial associations in the North, East and West. However, a boost to its fortunes arrived just after the May 2003 elections with Clackmannanshire and then Glasgow voting to return to COSLA.

In many respects the membership withdrawals (and then partial returns) have had a galvanising impact on COSLA. Now representing 31 of the 32 Scottish councils (only Falkirk remains outside), it is very keen to improve its communication with members. An important factor in this regard has been the integration of the Scottish Local Government Information Unit (SLGIU) into COSLA. A monthly publication entitled *COSLA Connections* began in June 2003 and already seems to be a very useful source of communication to the membership. The commitment of the Labour-Liberal Scottish Executive to PR for local government has also had something of a unifying impact on councils. COSLA can no longer be accused of being a comfortable 'insider', given its trenchant opposition to PR – as well as its recognition that a small number of councils are actually in favour of electoral reform. A full or near full-strength COSLA seems here to stay. Indeed, given the economies of scale it offers and the value for money offered to most of Scotland's smaller councils, it is difficult to imagine local government life in Scotland without COSLA or some other national equivalent. The creation of smaller associations would in all likelihood be a 'gift' to the Scottish Executive if it sought a divide-and-rule strategy over Scotland's councils.

Relations with the Legal System and Associated Bodies

All legal systems in liberal democracies bring both rights and obligations. For local authorities in Scotland, the first priority is to operate within the law. All local authorities employ solicitors: usually within the Chief Executive's department or a Corporate Services department. Their main roles are to advise departments and deal with the legal affairs of their council, often involving substantial external contacts. Taking Dundee City Council as an example, figure 2.3 outlines some of the internal and external work carried out by its Legal Services. It includes contacts with the district court, procurator fiscal, employment tribunals, fatal accident inquiries, public services ombudsman, insurance companies and private solicitors. The regular output of Scottish legislation affecting local government means that legal services divisions or sections continually expand their remits (and their contacts) into areas such as housing stock transfers, public private partnerships and human rights. One of the most important and more recent areas of activity is the right of local authorities to promote the 'well-being' of their area and/or individuals within it. This is liable to place considerable demands on legal services as councils seek to use their new powers but need clarification of the multiple limitations to this power.

Conclusion

This chapter has mapped the main networks and relationships in which Scottish local authorities are involved. From the outset, its sheer complexity is evident. A veritable 'spider's web' of networks brings it into contact with Scottish Executive departments, quangos and other public bodies, local communities, interest groups, political parties, elected representatives, the legal system, the media, auditors, sheriffs officers and self-representing bodies such as COSLA and SOLACE (Society of Local Authority Chief Executives and Senior Managers). Most of these relationships will be explored in more detail throughout subsequent chapters. In the meantime, we can turn our attention in a detailed way to the historical development of local government in Scotland, from the very earliest burghs of the twelfth century to the

Figure 2.3   A sample of the work undertaken by the Legal Division of Dundee City Council.

Anti-Social Eviction: Advising client department, serving Notice of Proceedings, raising court actions, preparing and conducting hearings.

Bequest: All legal work in connection with various trusts administered by the Council.

Bye-Laws: Advising client departments, preparing bye-laws, carrying out statutory requirements and all matters arising.

Court Action: Advising client departments, raising or defending miscellaneous court actions, carrying out all necessary court procedures, preparing and conducting proofs and hearings.

Contract: Advising on and preparing contracts of all descriptions and all associated legal work.

Compensation: Carrying out conveyancing procedures and all matters arising.

Custody Dispute: Advising client department, carrying out court procedures and appearances and all associated work.

District Court Clerking: Acting as legal assessors to Justices of the Peace.

Stated Case – District Court: Preparing stated case and dealing with all correspondence arising.

Deed of Servitude: Advising on and carrying out conveyancing procedures.

EU: Advising on contract procedures and statutory requirements.

Endowments: Advising on legislation, trust schemes and related matters.

Enforcement Notice: Advising on legislation, preparing Notices, carrying out statutory procedures, including dealing with appeals and reports to the procurator fiscal.

Fatal Accident Inquiry: Advising client departments and appearing for the Council.

Grievance Procedures: Advising on legal issues arising.

Health and Safety: Advising on legislation and matters arising, drafting and reviewing documentation and associated work.

Council House Sales: Carrying out all necessary conveyancing and statutory procedures.

Insurance Claims (3rd Parties): Advising client departments as necessary.

Interdict: Advising Client Departments and raising court actions, preparing and conducting hearings.

Employment Tribunals: Providing advice on appeals and preparing and conducting hearings.

Judicial Review: Advising client departments, instructing Counsel and all matters arising.

Loan Arrears: Carrying out debt recovery procedures including service of statutory notices.

Loan: Carrying out all necessary legal procedures and preparing deeds.

Ombudsman: Advising client departments, preparing composite responses, attending investigations.

Planning Appeal: Advising on, producing written submissions, preparing and conducting public inquiries.

Property Acquisition/Property Disposal: Advising on and carrying out all conveyancing procedures.

Reparation Claim: Advising on and preparing and conducting defence, including instructing Counsel for Court of Session actions.

Source: Adapted from information provided by Legal Services, Dundee City Council.

present system of 32 single tier authorities supplemented by community councils and a range of boards and public bodies.

?	Key Questions	?

1. Scottish local authorities have relationships with many sets of actors. Is there any single relationship that is more important than the others?
2. Can we argue legitimately that local authorities are so constrained by the multiple relationships they are involved in that they have very little freedom of action?
3. To what extent do local authority interactions with other bodies represent both a strength and a weakness?

📖	Further Reading	📖

Mapping the networks and relationships of post-devolution Scottish local authorities relies heavily on official reports and the occasional journal article rather than textbooks. A useful starting point is *How Government Works in Scotland*, produced by Audit Scotland (2002a). Another particularly useful source on the wider interactions with a system of local governance is *Mapping the Quango State*, a report by the House of Commons Select Committee on Public Administration (HC 367 2001). An article by Midwinter and McGarvey (2001) in *Public Administration* provides an excellent overview of the regulation of Scottish local authorities.

💻	Useful Websites	💻

http://www.scottish.parliament.uk
The Scottish Parliament. The research papers on various aspects of local government in Scotland give a very good sense of just how complex local government actually is.

http://www.scotland.gov.uk
The Scottish Executive. Follow the publications links through to

'Local Government' where you will find a staggering number of policy initiatives and details of the many bodies and groupings involved in these.

http://www.cosla.gov.uk
The Convention of Scottish Local Authorities. Particularly useful is the new *COSLA Connections* newsletter for details of what's happening in the world of Scottish local government. You will also find information on how COSLA works and interacts with its members.

http://www.audit-scotland.gov.uk
Audit Scotland, which carries out work on behalf of the Accounts Commission to audit the work of councils (as well as the NHS). Follow the links to 'Publications' where you will find detailed investigations of particular policy areas in Scottish local government.

CHAPTER THREE

Scottish Local Authority Structures: From Feudal Burghs to Single Tier Authorities

We could be forgiven for thinking that the structure of local government is not something worthy of prolonged political debate. The number of tiers (or levels) of local government hardly seems the most enthralling of issues. This is especially the case when we adopt a working definition of a 'tier' as a grouping of local, administrative units with broadly similar responsibilities and functions. In reality, however, appearances can be deceptive. The structure of local government in Scotland brings with it a number of issues regarding local democracy, accountability, cost and quality of local services. This chapter explores these issues, particularly in terms of the development of the present single tier (or unitary) system. First, it outlines the historical development of early structures from feudalism, via industrialisation, to the middle of the twentieth century. Second, it examines the Wheatley reforms of the late 1960s and 1970s which gave birth to the two tier, region-district system in 1975. Third, it explores the emergence of the current single tier system under the Conservatives in the early to mid 1990s, before providing a critique of (1) the Conservatives' underlying assumptions about the failings of the old two tier system and (2) the benefits of single tier authorities. Fourth, it examines the extent to which Scottish structures are distinct from structures in England, Wales and Northern Ireland. Finally, it concludes by suggesting that local government structures need to be seen in the wider context of the purpose they serve for dominant interests within society.

From Feudalism to Capitalism: Early Local Authority Structures in Scotland

There are very few records of life in Scotland before the eleventh century. What evidence there is points to largely self-sufficient peasant communities, subject to various aggressive incursions by the armies of the kings of the Picts, Britons, Gaels and Angles (Duncan 1975; Clancy and Crawford 2001). We can infer, therefore, that local administration was more or less non-existent in the evolving kingdom of Scotland. This changed in the twelfth century as a feudal system began to develop, co-existing with existing patterns of land tenure and social organisation. Under feudal law, the king created estates (fiefs) held by vassals in return for military services and common duties (Mitchison 1982). The feudal settlements established under David I (1124–53) were highly uneven but a basic power structure was being established: a Scottish nation ruled by kings, forging alliances (often less than secure) with the church and the nobility.

What type of local administration emerged in the context of these developing social relations? The answer flows from the ruling interests of the king and to a lesser extent the church. To understand the former we need to recognise that David I granted special trading status to some settlements (known as 'free burghs'), with monopolies on local and foreign trade. The first four burghs were Roxburgh, Berwick, Edinburgh and Stirling (Marwick 1904; Pryde 1965). Not only did the Crown receive benefit in terms of tolls and duties, but granting privileged status to some settlements was also a means of attempting to gain regional military and political control over unstable elements in Scottish society (Duncan 1975; Rodger 1983). Initially, the burghs had little independence and were subject to control by the sheriff, burgh lord's officers or other officials – particularly bailies who collected revenues on behalf of the lords (Marwick 1904; Ewan 1990). As trade developed and population increased, burgh administration became more complex and developed a greater local autonomy as new positions came into being. The alderman, mayor or provost was typically the head of the community (Marwick 1904). He had dual loyalty to the king and to the burgesses (freemen of the burgh) who elected him (Ewan 1990). Sergeands, who were chosen by the burgesses, had similar dual allegiances and were responsible for the settling of debts and the examining of bread and ale. More independent were the 'liners', often trustworthy burgesses who were responsible for lining property and burgh boundaries (Marwick 1904; Ewan 1990). Burghs also developed treasurers who were responsible for the Common Good (revenues from petty tolls and customs) as well as clerks who were responsible for written records, and officials responsible for the burgh 'seal' to authorise charters and other agreements.

As burgh administration became more significant, advisory bodies were needed: in effect, early town councils. They started on piecemeal basis and developed in terms of frequency of meetings and permanency of membership. Members were drawn from the ranks of the freemen (or burgesses) who had exclusive rights to participate in municipal affairs (Murray 1924). Burgh administration, therefore, was the privileged responsibility of the Merchant Guild and councils of burgesses (Scottish Office 1958; Mackie 1964; Rodger 1983) to the exclusion of craftsmen and other lower classes (Marwick 1904). Specifically, they oversaw the primitive, *ad hoc* and geographically diverse administration and regulation of burgh tolls, burgh laws and trading practices (Scottish Office 1958; Mitchison 1982; Lynch 1992). In the twelfth and thirteenth centuries, local administration was to become even more complex with the development of 'burghs of barony' and 'burghs of regality', established by nobles and prelates on their own land (Bell and Paton 1896; Marwick 1904; Scottish Office 1958). The first was Strathaven in 1450 and then Biggar in 1451 (Pryde 1965). There is also evidence to suggest that the parish, a feature of the power and influence of the church, formed the basis for another, co-existing form of local administration by providing an early form of education and poor relief (Shaw 1942). In this formative period of Scottish history, therefore, a primitive and *ad hoc* system of local administration was primarily a vehicle for securing and maintaining core feudal relations: domination by kings of Scots and the nobility in the localities of Scotland.

The progressive rise of capitalist relations from the sixteenth to the twentieth centuries was the main driving force for change. The ascendant agricultural, commercial and (latterly) industrial classes were part of a system based on private property, wage-labour and market relations. In essence, local administration developed to serve the interests of the new ruling classes. In the short-term, land enclosures created an estimated 200,000 rootless men begging from door to door (Turner 1908: 10–11). A harsh and primitive Poor Law system emerged via an Act of Parliament in 1574 for the stated purpose of 'the punishment of strong and idle beggars, and provision for the sustentation of the poor and impotent' (quoted in Turner 1908: 14). This was financed through the levying of a 'poor rate' on occupiers of property (McConnell 1999). As the needs of the new capitalist classes extended (particularly with regard to infrastructure for transport, policing of the working classes, sanitation and education), so too did systems of local administration. They developed through largely self-selecting and often corrupt boards, each with a particular focus, such as turnpike trusts, county road trustees, police, prisons, school boards. Most were financed through additions to the poor rate. It is misleading, however, to talk of such a thing as a typical locality (Lynch 1992). Indeed, the patchwork of local boards was overlain at times by a virtually incomprehensible combination of shires, sheriffdoms, parishes, towns and counties.

If the initial driving force behind the development of local structures was the interests of the new capitalist classes, the next series of developments was a consequence largely of the growing dominance of industrial capital (over agricultural interests and the churches) and the integration of the working classes into the running of the state. In 1833 via the Burgh Reform Act, burghs became subject to annual election with the restricted franchise based on a £10 property qualification. By the time further Reforms Acts had been passed in 1868 and 1884, the franchise had been extended to roughly two-thirds of the Scottish adult male population. In 1845, the church lost power to parochial boards (elected by ratepayers) who took over responsibility for poor relief. When school boards were established in 1872 (elected and without preferential status for landowners through their property holding), this was a further and major blow to Scotland's churches and their role in Scottish political and civil society.

By the late 1880s, local structures needed to change further to cope with the pressures of industrialisation and urbanisation. Elected county councils were established in 1889 and took over many of the functions of boards and commissioners. Elected parish councils were set up in 1894, taking over the poor law responsibilities of the parochial boards. By the very beginning of the twentieth century, therefore, a slightly more simplified but nevertheless exceptionally complex and diverse system of local government was in place. It comprised 869 parish councils, 33 county councils and 200 burgh councils. These co-existed with a proliferation of boards and commissions, and it was only in 1918 (when school boards were replaced by elected education authorities) and then 1929 (when parish councils and numerous other boards were abolished, as well as the creation of district councils in many areas) that further rationalisation took place. Nevertheless, the system was still highly fragmented. It comprised:

- 21 large burgh councils.
- 176 small burgh councils.
- 33 county councils.
- 196 district councils.

In addition, there was a multiplicity of boards and joint arrangements in areas including police, fire, valuation and social work. The Representation of the People Act (1918) had also extended the franchise to just under half of the female population and so the constitutionally 'democratic' basis of councils was at a more advanced stage (if not fully in terms of either the female franchise or the plethora of unelected boards). In essence, however, this was still a system which lacked any real coherence. It was designed for low levels of state intervention and capitalist classes who hadn't yet moved on from *laissez-faire* as the core assumption about the role of the state.

1966–75: Wheatley Reforms and the Advent of the Two Tier System

In the first few decades of the post-war period, the role of the state increased dramatically. The legitimating framework for this new era of intervention was Keynesian economic ideas which placed state expenditure at the heart of government policy, coupled with the interventionist philosophies of the post-war consensus. Local government was a vital component of this new state strategy (Rhodes 1988). It took on a host of new responsibilities in housing, education, town planning, social services, economic development and others. In common with other municipal systems throughout western Europe, a more rational and coherent system was needed to cope with the demands of this increased role for the state at local level. The situation was given added impetus because the focus of the post-1964 Labour Governments was very much on long-term planning and intervention in local and national economies (see Pollard 1983).

A Royal Commission was established in 1966 under the chairmanship of Lord Wheatley, and its report in 1969 started with the words: 'Something is seriously wrong with local government in Scotland . . . At the root of the trouble is the present structure' (Cmnd. 4150 1969: 1). The basic problems were described as:

- *Structure:* Too many authorities, irrational boundaries, fostering conflict and inhibiting planning.
- *Functions:* Unnecessarily small authorities causing poor service delivery and wasting resources.
- *Finance:* An unequal spread of rateable resources, requiring to be bolstered by equalisation grants and creating an excessive dependence on the Exchequer.
- *Membership and internal organisation:* Low public standing and a difficulty in attracting good-quality candidates. The archaic committee system also inhibits a wider perspective on local affairs.
- *Relationship with Central Government:* The balance of power has gone wrong and rests far too much with the centre. (Cmnd. 4150 1969: 32–4)

The tone of the Wheatley report was not only supportive of a more integrated system, but was also in favour of shifting the balance of power away from the Scottish Office and Westminster, towards local authorities. The context to this is important. By the late 1960s, Britain was experiencing civil unrest. A series of unofficial strikes led the Wilson Government down the route of attempting to tackle the trade unions. Also, the reality of public services had not matched the post-war aspirations: poverty still existed and was on the increase; working-class children still performed relatively poorly in schools; impersonal high-rise flats became more like huge cages for the working class; and unemployment was increasing. It can be argued that the Wheatley philosophy was very much one of encouraging community power and local involvement; essentially a strategy of social control via integration rather than attack.

The practical outcome of Wheatley's proposal was for a two tier system, namely a combination of:

- 7 large regional councils exhibiting economies of scale in service provision and corresponding to genuine communities. Functions included major planning, water and sewerage, education, social work, housing, police and fire.
- 37 district councils concentrating on more localised service provision, tailored to smaller communities. Functions included local planning, housing improvement, parks and recreation, libraries, environmental health and licensing.

The report also proposed to supplement this two tier system with non-statutory community councils – emerging only in neighbourhoods who wished to have them. They would have no legal powers and would exist only to give expression to community views.

The core philosophy of Wheatley was accepted, although inevitably the precise configuration of authorities changed as a consequence of lobbying and debate (see McVicar et al. 1995). The Local Government (Scotland) Act 1973 resulted in a re-organisation in 1975, creating 9 regions and 53 districts. There were only two exceptions to this two tier system. The first was the creation of three all-purpose island councils in Orkney, Shetland and the Western Isles, a move previously rejected by Wheatley on the grounds that island survival depended on a comprehensive and strong planning system for the Highland region. The second, as Wheatley recommended, was a system of community councils to represent grassroots opinion, rather than discharge functions and be called a tier of local government. By 1983 these would be 1,131 in number and cover 80 per cent of the population (Midwinter et al. 1991: 141).

In the few years immediately succeeding reorganisation, the new structures came under some criticism particularly from the SNP, Liberal Party and some sections of the media. The arguments focused particularly on the regions being too remote from local people, having grown excessively in terms of the costs and numbers of administrators, and generally being expensive to run, placing undue burdens on ratepayers. Research undertaken by Page and Midwinter (1979) undertook a detailed test of a number of hypotheses surrounding remoteness, efficiency and cost. Ultimately it recognised that no system was perfect and that a lack of suitable pre- and post-reorganisation data created methodological difficulties, but there was little evidence to support the critics. In many respects, the post-reorganisation criticisms seem to have been little more than political froth linked to the debates surrounding a possible Scottish Assembly.

After the 'No' vote in the 1979 referendum, the only areas of activity were the Stodart Report's 'tidying-up' exercise (Cmnd. 8115 1981) and the Montgomery Report (Cmnd. 9216 1983) into the island councils. These generated only short-term and fairly low profile Scotland-wide debate. The reason is that the minds of Scottish Office ministers, opposition parties and grassroots activists were occupied in the early 1980s by Compulsory Competitive Tendering (CCT), cuts in grants, and rate-capping. This was

followed later in the decade by further extensions of CCT, the Poll Tax, centralisation of business rates and other reforms. It was not that debates about structures had subsided completely. Rather, a reaction against the Thatcher Government had galvanised opposition forces in a revived momentum towards advocating either devolution or independence (Levy 1992, 1995; McConnell 2000b). Local authority structures were simply a by-product of the debates among the opposition parties. The Scottish Labour Party, Scottish Liberal Democrats and Scottish National Party all favoured single tier councils, essentially on the grounds that a Scottish Assembly would render two tiers redundant because it would take over some functions whilst enhancing others at the local level. Labour was particularly keen to avoid charges of 'over governing' and so by advocating single tier councils, it could avoid the charge of creating an extra layer of government (McVicar et al. 1994). The Scottish Conservative Party had some sympathies with the idea of abolishing the large regions, especially because most were a power base for Labour opponents – Strathclyde in particular. Ultimately, however, the Scottish Conservatives were wary of unitary authorities as a 'Trojan horse' for devolution. Thus, for all intents and purposes, by 1990 the structure of local government in Scotland was only the most marginal of issues because it had not been able to break through onto the Conservative Government's political agenda. It would not stay this way for very long.

1991–6: The Creation of a Single Tier System

Moves for reform came swiftly, driven by the Environment Secretary Michael Heseltine. He felt that local government reform north of the border, unlike the situation in England, should not be too difficult because the Conservatives had few councillors to worry about (Heseltine 2000: 393). A consultation paper was issued (Scottish Office 1991) proposing single tier councils. The consultation paper criticised the existing system from two angles. First, it suggested that the two tier system was flawed in itself because:

- it is not readily understood;
- the public are confused about the responsibilities of each tier, causing accountability to be clouded;

- old allegiances live on, particularly in old counties and county towns;
- some regional councils are too remote from local communities;
- there is duplication and waste in central administrative structures (such as personnel and legal services) as well as in concurrent functions (for example, urban renewal and industrial development); and
- there are delays and friction in areas of joint working. (Scottish Office 1991: 7)

Figure 3.1   Advantages of a single tier system as proposed by Scottish Office ministers, June 1991.

- Simple to understand
- Removes confusion among the public about the responsibilities of each tier
- Clarifies local accountability
- Removes the potential for duplication, waste, delay and friction
- Offers free scope for sensible and imaginative co-ordination of functions
- Increases the ability of authorities to act as enablers
- Facilitates flexible responses
- Makes best use of scarce financial and human resources

Source: Scottish Office (1991: 9).

Second, it suggested that the system was unsuited to wider changes that had taken place in society. Government had encouraged a much greater consumerist approach to local services, as well as an emphasis on value for money and strong financial management. Also, the growth of bodies such as Scottish Homes and Scottish Enterprise had taken away many local authority functions. In essence, local government had taken on much more of an enabling role, rather than being simply the provider of services. Therefore: 'The Government believe [sic] that the present two-tier system presents real obstacles to local government in meeting the challenge of change successfully and acts as a brake on desirable and necessary initiatives' (Scottish Office 1991: 9).

The Government's rationale for a single tier system is contained in figure 3.1; these arguments were taken further in a second consultation paper the following year (Scottish Office 1992). The tone of the paper and the messages emanating from Scottish Secretary Ian Lang and the Conservative hierarchy in Scotland were that the need for

---

Figure 3.2 Community councils in Scotland – the basics.

- The Local Government (Scotland) Act 1973 requires local authorities to prepare schemes for establishing community councils in their area.

- Receipt of a petition from 20 electors in an area triggers arrangements for the formation of a community council.

- The Local Government (Scotland) Act 1973 defines the role of community councils as: 'to ascertain, co-ordinate and express to the local authorities for its area, and to public authorities, the views of the community which it represents, in relation to matters for which these authorities are responsible, and to take such action in the interests of that community as appears to it to be expedient and practicable'.

- They have no statutory powers to deliver services or raise funds. Thus, they do not constitute a tier of local government.

- The last available figures (1999) indicate that there are 1,152 community councils in Scotland. They cover 83 per cent of the population and are more prominent in rural areas (93 per cent) than urban (69 per cent).

- They are funded by the unitary authorities, usually on the basis of population coverage.

- Community councils have freedom to decide on how members will be elected or appointed. Almost 9 out of every 10 councils use direct elections, although elections are not common because the number of nominees rarely exceeds the places available. When elections do take place, turnout tends to be very low. No comprehensive figures exist although a reasonable estimate is between 5 and 25 per cent.

Source: Based on Goodlad et al. (1999).

---

unitary authorities was not negotiable. The core issue for consultation was how many authorities there should be. The second paper discussed four illustrative options: 15, 24, 35 and 51. By the time a further White Paper was produced and the relevant legislation had been passed in the Local Government etc. (Scotland) Act 1994, the number of authorities had become 32: in other words, 3 existing island councils plus 29 new authorities. The final configuration is contained in table 3.1. Shadow authorities came into operation in April 1995 and a complete changeover to the new unitary system occurred on 1 April 1996. The system is supported by a system of community councils as detailed in figure 3.2.

A Flawed Case for Change?

Leaving aside (for the moment) the merits or otherwise of the unitary system, many argued that the Conservative Government exaggerated the problems with the two tier system in order to justify reform. In particular, the various consultation papers did not provide any supporting evidence because what research existed did not offer support for the Government's claims regarding the inadequacies of the two tier system. A few examples will suffice.

First, Midwinter (1992: 46–8) produced figures for the 1975–89 period which indicated that regional councils did not have the high bureaucratic costs attributed to them by the Conservatives. He used the percentage of total budgets spent on administration as a surrogate for 'bureaucracy'. His findings were that:

- The three all-purpose island councils were above average in terms of administrative costs.
- Larger regions tended to have lower costs than small regions.
- Regions spent 2.4 per cent on administration whilst districts spent 8.9 per cent.

Indeed, the alleged waste and inefficiency because of a regional-district overlap in service provision was only 2.2 per cent of total expenditure (Midwinter 1992: 48). The regional councils, Strathclyde in particular, were also able to generate economies of scale in terms of staffing and purchasing power. Furthermore, the size of the regions also made them politically powerful in bidding for funding from the European Regional Development Fund and the European Social Fund. Strathclyde was also the first council to integrate its operations over several European funds and have a permanent representation in Brussels (McTavish 2002: 260). Over the 1975–86 period it obtained a total of £311m from the structural funds and the European Investment Bank (Sutcliffe 1997: 46).

Second, the argument that region-district co-ordination of inter-related services (such as housing and social work) is a major problem certainly has an element of truth because inter-organisational co-operation may be difficult because of competing values, priorities, political control and decision-making processes. Nevertheless, the Conservative Government seemed to operate double standards. On the one hand, it presided over and supported the fragmentation of local services through CCT, housing associations, local enterprise companies and so on. On the other hand, this support for diversity in local service provision did not extend to support for two sets of elected local authorities.

Table 3.1   Scotland's 32 unitary authorities post-1996.

Old council areas	New unitary authorities	Population	Number of councillors
Aberdeen District Council	City of Aberdeen	211,910	43
Banff and Buchan District Council; Gordon District Council; Kincardine and Deeside District Council	Aberdeenshire	226,940	68
Angus District Council; Tayside electoral divisions of Monifieth and Sidlaw (some parts excepted)	Angus	108,370	29
Argyll and Bute District Council; Strathclyde electoral divisions of Helensburgh and Vale of Leven (part)	Argyll and Bute	91,300	36
Kilmarnock and Loudoun District Council; Cumnock and Doon Valley District Council	East Ayrshire	120,310	32
Cunninghame District Council	North Ayrshire	135,820	30
Kyle and Carrick District Council	South Ayrshire	112,160	30
Borders Regional Council	Scottish Borders	106,950	34
Clackmannan District Council	Clackmannanshire	48,070	18
Clydebank District Council; Strathclyde electoral divisions of Dumbarton and Vale of Leven (except the areas included in Argyll and Bute)	West Dunbartonshire	93,320	22
Dumfries and Galloway Regional Council	Dumfries and Galloway	147,780	47
Bearsden and Milngavie District Council; Strathclyde electoral divisions Kirkintilloch, Strathkelvin North and Bishopbriggs, and the South Lenzie/ Waterside district ward in the Strathclyde electoral division of Chryston	East Dunbartonshire	108,250	24
City of Dundee District Council (except the Tayside electoral division of Monifieth and those parts of Sidlaw which are in Angus or Perthshire and Kinross)	City of Dundee	145,460	29
City of Edinburgh District Council	City of Edinburgh	449,020	58
Falkirk District Council	Falkirk	145,270	32
Fife Regional Council	Fife	349,770	78

Table 3.1 *continued opposite*

Table 3.1 *continued*

City of Glasgow District Council (except Strathclyde electoral divisions of Rutherglen/Fernhill, Cambuslang/ Halfway and parts of King's Park/ Toryglen)	City of Glasgow	578,710	79
Highland Regional Council	Highland	208,920	80
Inverclyde District Council	Inverclyde	84,150	20
Cumbernauld and Kilsyth, Motherwell and Monklands District Councils; Strathclyde electoral division of Chryston (except South Lenzie/Waterside district ward)	North Lanarkshire	321,180	70
Clydesdale, Hamilton and East Kilbride District Councils; Strathclyde electoral divisions of Rutherglen/Fernhill, Cambuslang/ Halfway and parts of King's Park/Toryglen	South Lanarkshire	302,340	67
East Lothian District Council	East Lothian	90,180	23
Midlothian District Council	Midlothian	80,950	18
West Lothian District Council	West Lothian	159,030	32
Moray District Council	Moray	87,000	26
Orkney Islands District Council	Orkney Islands	19,220	21
Perth and Kinross District Council and parts of the Tayside electoral division of Sidlaw	Perth and Kinross	134,950	41
Eastwood District Council; Strathclyde electoral division of Barrhead	East Renfrewshire	89,410	20
Renfrew District Council (except Strathclyde electoral division of Barrhead)	Renfrewshire	177,830	40
Shetland Islands Council	Shetland Islands	21,960	22
Stirling District Council	Stirling	86,200	22
Western Isles Islands Council	Comhairle nan Eilean Siar (Western Isles)	26,450	31

Note: The total population of Scotland based on the 2001 census is 5,064,200 and the number of councillors in the new unitary authorities is 1,222. This is a reduction from 1,695 councillors under the previous two tier system.

Source: Adapted from Local Government etc. (Scotland) Act 1994 and updated via 2001 Census Statistics from http://www.gro-scotland.gov.uk/grosweb/grosweb.nsf/pages/file4/ $file/01mpe_t6.pdf

Third, there are difficulties with the Government's argument that councils (particularly the regions and notably Strathclyde Region) were badly understood and remote from the needs of local people. Research conducted for the Widdecombe Report found that 52 per cent of the sample electorate were 'well' or 'quite well' informed about local government (Cmnd. 9800 1986: 25). Also, 62 per cent could correctly name the political party controlling their region or county, with Scottish voters having the highest percentage (42 per cent) able to name their regional councillor (Cmnd. 9800 1986: 34). On the matter of local satisfaction, a survey in 1994 of 1,501 individuals was conducted by MVA Consultancy for the Scottish Office. It received little publicity but contained interesting findings. The survey revealed that 80 per cent of respondents found the quality of service provision to be good or very good (Scottish Office Central Research Unit 1995: 19). The MVA research also found a reasonably high knowledge of local services. Between 71 and 73 per cent of respondents could correctly name, respectively, the Region and the District as being responsible for particular services (Scottish Office Central Research Unit 1995: 14–17). Undoubtedly some confusion existed, but on balance the figures tended to support the idea of an electorate who were reasonably knowledgeable and satisfied about the services provided by their regional and district councils.

The final category of criticism levied at the Conservative Government and Scottish Office ministers in terms of the case for change was the manner of the policy-making process. In complete contrast to the deliberative, evidence-based approach of Wheatley, the consultation papers (especially the first) were the flimsiest of documents. Not a single shred of research evidence was put forward to justify either (1) criticism of the two tier system or (2) the rationale for unitary authorities. As Jean McFadden (1993: 24), the then Leader of Glasgow City Council, suggested: 'Any first-year student who produced such intellectually slipshod work would not rate a pass mark'. Furthermore, unlike the situation south of the border where an independent Local Government Commission was set up to conduct rolling consultations in each area, ministers in Scotland explicitly rejected such an option. They argued that a basic consensus existed on the need for unitary authorities and that national consultation was needed only on the fine detail.

In many respects, the ministerial vision of local government was a 'top down' one, based on its perception of local government's proper role as being an 'enabler'. It did not start from the 'bottom up' and reflect on the multiple roles of local government in Scottish society (see Chapter 1 for further discussion). Stoker (1993) has argued, therefore, that the Conservative approach fits the Garbage Can model of policy-making put forward by Cohen et al. (1972) and reinforced by Kingdon (1984). According to Stoker, the process did not proceed 'rationally' from an identification of problems leading to solutions. Instead: 'Solutions appear to be chasing problems. The weaknesses of local government are defined and redefined as participants seek to specify the problem so that their "pet" solution appears to fit' (Stoker 1993: 4–5).

We should not forget, of course, that many critics of the government favoured a single tier system, although most favoured doing so as part of a package of constitutional reform involving a Scottish Parliament. In the absence of reform being part of a wider constitutional package, however, opponents were sceptical of the benefits, not least from a Conservative Party which had previously rejected the option of unitary authorities. Indeed, the zeal with which Ian Lang and his Scottish Office team promoted reform was a surprise to many grassroots party workers. The message emanating from diverse opinion within Scottish society accorded with the old American adage 'if it ain't broke don't fix it!'. This leaves us with the only real rationale for reform – political. None of the regional councils were controlled by the Conservatives and four were under Labour control (Fife, Lothian, Central and Strathclyde) with a further two (Tayside and Grampian) where Labour was the largest party. Abolishing the regions offered the Conservatives the chance to remove powerful sources of opposition to the Conservatives in Scotland, especially what John Major had famously described as the 'monstrosity' of Strathclyde Region.

Single Tier Authorities, Conservative Style: A Critique

The arguments in favour of unitary authorities have already been outlined. They amount in effect to a more cohesive, simplified, accountable, effective and cheaper system. For many critics, however, reality is far removed from the rhetoric. We can examine the single tier system from a number of different angles.

Enhancing Democracy and Accountability?

Despite the Conservative Government's argument that services in each area would be 'under one roof', this did not transpire. Four particular categories of activity make the system not as straightforward as suggested. First, there are contract arrangements, where one council enters into a contract with another in order to assist in the discharging of certain functions. This happens particularly in specialist psychology, educational and social work areas where some councils are too small to be able to employ full-time permanent staff in these fields. Second, there are joint committees where authorities share the costs and responsibilities for particular roles. For example, 13 local authorities in the east of Scotland have created the non-statutory East of Scotland European Consortium to co-ordinate and maximise their access to EU funding. Third, there are joint boards with cross-authority membership and which share statutory provision for certain services. Notable examples are fire boards and police boards. Fourth, some services were removed completely from the remit of elected local authorities. The highest profile is water and sewerage which was removed to three independent water authorities (latterly amalgamating into Scottish Water), despite a ballot in Strathclyde Region with a remarkable 97 per cent favouring the service being kept under council control (*The Herald*, 23 March 1994). Other non-elected bodies were based around functions previously conducted by local authorities including the Scottish Environment Protection Agency (SEPA) and Scottish Children's Reporter Administration (SCRA).

In sum, the two tier system has been abolished and replaced with a different form of two tier system, namely a surrogate upper tier rather than a directly elected one. As Hayton (1993: 7) suggests: 'two into one won't go'. This accords with the view of Newton (1982) who argues that some form of large-scale local government is inescapable in complex urban industrial societies, because some services such as transport and water are too large to be the responsibility of individual authorities.

Further discussion of the 'democratic' nature of quangos is contained in Chapter 6. For the moment, it can be suggested that a surrogate upper tier (particularly joint board and independent quangos) stretches the idea of 'democracy' rather more than many would think justified. It removes aspects of the system of local governance, partly or wholly away from the direct control of elected representatives. This is not to suggest that traditional systems of local democracy in Scotland are ideal – far from it (see Chapter 5). Some even view non-elected bodies as a 'democratic gain' because they are accompanied by systems of accountability and control. For example, SEPA operates its own code of practice on openness and is bound by the Code of Practice on Access to Government Information issued by the Lord Chancellor's Department. Also, Scottish Water is held to account by five Water Consultation Customer Panels, as well as other bodies including the Water Industry Commissioner for Scotland, the Drinking Water Quality Regulator for Scotland and SEPA. Others would argue, however, that ministerial-appointed bodies (or Convenors of such bodies) overseeing other ministerial-appointed bodies hardly constitutes local democracy. Customers' panels have (the Convenor aside) only four members each – often lecturers, business persons or community activists. In effect, the notion of democracy is being reconstituted – based on community representation as being reflected predominantly in customer 'elites' representing the interests of consumers, rather than political elites representing the interests of a citizenry.

The new system is also exceptionally complex – far more so than the 'two into one' philosophy would imply. As the Scottish Local Government Information Unit (1996: 2) suggests, there is the 'illusion of unitary status'. Focus group research by the Scottish Executive Central Research Unit (1999) found that participants tended to view the remit of local authorities as wider than they actually were. Therefore, if a reasonably high standard of public knowledge of government is a prerequisite for accountability, it is difficult to avoid the conclusion that the system of local governance emanating from the 1996 structural reforms is found wanting.

Encouraging Greater Co-ordination and Coherence?

No studies have been undertaken which would provide a wide-ranging answer to this question. Certainly, there is valid logic in assuming that coherence might be improved by placing all services under 'one roof'. This might especially be the case where related services were previously under the control of different political parties (or independents) at the regional and district level. The Conservative argument, however, becomes questionable once we move beyond this basic point. There are two main reasons for this.

First, as the previous point indicates, the system is far more complex than we might think. Contract arrangements, joint committees, joint boards and non-elected quangos have produced a system which in many respects is much more disjointed than before.

Some might go further and argue that the two tier system, for all its faults, had a much stronger political identity and hence an ability to act as a cohesive factor. Second, the 'under one roof' argument fails to recognise that there are many other conflicts and rivalries which inhibit the co-ordination and coherence of policy-making and provision. Variables include inter-party relations (especially within ruling party groups), inter-departmental influences (including professional differences), intra-departmental influences, and inter-party differences (especially the relations between party groups in hung councils) (Wilson and Game 2002: 303). For example, Kendrick (1995) in his study of social work services in Scotland quotes Bruce who recognises the fundamental differences between educationalists and social workers. The situation is akin to 'an anthropologist, a hundred years ago, aiming to document and describe the confrontation between two widely differing cultures' (cited in Kendrick 1995: 627).

Reducing Costs and Improving Services?

Local government reorganisation involved a number of activities with financial implications. These included the costs of:

- Relocation and recruitment.
- Early retirement and redundancy (roughly 11,000 staff).
- Planning for change (such as rationalising systems and practices, including IT).
- Materials, equipment and new corporate identities (for example, stationery, vehicles and public relations).

The Scottish Office commissioned management consultants Touche Ross to conduct an initial assessment of the costs of the 15, 24, 35 and 51 unit structures. The figures as cited in table 3.2 did give some comfort to critics of the Government's approach because they indicated that larger authorities tended to be the most efficient. Indeed, the 15 unit structure was based substantially on an adaptation of the existing regions. This matter aside, the Touche Ross report came under severe criticism. Hayton (1993) and Midwinter (1995) provide a thoroughgoing critique of Touche Ross's underestimation of key costs and inappropriate methodology. Nevertheless, the Scottish Office used the figures as the broad basis for assuming that reorganisation would not only be relatively inexpensive, but would also generate annual cost savings. Scottish Secretary Michael Forsyth assumed that the new councils would generate savings of £20m in 1997–8 and £40m in 1998–9. Correspondingly, the financial support from the Scottish Office was much less than councils needed. A report by the Accounts Commission in 1998 pointed to a disparity between the estimate of the Scottish Office that reorganisation would cost £76m, compared with COSLA's estimate of £281m. Controller of Audit Bob Black stated:

> ... it is difficult to avoid the general conclusion that the actual costs were significantly greater than the estimates provided for by the Scottish Office. It is striking that in 1995/96, the Scottish Office made no explicit provision for redundancy costs incurred by the outgoing councils whereas these councils, according to COSLA figures, incurred severance costs of some £80m in that year. (Controller of Audit to the Accounts Commission 1998: para. 7.2)

In actual fact, the final figures seem to be even greater. The most comprehensive study to date of the costs of reorganisation in Scotland, England and Wales estimates that Scottish costs were approximately £400m at 1996–7 prices (Chisholm 2002: 259).

Table 3.2 Touche Ross Report (1992) on the predicted costs and savings of local government reorganisation.

No. of authorities	Annual costs/savings	% of current spending
15	– £192m	–2.6
24	– £120m	–1.6
35	–£55m	–0.7
41	+£58m	+0.8

Source: Quoted in Midwinter (1995: 101).

Paradoxically, the burden of financing reorganisation was placed on local people via a combination of tax rises and cuts in services. Whereas Council Tax levels rose by 3.7 per cent in the financial year 1995–6 prior to reorganisation, the rises for the first two years of the new councils were 13.4 per cent (1996–7) and 10.6 per cent (1997–8). Indeed, the first of these increases would have been much higher had it not been for an unprecedented last-minute intervention by the Scottish Secretary and an additional £100m funding for councils (Midwinter 1998: 57). Figures from COSLA indicated widespread cuts of over £400m in 1996–7, especially in social work services, education and libraries. For example, the financial year 1997–8 in Glasgow produced cuts in education (over £10m), social work (over £10m), roads (almost £4m), parks and recreation (over £3m), environmental services (£2.9m), arts and culture (£2.4m), social strategy (almost £6m), property services (over £3.4m) and an additional cut across all services of £10.7m (*Glasgow Herald*, April 1997: 4–5).

If service provision suffered in the short-term, it is difficult to judge the long-term impact, although perceptions of local service provision could be more positive. Figures from the 2001–2 Scottish Household Survey found that only 43 per cent 'agreed' or 'tended to agree' that their council provided high-quality services (Scottish Executive 2003f: 163). Service cuts in Scottish local government tend to operate on the basis of a ratchet effect (cuts unable to be restored) but a thorough evaluation would need information that is impossible to obtain: what would have happened in the absence of reorganisation? What we can say, however, is that all the major political parties now support the unitary system. They may disagree on a number of matters, particularly the status of non-elected governance and the balance of power *vis-à-vis* local government and the Scottish Parliament, but the single tier system in Scotland seems here to stay. Ironically, the Conservatives may have done Labour and the Liberal Democrats a favour. They pushed through a controversial reorganisation and took substantial political flak in doing so, but paved the way for a Scottish Parliament.

Scottish Structures: Distinctiveness in the UK?

The structures of local government in Scotland, England, Wales and Northern Ireland each have separate histories that coincide from time to time. They exhibit both differences and similarities in a number of respects. Each of these dimensions can be considered in turn.

UK Differences

The most obvious differences are that structures differ throughout the UK. Between 1974 and 1995, England (except for London) operated on the basis of a three tier system. Counties and districts were the principal authorities but there also existed approximately 8,000 parish and town councils, covering about 30 per cent of the population in mostly non-urban areas (Elwood 1999). Unlike community councils in Scotland, they constituted a third tier because they had (and continue to have) minor statutory powers, usually concurrent with functions of principal councils. These include responsibilities for burial grounds, bus shelters and common pastures. A further reform over the 1995–8 period produced a hybrid system. In some areas such as North Yorkshire, Norfolk, Kent and Dorset, a two tier system operates. Conversely, 46 areas have unitary authorities, in predominantly urban areas such as Luton, Reading, Slough, Bristol and Nottingham City. Parish and town councils (now roughly 10,000 in number) were left unchanged. Depending on the particular area, therefore, there may be either one, two or three tiers of local government in England (Wilson and Game 2002).

Structures in London have developed a life of their own within the English system. This is unlike structures in Edinburgh and Glasgow which have always fallen into line with Scottish-wide developments. The London Government Act 1963 created a Greater London Council (GLC) as an upper tier, and 32 London boroughs (plus a continuing City of London Corporation as a lower tier). In 1986, the Thatcher Government controversially abolished the directly elected bodies of the GLC and six metropolitan county councils – baulking at the 'socialist' nature of these councils and their alleged inefficiency (Duncan and Goodwin 1988). Powers were removed to an exceptionally complex system of joint boards, committees and central departments. This left London as the only major capital in Western Europe without a democratically elected strategic authority. The situation was remedied eventually in 2000 with the creation of the Greater London Authority (GLA). It comprises a directly elected Mayor and 25-member assembly with strategic responsibilities for (notably) transport, police, fire and emergency planning, economic development, and planning. Many of its functional responsibilities are conducted through 'quangos' such as Transport for London and the London Development Agency (see Pimlott and Rao 2002; Travers 2004). Nevertheless, the formal differences remain vis-à-vis cities in Scotland; two tiers in London but single tier in Scotland's two largest cities of Glasgow and Edinburgh.

The structure of local government in Wales seems initially to have more in common with Scotland. Over the period 1974–96, it had 8 upper tier county councils and 37 district councils. Subsequent reforms in 1996 produced a system of 22 unitary authorities, although this is something of a misnomer. The pre- and post-1996 structures exist alongside community councils, covering 68 per cent of the population and not being confined to rural or suburban areas (Woods et al. 2002: 22). Unlike their Scottish namesakes, they can choose to exercise minor statutory powers, similar to those for parish councils in England. Thus, the apparent unitary system in Wales is actually a two tier system in many areas.

Local government structures in Northern Ireland have largely been isolated from the various reforms on mainland Britain. The Local Government (Northern Ireland) Act 1972 created 26 single tier district councils and the format has stayed the same ever since. Structures in Northern Ireland are linked to the unique social and political circumstances there (Carmichael and Knox 1999). The functions of districts have been heavily delimited to avoid sectarian bias, whilst 'traditional' local authority powers in areas such as education, housing and social services are the responsibility of various boards, agencies and departments of the Northern Ireland Office (Wilson and Game 2002: 59–60). In some senses, therefore, there are similarities to Scotland because a single tier system is supplemented by a surrogate upper tier, although the crucial difference is that councils in Scotland have much more substantial powers.

Another difference in terms of Scottish structures in relation to the rest of the UK is not the structures themselves, but the decision-making processes which have produced these structures. Although local government structures are now entirely within the remit of the Scottish Parliament, all reorganisations to date (in Scotland and elsewhere) have been the responsibility of government at Westminster. While all reorganisations have contained elements of consultation, a difference can nevertheless be discerned. In essence, structural reforms in England tend to be more consultative. The reforms of the 1990s are the best examples of this. The Local Government Commission was established in 1992 to conduct rolling evaluations of opinion throughout each area of England. Although unitary authorities were still the government's preferred option, the exercise was less prescriptive from the start and recognised that some areas might wish to retain two tiers. This was unlike the situation in Wales and Scotland where the Scottish Office and Welsh Office considered the principle of single tier authorities to be non-negotiable.

UK Similarities

Paradoxically, we can go some way to explaining all these differences if we consider the similarities of local structures in the

UK. Taking the post-war period as an example, each reorganisation of local government has come at a time when the Westminster state perceives a threat to its political and economic dominance (and the various interests which it represents) if local government is not reorganised. For example, Dearlove (1979) argues that moves in Britain towards local government structural reorganisation in the 1960s and 1970s need to be seen in the context of a fiscal crisis whereby dominant business interests could not afford to sustain a system where its expenditures tended to outpace its ability to raise the necessary income. Therefore:

> . . . the essential object of reorganisation has been to make local government more functional for dominant interests, by restructuring it to facilitate their direct control of its expenditures and interventions. The study of the reorganisation of British local government has to be undertaken as a study of the struggle to counter its relative autonomy from dominant interests and the state in order that closer links might be asserted between economic and governmental power. (Dearlove 1979: 245)

The situation in Northern Ireland in 1972 has a similar resonance. The introduction of direct rule from Westminster produced a counter tendency to the recommendation of the McCrory review of 1970s which proposed regional tiers of local government – similar to Wheatley's proposals for Scotland. To do otherwise would have left too much power in Northern Ireland and rendered direct rule from Westminster severely blunted. The abolition of the GLC in 1986 fits this same pattern. With its high media profile and interventionist policies based on equity and social justice (such as subsidised public services for pensioners, support for minority groups and strategic planning), it symbolised a 'socialist' alternative to Thatcherism (Duncan and Goodwin 1988) with its expenditures posing a threat to the centre's economic strategy (Rhodes 1988).

Moving into the 1990s, similar patterns appear once again. The two tier or three tier systems were viewed as obstacles to the Government's agenda. Not only did the Conservatives consider these systems to be economically damaging to Britain's interests because they encouraged waste and inefficiency in state expenditures, but they also considered them to be politically damaging. The Government perceived multiple tiers and the entrenched political and bureaucratic interest therein to be an obstacle to the 'enabling' role of government in overseeing others such as private companies, independent boards and associations. Furthermore, in some areas – Scotland in particular – it saw large (typically Labour-controlled) councils as major critics of the Conservative programme.

An explanation of this combination of differences and similarities can be found in the argument that the UK is a 'union state' (Mitchell 1996; Mitchell 2003). This allows for considerable regional autonomy based on historical, social, economic and political differentiation, whilst recognising the common Union element. It is hardly surprising, therefore, that local government reorganisation throughout the UK has varied in terms of timing, structures and policy processes. Equally, it not surprising that there is a common link to state power at Westminster. Thus, Scotland may differ from the rest of the UK in terms of the specific structures of local government, but we can be fairly confident that structural reforms have and will continue to take place when the strategies of the 'centre' (whether this is at the levels of the Westminster Parliament or Scottish Parliament) seem to be under threat.

Conclusion

We have come full circle. It can be argued that the best way to understand the structure of local government in Scotland from feudal times to the present is by recognising its link to dominant interests. Just as burgh administrations in the twelfth and thirteenth centuries helped maintain the dominance of the king, in conjunction with the church and the nobility, so too did the reforms of the mid 1990s. They attempted to take local authorities further down the road of compatibility with 'business' interests by seeking:

- greater efficiency leading to reduced tax burdens, lower public expenditures and lower inflation;
- greater flexibility in service provision with a role for the private sector in direct service provision via public-private partnerships; and
- smaller councils with less of a nationwide public presence should they wish to promote 'alternative' views.

How to understand the nature of these ruling interests is another matter. Debates about modern local government as a local state are incorporated within models dealing with post-Fordism, regulation theory, uneven development, sub-national governance, globalisation and others (for example, Cochrane 1993; Duncan and Goodwin 1988; Painter and Goodwin, 2000; Leach and Percy-Smith 2001; John 2001). Even at the most basic level, such theories make us realise that the structures of local government in Scotland and elsewhere in the UK need to be seen in context. As Leach and Percy-Smith argue:

> . . . much of what we associate with local governance is not so much the consequence of deliberative choice by local communities on the one hand or national governments on the other, but the manifestation of much broader economic and societal trends, a distant consequence of developments in global capitalism. (Leach and Percy-Smith 2001: 39)

The 'bigger picture' of Scottish local government in the context of a system of multi-level governance within the EU and globalisation will be considered in Chapter 10.

? Key Questions ?

1. To what extent does the structure of Scottish local government 'change with the times'?
2. Is it inevitable that Scotland has some form of non-elected local governance?
3. Was the two tier system of regions and districts so 'bad' after all?
4. By what standards should we judge the success of the single tier system in Scotland and to what extent are these standards being met?
5. Are Scottish local government structures really that different from other areas of the UK?

Further Reading

The historical development of local government structures in Scotland necessitates delving into historical texts rather than those grounded in politics and public policy. *Townlife in Fourteenth-Century Scotland* by Elizabeth Ewan (1990) is particularly good for the period covered in the title and beyond. A more wide-ranging and very useful source is J. E. Shaw (1942), *Local Government in Scotland.* The Wheatley Report (Cmnd. 4150 1969) is worth revisiting for the impressiveness of its research and its thoughtful approach. For different reasons (the flimsiness of the evidence and argument), it is worth looking at the first two Scottish Office (1991, 1992) consultation papers which criticised the two tier system and proposed single tier authorities. The best overview and critique of the introduction of the single tier system can be found in Midwinter (1995), *Local Government in Scotland: Reform or Decline?* For structures in England and Wales, *Local Government in the United Kingdom* by David Wilson and Chris Game (2002) is an excellent overview.

	Useful Websites	

http://www.cosla.gov.uk
The Convention of Scottish Local Authorities. Follow links to access the websites of every local authority in Scotland, as well as a multitude of bodies operating in the field of Scottish government and politics.

http://www.audit-scotland.gov.uk
Audit Scotland. It doesn't deal (except indirectly) with the democratic nature of the single tier system but it does produce periodic reports on aspects of economy, efficiency and effectiveness.

http://www.unison-scotland.org.uk/
Scotland's largest trade union, representing workers in local government and other areas of the public sector. Its regular campaigns and publications help highlight the 'deficiencies' of Scottish local government.

CHAPTER FOUR

Council Decision-Making Structures: From Traditional Administration to Post-Devolution Modernisation

The way in which a local authority organises its internal structures in order to make decisions 'may appear initially to constitute a technical management issue [but] it is also a fundamentally political one' (Atkinson and Wilks-Heeg 2000: 162). We can understand the reasons for this by briefly mapping out key issues. In a formal sense, executive decision-making in Scottish local authorities is the responsibility of democratically elected councillors (organised through the committee system), assisted by officers (organised through departmental structures). The long-standing tradition in local government north of the border (and elsewhere in the UK) is that the full council, as a corporate body, is legally responsible for taking executive decisions. There are some matters which legally must be undertaken by the full council itself (such as the annual budget and appointing the Head of Paid Service) but otherwise councils have considerable freedom to delegate decision-making to committees of councillors or (occasionally) officers. There is no provision for decisions to be taken by individual councillors.

The decision-making structures adopted by councils have evolved over time and exhibit varying balances of central prescription, central encouragement and local discretion. There is no 'ideal' decision-making structure because several very difficult issues arise:

1. Should some councillors have executive functions (the power to take decisions) whilst the remainder have only scrutiny functions?

2. Should all parties be represented in decision-making forums or should representation be limited (similar to Westminster) to the party with an overall majority on the council?
3. To what extent do councils require leadership, and to what extent should leadership be a strategy role or a full-blown executive role?
4. If councils do require leadership, should this be vested in senior councillors or a single individual?
5. Should citizens have an active say in selecting individual leaders (for example via electing mayors) or should they be selected by a body of elected councillors?

Such issues are complicated further because the way in which councillors are organised via the committee system is often linked to the way in which officers are organised in departmental structures. A further and vitally important complication is that it is by no means certain that councillors (whichever way they are organised to take decisions) are the real source of power in councils. As discussed in more detail in Chapter 5, party groups and officers are alternative sources of power. What we can say, therefore, is that the structures and processes of local authority decision-making are political dynamite. They strike at the heart of who wields power in local authorities – in Scotland and elsewhere. For every reform that gives power to certain groupings or individuals, it must take power away from others.

This chapter explores the development of council decision-making structures in Scotland, focusing particularly on the tensions produced in each new system. First, it outlines the 'traditional' approach to decision-making which operated in the first few decades after the Second World War. Second, it focuses on the rise and implementation of corporate decision-making and management from the mid 1970s to the early 1980s. Third, it examines pressures placed on the corporate approach by Conservative Governments in the post-1979 period, particularly the fragmentation encouraged by CCT and the attempted 'depoliticisation' subsequent to the Widdecombe Report. Fourth, it outlines the council modernisation agenda pursued since the advent of single tier authorities in 1996. A particular focus is on the modernisation programme of the Scottish Executive and the way in which Scottish structures have evolved differently from those in England and Wales. Finally, it concludes by suggesting that despite numerous changes in local authority decision-making structures and processes over the past 50 years or so, there is more continuity than we might think.

1950s–60s: The 'Traditional' Approach to Council Decision-Making

Core Assumptions of the 'Traditional' Approach

The internal arrangements of Scottish councils in the immediate post-war period were a relic of the past. Decision-making structures adhered to a logic which made sense in a system (1) designed for relatively minimalist state intervention at the local level and (2) whose only reference point was the functional specialism of *ad hoc* boards. Stanyer (1976: 133) notes that the traditional system was based on the simple principle of:

one service → one committee → one chief officer → one department

Figure 4.1 outlines the stages of decision-making under the traditional system, these being normative as well as descriptive. Two particular implications are important. First, party politics and political decisions by councillors played only a marginal role. The real source of power was senior officers, who set committee agendas and advised councillors how to deal with each item. As a consequence, the role of councillors was limited primarily to thinking about the political reactions to the decisions made. A second implication is that councils were much more suited to the administration of services than the governance of their areas (Midwinter 1982: 3). The outcome was a system of local authority management which was fragmented, departmentalised, lacking in co-ordination and driven largely by professional and bureaucratic interests.

Dearlove (1979: 146–9) suggests that some caution is needed before adopting the above as an accurate portrayal of councils in the few decades after the war. He rightly notes the shortage of empirical research in this area, and suggests that 'insider' accounts of the time ignored important aspects of local government and politics. This is

Figure 4.1   The 'traditional' approach to council decision-making processes.

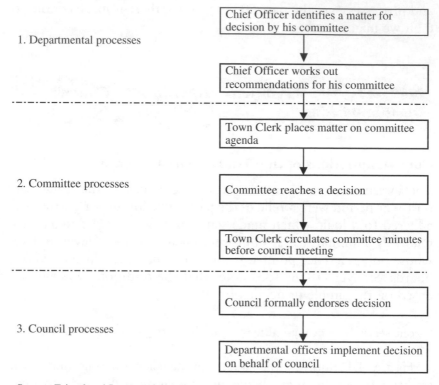

Source: Friend and Jessop (1969: 48).

certainly a point to bear in mind, but it does not stop us from getting a sense – albeit possibly a crude one – of council affairs in the early post-war years. We should note that political control of Scotland's councils was much less than it is today. In 1955, a survey by the *Municipal Yearbook* found that only 25.4 per cent of Scottish burgh councils and 9.5 per cent of Scottish county councils were under the control of a political party (Gyford et al. 1989: 24–5). We must also remember the context of the post-war consensus and a relative congruence on fundamental principles between the main parties. Thus, a powerful role for bureaucratic interests probably captures the essence of the age. An example can be found in the work of McTavish (2002), which covers the management of education in Glasgow Corporation. He quotes the Director of Education in 1955 who sought in a report to rebuff a proposal to separate educational policy-making and administration:

the recommendations are founded on the fallacy that it is possible to divide educational administration into two separate spheres – matters which have a teaching implication and those who [sic] do not – educational administration exists to meet the needs of the children in our schools and therefore must be directed by officials who have first hand experience of these needs. (Quoted in McTavish 2002: 241)

The 'Traditional' Approach Under Pressure

The system of internal decision-making in councils could not survive the expanding role of local government in the post-war age. As local authorities took on more responsibilities in areas such as housing, education and planning, so the number of committees and sub-committees mushroomed. In the same vein as local government structures (see Chapter 3), something had to change. The 1964–7 Maud Committee was the first major investigation into the weaknesses of the traditional system. Its focus and research evidence was based on local government in England and Wales, although its findings do not seem unrealistic in the Scottish context. The report found that most county boroughs had approximately 20 full committees and between 40 and 50 sub-committees. Membership typically fell into the range 10 to 13 although committees of over 100 were not unknown (Maud 1967: 14). The consequence was a lack of uniformity throughout the country and a lack of co-ordination in decision-making. The report also recognised (but found it difficult to provide details of) the importance of political parties in council decision-making, particularly in urban areas. Similar views to Maud were contained in the 1967 Hughes Report for Scotland and the Mallaby Report for England and Wales, both examining the recruitment, training and employment of local government officers.

Maud's specific proposals were for management boards (similar to local cabinets) and a streamlining of committees and departments, but these recommendations did not find widespread support among back-bench councillors. Not only did the reforms transfer substantial power to a chief officer, but they also relegated most councillors to deliberative roles in non-executive committees. The Wilson Government did not legislate to introduce the Maud recommendations. It had enough to contend with in the form of the devaluation of the pound in 1967, budgetary cuts and a battle with the trade unions. Nevertheless, some English authorities embraced aspects of the recommendations by instituting central, co-ordinating committees. By 1970, the level of adoption was county councils 47 per cent, county boroughs 83 per cent and London boroughs 83 per cent (Rhodes and Midwinter 1980: 23). Scotland, however, was much less enthusiastic. There were over 400 councils in Scotland but only 4 councils had adopted some form of policy committee and only 9 or so had a designated head officer (Paterson Report 1973: 12–13). Glasgow Councillor Ron Young (1977: 89) suggests that an imminent reorganisation and lack of training opportunities in Scotland led Scottish councils to exercise caution. Nevertheless, the impetus for change could not disappear. The Wheatley Report in 1969 stated that 'what is missing in local government is unified management. Drive and co-ordination are difficult to achieve. Some organ is needed beside the council itself in which aims can be formulated for the authority as a whole . . .' (Cmnd. 4150 1969: 229).

In 1969, similar statements were made in the Redcliffe-Maud Report on local government structures in England and Wales. Why, therefore, was there a nationwide trend towards reforming the internal structures of councils in the direction of a more integrated, corporate approach? A 'rational' straightforward explanation is offered by Elcock. He suggests that the pressures for change were:

- an acute lack of co-ordination between services;
- a lack of efficient use of resources (despite the availability of large mainframe computers with the capacity for assisting in the management of finances); and
- a lack of forward planning. (Elcock 1982: 234–41)

Dearlove suggests, however, that 'rational' explanations only scratch the surface. He argues that:

> The organizational experts concerned to introduce the corporate approach speak a language which hides the ultimate meaning of their actions from ordinary citizens at the same time as it places them beyond easy critique. There is the presumption that knowledge, information and experts can transcend ideology and interests . . . The firm entrenchment of this perspective on reorganisation is crisply situated within the prevailing ideology of science and technology. (Dearlove 1979: 254–5)

Dearlove frequently and favourably cites the work of Cockburn (1997) and her study of Lambeth as offering a perspective which gets to the heart of the drive to move beyond traditional structures and adopt a corporate approach. She suggests that 'The moment when a new style of management is looked for is the moment when existing means of control are under pressure' (Cockburn 1977: 7). The specific problems for the capitalist state as the 1960s progressed were the need to (1) keep down local state expenditures and avoid unnecessary costs which inhibited the process of capital accumulation and (2) deal with the 'legitimation crisis' which was a product of growing working-class militancy in response to failings in education, housing, the workplace and so on. Therefore, the 'traditional' approach is ultimately a barrier to the conditions under which successful capitalist accumulation can take place. Arguably, the muted language of the Wheatley Report contained similar seeds. It suggested that local government had become fragmented, marginalised and subject to excessive central control. As a consequence:

> . . . local government lacks the ability to speak with a strong and unified voice . . . The electorate are aware of this. They are increasingly sceptical whether local government really means government. The question is being asked – and it is a serious question – whether, as an institution, local government is worthwhile maintaining at all. (Cmnd. 4150 1969: 1)

1970s: The Corporate Approach in Scotland

Origins of the Corporate Approach

Corporate management is an integrated approach to the management of local authority affairs. It aims to transcend all the various departmental, political and public interests in order to bring order, priorities, strategy, planning and suitable resource allocations to the decision-making and governance of local communities. Its origins as a managerial philosophy lie in the United States private sector. The development of the Planning, Programming, Budgeting (PPB) system in the Department of Defense in 1961 was one of the earliest moves (Dearlove 1979: 139–40). British companies such as GKN and

Smiths were developing Management by Objectives (MbO) in the late 1950s and early 1960s (Cockburn 1977: 8), and in 1964 the PPB system was adopted in the UK by the Ministry of Defence. The Public Expenditure Survey Committee (PESC) system was also introduced by the Treasury in an attempt to take an integrated approach to the expenditures of Whitehall departments (Thain and Wright 1995). Policy analysis literature helps us understand the philosophy underpinning the corporate approach. The traditional approach was based very much on bottom-up 'incrementalism' (Lindblom 1959). Policy lacked any fundamental examination of services or costs. Therefore, typical developments were for services and costs to expand 'incrementally' on an annual basis. As Wildavsky (1984: 221) suggests, the incremental approach ' . . . makes calculations easily because it is not comprehensive . . . it is neutral in regard to policy'. By contrast, corporate management is based much more on a top-down 'rational' approach which its proponents tend to see as apolitical (see Simon 1976: chap. iv). Corporate planning (to use the name by which it was originally called) involves identifying needs, setting objectives, considering ways of meeting these objectives, evaluating the impacts, taking decisions, translating into management action and monitoring outcomes (Stewart 1971: 30).

The benefits of a corporate approach filtered through to the Maud, Wheatley and Redcliffe-Maud investigations. Some councils such as the GLC and Coventry had already experimented with PPB systems. However, specific development work was needed to examine the issues in more detail. As a consequence of the Wheatley Report, the Paterson Committee was established (under the chairmanship of the County Clerk of Lanark) to examine the organisation and management structures of Scottish councils (Paterson Report 1973). Based on the recommendations of the Redcliffe-Maud report, a similar investigation was conducted south of the border in the form of the Bains Committee (Bains Report 1972). The recommendations of both were remarkably similar, although there were some differences and Paterson was more sceptical of PPB-style systems (Rhodes and Midwinter 1980). A summary of Paterson's recommendations are contained in figure 4.2. While legal powers were to remain vested in the council as a whole, internal processes were to be reorganised on hierarchical lines to bring leadership and direction on both the councillor and officer sides. For councillors, a rationalised committee system would be given direction by the powerful Policy and Resources

(P&R) committee of senior councillors. In parallel, officers would be given direction by a Chief Executive and a Management team.

Figure 4.2   A summary of the main recommendations of the 1973 Paterson Report into the organisation and management of councils in Scotland.

Policy and Resources Committee: Responsible for: setting out fundamental objectives of the council; co-ordinating the work of other committees; monitoring and reviewing service committees and departments.

Programme Area Committees: Where possible, committees and departments should group together their activities on a 'programme area' basis, i.e. activities closely related in purpose or end result.

Chief Executive: Appointed as the head of an authority's paid service. He would be the principal advisor on general policy matters, would co-ordinate advice with regard to forward planning of objectives and services, and provide leadership of the management team in order to deliver a corporate approach to the affairs of the council.

Management Team: To act as a focus for preparing and presenting to the council co-ordinated advice on individual policies and more general programmes of work.

Note: Paterson recognised that authorities varied considerably in size, functions, population, location and geographical area covered. As a consequence, it was envisaged that the specific application of corporate structures would vary from council to council.

Source: Paterson Report (1973).

The Heath Government did not legislate to introduce corporate structures. It had other priorities such as the imposition of an unpopular prices and incomes policy, the coal dispute, and a sharp rise in world oil prices (McConnell 1995: 49–51). Ministers felt that councils would voluntarily take on board the main thrust of the recommendations for a corporate approach. There seemed to be broad support for the move from many Conservative councils (who welcomed a greater role for private sector practices in the running of councils) and from Labour councils (who saw corporate management as a means of strategic planning for community needs).

Implementation of the Corporate Approach

In practice, most councils in Scotland adopted Paterson-type corporate structures. A survey by Midwinter found, based on responses from 62 of the 65 councils, that:

- 90 per cent of councils had adopted a corporate management approach in principle;
- 80 per cent had wholly or partly changed their departmental structures in line with Paterson principles; and
- 85 per cent had a Policy and Resources/Policy and Finance/Policy Committee. (Midwinter 1978: 24–8)

In reality, this apparent conversion to corporate decision-making and management was not quite what it seemed. Rhodes and Midwinter (1980: 103) suggest that in the majority of cases, this conversion was only 'skin deep'. Unifying corporate structures had been introduced but authorities continued to operate largely in the old, entrenched, departmental ways. The post-1976 pressures on local authority funding had put an end to incremental growth in local authority budgets. Therefore, the financial and political uncertainties of this new climate made it very difficult to engage in long-term strategic planning. The internal logic of corporate management also contained a number of contradictions. Any system based on hierarchy and leadership is, by definition, exclusive of those interests below the apex. Many back-bencher councillors were reluctant to see their power siphoned off to a P&R committee, Chief Executive and management team. Equally, many professionals saw it as 'a threat, invading areas of operation previously regarded as sacrosanct . . .' (Young 1977: 90). This is especially the case in a climate of fiscal retrenchment where difficult choices had to be made about service priorities and budgetary restraint. A survey by a Scottish District Councils Working Party set up by the Local Authorities' Management Services Advisory Committee (LAMSAC) summarised the problems:

> Authorities have not found it easy to secure a methodical and objective application of the corporate approach . . . It has not emerged that the establishment of priorities among very diverse services can be resolved with mathematical precision. Judgement, that is to say, political decision, is required but it has been found difficult to involve elected members in the early stages of the corporate processes. As a result, policies already far advanced may be subjected to changes when their practical implications turn out to be politically unacceptable. (LAMSAC 1980: 8)

Why, in this context, did the vast majority of Scottish local authorities actually adopt corporate structures? As Rhodes and Midwinter (1980: 97) suggest: 'The Paterson proposals were adopted because they were available at a time when local authorities required quick solutions to problems.' The reorganisation in 1975 resulted in enormous upheaval and the corporate approach seemed like a unifying force. Also, in the economic climate of the mid to late 1970s – high inflation, rising unemployment, public expenditure cutbacks – councils could no longer be complacent about their future. Therefore, adopting corporate structures seems to have been something of a coping strategy on the part of most Scottish councils. Some did genuinely engage with the new philosophy, and there were variations based on size, internal politics, functional diversity, degree of change required and relative costs of implementation (see Rhodes and Midwinter 1980). Nevertheless, available evidence seems to indicate that changes in structures were not accompanied by equivalent changes in processes (Scottish Office Central Research Unit 1997). Indeed, a corporate approach to decision structures seemed to wane. By the early 1990s, a study found with regard to P&R committees a mixture of councils with (1) no committee (2) a committee with little or no power (3) a committee with limited power and (4) a powerful committee (Scottish Office Central Research Unit 1997: 15–18).

In many respects, the Paterson Report was more modest than Bains in terms of the benefits of a corporate approach. It saw it in gradualist terms: more as an aid to improving decision-making rather than a quick fix for all the problems of local authorities (Midwinter 1982). Perhaps, therefore, its limitation as a 'useful side effect . . . on decision-making' (Ferguson 1984: 29) is not so surprising after all.

1979–97: The Impact of the Conservatives: Fragmentation and 'Depoliticisation'

As Stoker argues:

> What happened to British local government during the period of Conservative government from 1979 to 1997 was in many respects a brutal illustration of power politics . . . The spending, functions and

> structure of local government had been restructured at the behest of a central government capable of imposing its will against considerable but limited resistance from local authorities. (Stoker 1999: 1)

Many of the ideas supporting these changes can be encapsulated under the term New Public Management (NPM). In many respects its ideas may not be quite as coherent or as radical as we might think (Lowndes 1999), but they are reasonably consistent. NPM draws on the work of free market proponents such as Friedman and Hayek, has intellectual underpinnings in the 'public choice' approach of Downs, Buchanan and Tullock and Niskanen (Dunleavy 1991), and is influenced by think-tanks such as the Adam Smith Institute and the Institute of Economic Affairs. It aims to minimise bureaucracy, promote free markets, focus on performance, and decentralise power to citizens (John 2001: 99). Added to this is sheer gut-instinct politics against what Mrs Thatcher (1977: 2) described as 'the whole fallacy of socialism'. The outcome in terms of local government (apart from the general trends identified by Stoker) was to challenge the internal organisation of councils in a number of ways. The main aspects were UK-wide, but there was some variance in the Scottish dimensions. Three particular developments can be identified.

First, the advent and extension of Compulsory Competitive Tendering (CCT) in 1980, 1988 and 1992 created a tension at the heart of local authorities (see Chapter 8 for further details). As a consequence of having to bid for work which they had previously undertaken themselves, they took on a dual role: as a client (buyer of services) and a contractor (seller of services) (Mallabar 1991: 153–7). This had an impact on the internal structures of Scottish councils. It meant that the decision-making process surrounding the awarding and monitoring of contracts had to be kept separate from the process surrounding the bidding for and provision of services. Ministerial regulations prohibited conflicts of interest on the officers' side and discouraged such conflicts by requiring councillors to declare interests. There was, however, no legislative requirement to adopt specific organisational structures.

As a consequence, Scottish councils took guidance from the Accounts Commission and COSLA, and ultimately took their own decisions with regard to internal structures and procedures. Variability of practice was the result – typically affecting the organisation of departments as well as committee structures. The practice of separating the client–contractor roles was variable.

A study by Ogden (1994: 253) of 11 Scottish local authorities found councils operating Direct Service Operations (DSOs) that were single service DSOs, dual service DSOs, multi-service DSOs, and super DSOs covering all services. A later study by Kane (1996) of seven Scottish councils revealed substantial but varied fragmentation of departments in order to cope with these dual roles. For example, Tayside Region operated a full split within the context of a multidisciplinary DSO whilst Perth and Kinross operated a partial split because the heads of department were responsible for both sets of duties. The study also dealt with how the client-contractor split had an impact on committee structures. Midlothian District Council established a Contract Services Committee; another had a Contractor's Sub-Committee of the Resources Committee; and another developed client and contractor sub-committees for cleansing although the Convenor and Vice-Convenor were common to both. More generally, Kane (1996) found committee structures to be underdeveloped. The reasons include councils' political strategies and attitudes to workforce pay and conditions. In many respects, there seems to have been a reasonable degree of continuity from the past, as councils struggled to balance the central imperatives of CCT with the practical and political implications for the workings of the council. The general tendency, however, was for CCT to fragment council decision-making structures and processes.

Second, the Conservatives tried to remove what they considered to be the unnecessary 'politicisation' of council business. The context to this is the turmoil in central–local relations in the early to mid 1980s and a heightened resistance to the Thatcherite policies of rate-capping, penalties for overspending and so on (Duncan and Goodwin 1988; Butcher et al. 1990; Stoker 1991). Two particular concerns of the government with regard to council decision-making were (1) committee membership and chairmanship being allocated on the basis of party affiliation and (2) party groups deciding a policy line in advance of the full council and committee meetings. The Widdecombe Committee was given the responsibility of investigating the conduct of local authority business and it reported in 1986. To the dismay of many ministers, Widdecombe provided a classic defence of the virtues of local government (see Chapter 1). It also argued that the power of party politics had a long, worthwhile tradition in local government, and that it should not be replaced by a 'theoretical' model 'transplanted' from elsewhere.

The Government ignored the more 'localist' leanings of Widdecombe and concentrated on putting an end to what it perceived as unnecessary political biases in local decision-making. The means of doing so was the Local Government and Housing Act 1989. It introduced a number of measures such as a new code of conduct for councillors, the creation of 'politically restricted posts' for officers above a certain level on the National Joint Council pay scale, and the necessity for all officer appointments to be based on merit rather than political sympathies (Scottish Local Government Information Unit 1989). With specific regard to committees, it gave the Secretary of State the power to impose a set of model standing orders for the conduct of meetings. In Scotland, initial discussions between the Scottish Office and COSLA eventually faded away, in part due to the fact that councils in Scotland had their own standing orders which contained nothing of serious consequence that would antagonise ministers. A more lasting legacy of the Act was the requirement for all council committees and sub-committees to be comprised of groups as close as possible to the balance of groups on the full council (Scottish Local Government Information Unit 1989).

The sum total of the Conservative reforms was an attempt to introduce a particular set of values into local decision-making structures and processes. The Conservative Government saw it as preventing the unnecessary introduction of 'politics' into the running of councils. Opponents felt that the Government's notion of 'politics' effectively equated with councillors who might not agree with Government policies towards local authorities. Therefore, from this viewpoint, the legislation had more to do with suppressing political opponents than it did with genuinely trying to improve the workings of councils. When we add the fragmentation resulting from CCT, the shift (on the surface) seems to be from a more corporate approach to one which lacks coherence either from strategy or politics. Whether this happened in practice is another matter. Little research has been done on these issues in Scotland, although one study by Richard Kerley for the Scottish Office Central Research Unit (1997) entitled *Local Authority Organisation and Management in Scotland 1975–1996* contained interesting findings. Based on extensive interviews with councillors and officials, it found a remarkable continuity in the internal political management of councils. One of the major reasons for this was political inertia on the part of councillors who were generally quite happy with modes of working such as the committee system, confrontational politics, and clear lines laid down by party groups. Perhaps, therefore, the informal political interplay of actors at the local level in terms of their decision-making is much better placed than we might think to survive reforms inspired by the centre. We will return to this issue in the Conclusion.

Post-1996: Unitary Authorities and the Modernisation of Political Management Arrangements

In order to understand developments in Scotland, it is useful to provide a context by outlining developments south of the border. From 1997 onwards, a commitment to 'modernisation' of the public sector was at the forefront of the New Labour agenda as embodied in the White Paper *Modernising Government* (Cm 4310 1999). Modernisation is something of a catch-all term to cover a multitude of issues and this is exemplified in the modernisation of local government. It includes not just the rethinking of arrangements for council decision-making, but also reforms which encourage electoral participation, facilitate greater community consultation, encourage partnerships with community bodies, improve ethical frameworks, increase financial support for councillors, review central funding, encourage exchanges of ideas and develop IT capabilities (Pratchett 2002). In a sense, every single New Labour policy for local government might fall within the umbrella of 'modernisation' (see Stewart 2003 for an overview).

Our focus in the current chapter is councils' decision-making arrangements. The Conservatives had previously tackled this issue in the early 1990s as part of the proposals for wider structural reforms of councils (Stewart 1995; Stewart 2003). Secretary of State for the Environment Michael Heseltine was particularly keen on elected mayors as a means of increasing the accountability and transparency of decision-making in local authorities. A Scottish variant of the proposals was produced (Scottish Office 1993) although it came to nothing and reform possibilities languished in the background until New Labour came to office and developed its 'modernisation' programme. Issues were dealt with in a series of six initial consultation papers and then brought together in *Modern Local Government: In Touch With the People* (Cm 4014 1998). In a section providing the rationale for reform, it outlined perceived weaknesses with the existing system:

- Traditional committee structures result in inefficient and opaque decision-making. Many key decisions are not taken in the committees themselves, but by political groups or even a few elites within the majority group. As a result, many councillors are not influential in shaping council decisions.
- Councillors are burdened with too many meetings, often of little consequence because decisions have effectively been taken elsewhere.
- There is a lack of clear political leadership. The root problem is council structures rather than the quality of individuals.
- There is a lack of transparency in decision-making, and people do not know who to hold to account in the event of problems. (Cm 4014 1998: 18)

If a government reacts against the failings of a centralised system it will often seek to disperse it. If the problem is seen to be one of lack of cohesiveness and clarity, it will often seek some form of integration. In this instance, the solution was the former, a modernised version of corporate leadership. The Local Government Act 2000 requires that all local authorities in England with a population in excess of 85,000 adopt one of three structures:

- A directly elected mayor with substantial powers of decision and delegation, plus a cabinet executive, appointed by the mayor and drawn from the ranks of councillors.
- A leader who is appointed by the council, plus a cabinet executive, drawn from the ranks of councillors.
- A directly elected mayor to provide broad policy direction, plus a council manager who has executive powers. (Wilson and Game 2002: 100–3)

These initiatives represent a fundamental break from the tradition of local decision-making. For the first time in modern British local government, there is a separation of executive decision-taking from scrutiny roles. On the one hand, an identifiable political executive exists to facilitate quick decision-making, offer transparency, and promote accountability (Cm 4014 1998). On the other hand, non-executive councillors are freed up to 'represent their area or special interests, to scrutinise and monitor the political executive and administration and to challenge other organisations in the locality about their performance' (Stoker 1998: 126). As Stewart suggests (2003: 76–8), however, the distinction between these in practice is not as clear-cut. Authorities have interpreted the legislation in different ways and there has been some confusion on the part of many councils. The systems also contain weakness, including a danger of executive overload (having to deal with too many decisions) and too much scrutiny (because this function is already built into Best Value) (Stewart 2003: 78–82). It also fails to tackle the real source of power within councils – the party group (Copus 2001a; Midwinter 2001).

The Scottish pathway has been different to that in England and Wales. The McIntosh Commission was established in January 1998 to consider the building of relations between local government and the Scottish Parliament, as well as ways in which councils could make themselves more democratic and responsive to local communities. After extensive consultation with a wide range of interests including councillors, officials, community groups, trade unions, COSLA, the media, general public, and businesses, the McIntosh had sympathy for the public view that '. . . council and committee meetings are a charade; the business comes pre-packaged, usually from a party group, and the meeting is either a pure formality, finished in minutes, or taken up by political jousting' (Scottish Office 1999a: 26). It also concurred with the view that councillors were overburdened with paperwork. Its solution was the separation of the executive and scrutiny functions of councils, but it was more cautious (compared with the approach in England and Wales) as to how this should be done. It wanted to give councils the opportunity in the first instance to voluntarily change their internal structures. Therefore, it recommended that councils review their decision-making arrangements, paying particular attention to executive models and more simplified committee structures (Scottish Office 1999a).

Two investigations were established as a direct result of the McIntosh Report. The first was the Renewing Local Democracy Working Group, chaired by Richard Kerley of the University of Edinburgh (Report of the Renewing Local Democracy Working Group 2000). Its principle focus was on ways of making council membership more attractive to a wide cross-section of the community, and improving the representative basis of councils (see Chapter 5). With more emphasis on the workings of councils, the

Leadership Advisory Panel (LAP) was established under the Chair of Alistair McNish, former Chief Executive of South Lanarkshire. Its final report did not favour any particular option for decision-making structures. Its general tone was one of finding solutions which were based on local needs and circumstances. Nevertheless, it did set the agenda by clearly identifying the criteria against which councils should conduct self-reviews and measure their proposals for change:

- 'Council business should be managed in such a way that policy proposals and matters for decision by the Council are subject to open debate.'
- 'The Council must be able to effectively scrutinise the actions of the leadership or Executive and hold it to account for its performance.'
- 'The work of the Council should take place, as far as possible, in public and free from unnecessary constraints imposed by the use of the party whip.'
- 'Council business should be organised in such a way which allows as wide a cross-section of the community as possible to realistically consider becoming a councillor.' (McNish 2001: 9–11)

Ultimately, there was no enthusiasm within Scottish councils for an elected mayor or provost. It is difficult to be precise about the reasons for this. Perhaps the Scottish psyche is more sympathetic to collective endeavours than the 'cult of the personality' approach. Whatever the rationale, Scotland has not gone down the English and Welsh routes.

The final LAP report breaks down the emerging structures into three categories. First, the vast majority of councils (23) opted to streamline their committee structures. These included Glasgow, Stirling, South Ayrshire, East Dunbartonshire, West Lothian and Angus. Many did so by reducing the number of service-specific committees and focusing more on thematic areas such as criminal justice and health care. A small minority of councils combined committee rationalisation with executive structures (Dumfries and Galloway and Falkirk) although most did not favour this pathway, at least not in the short term. The McNish Report specifically rejected the idea that committee streamlining was an 'easy option'. It suggested that councils had engaged in genuine attempts to introduce reforms which would provide strategy on cost-cutting issues, reduce paperwork, and speed up decision-making.

Second, a total of six councils opted for executive structures: the City of Edinburgh, Midlothian, East Lothian, Scottish Borders, West

Dunbartonshire and East Renfrewshire. Under these arrangements, responsibility for the majority of strategic decisions is devolved by the full council to an executive comprised of between 5 and 13 elected members. As an illustration, the structure of the City of Edinburgh's committees is depicted in figure 4.3. In five out of the six councils mentioned above, the executive is limited to members of the ruling party on the council, although in one instance (East Lothian) the leader of the opposition is also included. A further two councils (Dumfries and Galloway, and Falkirk) did not formally declare that they had executive structures, but nevertheless adopted a streamlined committee or executive configuration in all but name. Regardless of the composition of the executive or the specific labels given to structures, a major function of non-executive councillors is a scrutiny function of the activities of the executive.

A third and final modernisation theme is the introduction of devolved or partially devolved structures. Three councils in remote and/or large areas (Argyll and Bute, Highland, and Fife) introduced area committees in order to devolve decision-making as close as possible to local communities. More generally, the McNish Report was keen to emphasise that local decision-making structures should not reach an 'end point'. They should be revisited regularly and adapted where appropriate. Further research is needed to ascertain the effectiveness of the post-McIntosh and McNish developments, but some provisional comments can nevertheless be made.

Will the reforms actually alter the dominance of political parties in council decision-making? Certainly, the climate seems to be conducive. The legal requirements for Best Value and Community Planning as prescribed in the Local Government in Scotland Act 2003 are designed to ensure that service improvement and community consultation are major priorities for Scottish councils (see Chapter 8 for further discussion). One would imagine that these are powerful forces working against political parties if they seek to adopt a relatively inward-looking approach. However, we should not rush to declare political parties to be in decline at the local level. A detailed survey of councillors and officials in Scotland by McAteer and Orr found that roughly half of the councillors from the three main parties felt that party whipping was necessary for 'tough decisions'. For councillors of the Labour Party, the dominant party in Scottish local government, the figure was 67 per cent (McAteer and Orr 2003: 72). The survey also found that

Figure 4.3 An example of executive decision-making structures – City of Edinburgh Council.

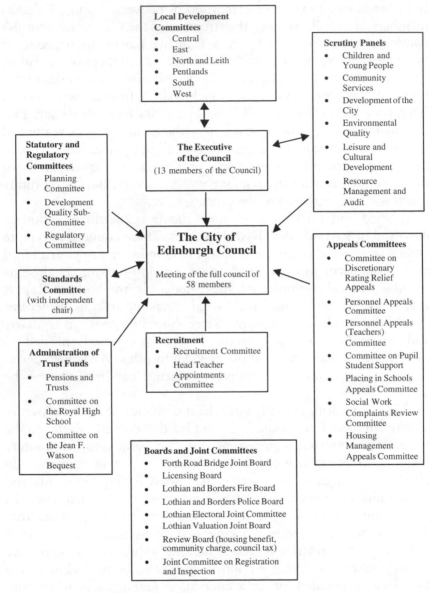

Source: City of Edinburgh Council,
http://www.edinburgh.gov.uk/CEC/Committee_Services/New_Cabinet_Style_Government/cabinetgov.html

council leaders, office bearers and non-office bearers were all of the opinion that raising an issue through the political group was the most important means of influencing council decisions (McAteer and Orr 2003: 76). The broad conclusion, therefore, is that 'the attempts to "modernise" Scottish local authorities has [sic] not resulted in the decline of political parties and diminution of the "political" nature of decision making' (McAteer and Orr 2003: 80). This accords with the view of Copus whose examination of party groups on a UK-wide basis leads him to conclude that:

> our council chambers will still remain controlled by blocs of councilors cohering around a party political label and largely developing policy, making decisions, distributing patronage and conducting council affairs with party label as the first point of reference and with party advantage as of prime importance. (Copus 2001a: 62)

This has further implications for the role of local people in decision-making forums (see Chapter 5 for more detailed discussion). McAteer and Orr (2003) found in their interviews with community activists a sense that access and influence had got better but there was still a long way to go. Midwinter (2001) goes further and argues that providing additional resources for councils is more liable to engage the public and improve local services than tinkering with organisational structures and processes. Midwinter's point is a valid one but there is a deeper issue. From the point of view of central government (in Edinburgh or Westminster), the modernisation of council decision-making processes enables it to get the best of both worlds. On the one hand, it confers additional legitimacy on local authorities (and the centre because it oversees the processes of change). After all, who would argue against local authorities being 'modernised', transparent and accountable? On the other, the processes of reform bypass the enormous power of party groups. 'Missing the target' in this way may or may not be intentional. Whatever the case, to legislate against party groups (such as banning the use of the whip) would be to destroy the grassroots cohesiveness of local parties – the building block for the success of parties at the national level (see Chapter 7).

Conclusion – Continuity rather than Discontinuity

Local decision-making structures and processes have undergone numerous changes from the immediate post-war period through to the 'modernised' arrangements adopted by the 32 single tier councils in the post-devolution era. Two particular issues are worth highlighting which suggest that the commonalities are more important than the differences.

Scotland has at times departed from developments south of the border. For example: it was less enthusiastic in adopting the proposals of the Maud Report in the late 1960s; it was more cautious about the benefits of corporate decision-making in the 1970s; and it was sceptical of the benefits to be gained from executive leadership residing in a directly elected mayor or provost. Despite these Scottish variations, however, the fundamental principles in each phase are common north and south of the border. There is a broad sharing in similar time periods of the experiences of tradition, corporatism, fragmentation and depoliticisation, and modernisation. The historical parallels, therefore, are more evident than the dissimilarities.

Second, we should distinguish between the formal and the informal sources of power and decision-making (Bachrach and Baratz 1970). Despite the fact that formal power resides with the full council as a corporate body, evidence suggests that actual decision-making power is much more complex than this. The traditional practices of the early post-war period masked the domination of officers, whilst subsequent reforms have altered formal structures but been unable to diminish the growing power of party groups. Officers are also a further source of power and their position in relation to councillors is explored in the next chapter. Only the limited adoption of elected mayors in England represents a serious threat to this long-standing informal source of power. Otherwise, it can be argued that changes to local decision-making structures may come and go, but the subterranean relationships between councillors, party groups and officers should be our real focus if we wish properly to understand who holds power over local decisions.

?	Key Questions	?

1. What are the main elements of continuity in council decision-making structures over the years in Scotland?
2. To what extent are Scottish councils truly 'modernised' in their approach to decision-making?
3. To what extent do the formal decision-making structures of Scottish local authorities mirror the real sources of power?

4. Would the English model of elected mayors be suitable for Scotland?

Further Reading

Dearlove (1979) provides an excellent example of how local decision-making and management structures can best be understood in their wider political context. The advent of corporate management in Scotland is given unrivalled treatment by Midwinter (1978, 1982) and Rhodes and Midwinter (1980). *The Changing Politics of Local Government* by Gyford, Game and Leach (1989) is based on work undertaken for the Widdicombe Committee and provides a thorough examination of local politics in the 1980s and the preceding years. A highly impressive book on New Labour's modernisation of local government is Stewart (2003), *Modernising British Local Government*. It includes not only the development of New Labour ideas in local government, but also a critique of them. The most up-to-date work on the Scottish situation is an article in *Public Policy and Administration* by McAteer and Orr (2003).

Useful Websites

http://www.scotland.gov.uk/library/documents-w10/clg-00.htm
The Report of the Commission on Local Government and the Scottish Parliament (McIntosh Report). This report started the process of modernisation in Scottish councils.

http://www.scotland.gov.uk/library3/localgov/rlap-00.asp
Report of the Leadership Advisory Panel, chaired by Alistair McNish.

http://www.scotland.gov.uk/library2/doc16/rldw.pdf
Report of the Renewing Local Democracy Working Group, chaired by Richard Kerley.

http://www.tagish.co.uk/tagish/links/localgov.htm
A directory of links to the websites of local authorities throughout the UK. Most contain some details of their decision-making structures.

CHAPTER FIVE

Councillors, Elections and the Electoral System: A Healthy Democratic Foundation?

It is generally recognised, as Beetham (1996: 4) suggests, that 'the model of elected local government has much greater intrinsic potential for realising democratic values than a centrally-organised system of local administration'. The benefits of local democracy include the spreading of societal power, the encouraging of participation, and responsive government based on local needs and preferences. The reality of local democracy is less straightforward. This chapter explores a number of issues surrounding the 'health' of local democracy in Scotland, focusing on its foundations: councillors, elections and the electoral system. It should be read in conjunction with Chapter 6 which examines the impact on democracy of non-electoral forms of public participation and the growth of non-elected local governance.

The Multiple Roles of Councillors: Representative, Politician and Manager

Scotland's 1,222 councillors are elected to office and have multifaceted roles although they have no specific legal 'job description'. Rather, their roles have developed historically, based around a variety of expectations and each councillor's personal interpretation. We can identify three broad roles of councillors in Scotland and examine each in turn: (1) representative role; (2) party politician role; and (3) management role.

Representative Role

Potentially, councillors may be representative in two particular respects. First, we may have expectations of microcosmic representation. Judge (1999) traces the arguments of Jeremy Bentham, John Stuart Mill, James Mill and others, suggesting that the social characteristics of elected representatives should reflect the social characteristics of the electorate as a whole. We may of course not have any such expectations, but if we do, local government (as with all levels of government) is found wanting. Scotland's councillors are not typical of the Scottish electorate as a whole. The last two surveys conducted were of the 1999 and 2003 intakes of councillors (Vestri and Fitzpatrick 2000; Scottish Executive Social Research 2003). In summary, the general profile of councillors exhibits a number of biases in comparison to the profile of the Scottish population. Councillors are overwhelmingly male. In terms of those elected in 2003, 78.2 per cent were male – a slight increase on the figure of 77 per cent for 1999 (Scottish Executive Social Research 2003: 9; Vestri and Fitzpatrick 2000: 63). Councillors also tend to be older than the population as a whole. In 2003, only 4.3 per cent of councillors were under 35 years of age, yet 25.1 per cent of the population is in this category (Scottish Executive Social Research 2003: 10). At the other end of the scale, 56.3 per cent of councillors were 55 years of age or older, whereas only 36 per cent of the population is in this age group (Scottish Executive Social Research 2003: 10). Indeed, trends seem to be getting worse. In 1999, the average age of Scotland's councillors was 53 and by 2003 it had increased to 55 (Vestri and Fitzpatrick 2000: 63; Scottish Executive Social Research 2003: 11). Councillors are more likely to be middle class and hold professional qualifications. In 2003, 72.4 per cent of councillors were from the employment categories of 'Managerial/Executive', 'Professional/Technical' or 'Lecturer/ Teacher/Researcher' (Scottish Executive Social Research 2003: 19). Furthermore, the data available for candidates in 2003 (as opposed to those elected as councillors) indicates that they are almost twice as likely to belong to the highest AB social grade than the population as a whole (Scottish Executive Social Research 2003: 24). Finally, although 2 per cent of the population belong to an ethnic minority and this same percentage stood as candidates, only 1.1 per cent of councillors were from an ethnic minority background (Scottish Executive Social Research 2003: 12–13). This is an improvement of the 1999 figure of 0.5 per cent, but it still suggests an under-representation in this area (Vestri and Fitzpatrick 2000: 66–7). The blunt conclusion, therefore, is that councillors in Scotland are overwhelmingly white, professional, middle class and male. These broad patterns are replicated in England and Wales. A National Census of Councillors in 2001 found, for example, that 71 per cent of councillors south of the border were male; 86 per cent were over 45 years old, 65 per cent of those employed were in managerial or professional jobs, and only 2.5 per cent were from an ethnic minority (IDeA and EO 2001: 2).

Why do such biases exist? To take gender bias as an example, no simple answer can be provided. The situation has improved to a reasonable degree since the 1970s but women can be discouraged from standing for office for many reasons. Institutional and systemic barriers may exist. The high workload and commitment involved in being a councillor revolves around typically inflexible agendas. These are less suited to women, who tend to be the carers within their families and require greater flexibility than council business can offer. Some research undertaken in the United States also suggests that women may feel more comfortable in contesting multi-member wards where 'positive campaigning' is the norm, rather than single-member wards where the tendency is towards adversary 'opponent bashing' (Rallings and Thrasher 1997: 70). Overlapping with these issues may be cultural barriers where political networking and advancement is done within pre-existing, more status-conscious, male-dominated networks.

As indicated earlier, our perceptions will determine whether we consider such biases to be problematic. For example, we could argue that the predominance of male councillors is undesirable because they are less able to represent and be sympathetic to the interests of women and the biases they face in the family and the workplace. By contrast, we could argue that gender bias is unimportant because a 'good' councillor will have sufficient cross-cutting experience and awareness to represent both sexes effectively. Indeed we could argue that other, non-gender differences are more important. In a working-class ward, for example, it could be argued that a male councillor from a manual, trade union background would be more effective in representing the interests of working-class women and their families than a middle-class professional woman. Whatever our views, it is likely that the profile of councillors will experience some change over the next few years. In August 2003, the Scottish Executive set up the Widening Access to Council Membership Progress Group, chaired by Rowena

Arshad, Director of the Centre for Education and Racial Equality at the University of Edinburgh. It will examine ways of making council membership a more attractive option for a broader cross-section of the community.

The primary form of representation to consider is the idea that councillors should be able to represent their wards. As Rao suggests, however:

> Although the dictates of democratic theory require that elected members as representatives should attend to the interests and well-being of those represented, there is no single definitive view on such questions as how representatives should behave, what constitutes responsive behaviour, or how far representatives can stray away from public preferences and still be responsive. (Rao 1994: 36)

Councillors can be active in vastly differing ways across a range of policy, service and resource issues, and still lay claim to represent their communities. They can act more or less as a delegate – simply transmitting and acting on the view from their wards – or they may use their Burkean trustee-type autonomy to go against the explicit wishes of voters but argue that the best interests of the local community are served by doing so (Judge 1999). An important issue, therefore, is councillors' perceptions of their roles. Figure 5.1 amalgamates and adds to numerous writings on this subject (Dearlove 1973; Newton 1976; Gyford et al. 1989) and identifies key issues upon which Scotland's councillors have to make judgements. These issues or variables are by no means always compatible and councillors often have to make difficult decisions as to where their priorities lie. For example, some councillors might see their primary roles as dealing with individual constituents and their grievances. Others might be prepared to sacrifice aspects of constituency representation in order to be loyal to their party and more generally seek advancement within the party.

Variability of attitude can be found in a study of councillors in five Scottish councils (Local Government Committee 2003c: 29) for the Scottish Parliament's Local Government Committee. In the survey, over 20 per cent agreed with the view that councillors should be bound by the outcomes of public participation exercises. Correspondingly, roughly 55 per cent felt that councillors should use their judgement to interpret and carry forward as they see fit. In terms of councillor priorities, 24 per cent felt that their most

Figure 5.1   The competing priorities of councillors in Scotland.

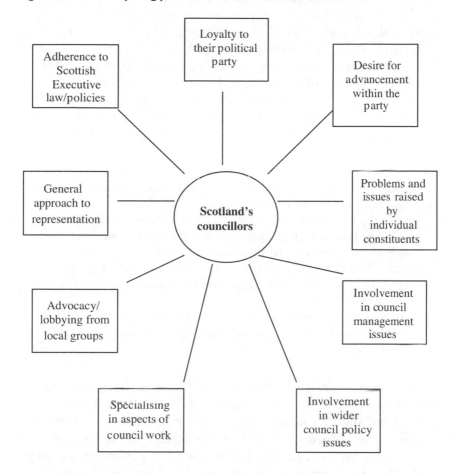

important role was giving support and advice to constituents. By contrast, representing a political party was considered the least important role. We will return to this point shortly.

If councillors' perceptions of representation vary from one individual to another, what *is* constant is a number of key factors which are potential barriers to councillors' abilities to represent their local communities. Four are worthy of particular mention. First, as detailed in Chapter 1, councillors must operate within the legislative and financial framework determined by the Scottish Executive. Thus, local authorities are not sovereign over their responsibilities. The freedom of councillors to 'represent' has clear boundaries within which they must operate or face penalties from the Standards Commission for Scotland. Second, there is the long-standing argument that the real source of power in councils is appointed officials rather than elected, generalist councillors. Kingdom (1991: 156) summaries the basis of officer power as being their permanence, expertise, numbers, social status, ability to control the flow of information, and role in implementation. Wilson and Game (2002: 303) counter this perspective and suggest that power within councils is determined by a series of factors which cannot be encapsulated by a simple 'technocratic' model. These are:

- *Intra-party influences*: Relations within local parties and between party groups and the wider party (such as party factions and back-bench influence).
- *Inter-departmental influences*: Relations between departments and professions (for example, departmental conflicts over corporate priorities, and professional rivalries).
- *Intra-departmental influences*: Relations within departments (such as friction within departments, and decentralisation of decision-making).
- *Inter-party influences*: Relations between party groups, especially in authorities with no overall control by a single party (for example, minority administrations).

The implication drawn by Wilson and Game is that power within councils is influenced by a multitude of factors. The outcome is a series of shifting alliances, varying from issue to issue and from time to time. One consequence is that the traditional divide between policy and administration is simply not as pervasive as we might think. Thus to varying degrees, the ability of Scotland's councillors to 'represent' local communities is compromised.

A third limitation is the Best Value regime (see Chapter 8). For all its actual and potential benefits, it is an enormous bureaucratic exercise for councils, involving highly detailed and specialist involvement in matters such as Best Value Plans, Performance Management Planning Systems, Public Performance Reporting, and quality management tools such as the Business Excellence Model, and the Balanced Scorecard. A strand running through some of the Best Value Task Force Reports and the periodic audits by the Accounts Commission on the progress of Best Value is the role of elected members. A second appraisal-round in late 1998 found that: 'To date, Best Value has been driven by officers' (quoted in SLGIU 2000: 1). A report produced on behalf of the Accounts Commission by Audit

Scotland (2001: 21–2) found that about one-third of councils didn't fully involve elected members in the Best Value regime in any systematic way: 'Where Best Value is seen as a managerial issue best left to officers, it is less likely to have a real impact in delivering cost-effective, user-focused services.' We should hardly be surprised if the complexities and specialisms required to implement Best Value create difficulties for member involvement. Indeed, an added complexity is that the Best Value regime requires a customer or citizen focus, resulting in council consultation with the public through area forums, questionnaires, citizens' juries, public meetings and so on. Whilst most of us would applaud such initiatives, they do present a further challenge to the power of councillors to 'represent' as they see fit. One additional point to note is the argument by Midwinter and McGarvey (1999) that Best Value is not a radical break from the past: it exhibits strong elements of continuity in terms of drives for efficiency and effectiveness. Perhaps, therefore, the constraint on councillor autonomy is less one of Best Value *per se* and more one of the new public management ethos which has bureaucratised and fragmented local service delivery in the quest for value for money – leaving many councillors disengaged on the sidelines.

A fourth potential limitation on the ability of councillors to represent their constituents is the expectation of their parties that they will adhere to the party line. On occasions, these two different sets of expectations may be perfectly compatible, but in others there may be what Copus (2001b: 152) describes as a 'crisis of representation'. Imagine the situation where a councillor is a member of a ruling party group that has a policy to support school closures because of over-capacity in the local authority area. If one of the schools is in the councillor's particular ward, they are faced with the situation of a clear choice as to which set of interests to support. A study of councillors in five Scottish local authorities found in excess of 66 per cent of councillors recognising that they are torn between representing party and representing ward in relation to public participation exercises (Local Government Committee 2003c: 40). The demands of 'party' are such that they form part of the general roles of most councillors. We can now explore this issue in more depth.

Party Politician Role

Most of Scotland's councillors stand for election on a party ticket and the trend is increasing. In 1974, 67 per cent of councillors were selected by a party (Bochel and Bochel 1998: 30). Subsequent figures are 1995 (86.3 per cent) and 1999 (88.2 per cent) (Bochel and Denver 2000: 123). In 2003, the figure fell slightly to 81.1 per cent (see Chapter 7 for further discussion). Councillors of the same party on each council form a party group. Byrne (2000) identifies the main role of party groups as being:

- Choosing committee members, party group leader and council convenor and other senior posts.
- Formulating council policies.
- Deciding the group's attitude to policy proposals emerging from sources such as chief officers and committee reports.
- Deciding tactics on debates and votes.
- Ensuring party discipline and unified voting.
- Keeping members informed on key issues.
- Scrutinising existing policy and administration
- Promoting co-ordination of the authority's policy and administration.

The demands of party discipline are considerable and at times formidable. The UK Labour Party has Model Standing Orders which Scottish Labour Party councillors are bound by (Copus 1999). There is little room for interpretation and manoeuvre. Indeed, there is no recognition within the Standing Orders that councillors have to perform ward-specific tasks. Model Standing Orders of the SNP are almost equally as firm. They do recognise ward-based representation activities and abstention is permitted. Other than this, failure to attend group meetings is a disciplinary offence and there must be no criticism inside or outside the chamber of group policy or members (Copus 1999). Slightly more flexible are the Model Standing Orders for Liberal Democrat councillors which come from the Association of Liberal Democrat Councillors rather than the Party itself. There is an explicit recognition of the right of councillors to deal with ward issues, although requirements for group loyalty are still remarkably similar to those of Labour and the SNP. In recent years, the Conservatives have moved away from a more decentralist approach, and adopted model rules which are roughly akin to those of the Liberal Democrats, attempting to balance party loyalty with distaste for central direction.

The national rules for local party groups may be slightly different but the importance of the groups themselves cannot be overstated.

Copus offers an astute observation of what goes on behind closed doors, away from public scrutiny in formal council meetings:

> local government in Britain is party government . . . local . . . representation is viewed by the councillor through the prism of the political party group. The majority of council chambers consist of organised, disciplined and publicly united blocs of councillors, cohering around a political party label and speaking and voting, largely as one. The experience of council politics shared by most councillors, irrespective of political affiliation, is one of party group meetings, debating policy options, exploring political problems, planning tactics and ensuring certainty of action amongst members in the public meetings of full council and committees. The Party group is arguably the most important forum for political deliberation and decision-making in British local government. (Copus 2001a: 53)

We should not think, however, that councillors in Scotland slavishly adhere to the party line simply because they are forced to. Rather, councillors in each group share broad common ideologies and they want to win votes. No matter how much some groups may be ridden by factions, they will tend to put differences aside at crucial times because they detest the opposition even more. Pragmatism is also important. Councillors have to deal with many complex issues and, even if they wanted to, they cannot possibly grasp the fine detail of every single issue upon which they have to make judgement. This is especially the case in full council when most of the work will have been done by colleagues on other committees or (more likely) senior party and officer elites. Thus, voting 'with the party' is often a convenient move for councillors because it is a means of cutting through the morass of complex issues.

Before we become too attracted to the notion that common ideas and pragmatism are the sole unifying forces, the political reality is that potential sanctions for failing to obey the party also come into play. There may be immediate threats such as removal from party posts or removal of the whip (in effect, being thrown out of the party group), or loss of candidacy at the next election. A more intangible sanction is the blocking of career prospects within the party. A study by Bochel and Bochel (1998) of councillors in Scotland found a surprisingly high number (48 per cent) indicating a preference for seeking election in a devolved Scottish Parliament, an independent Scottish Parliament, Westminster or the European Parliament. In the

1999 intake to the Scottish Parliament, 41 MSPs were or had been councillors at one time. The 2003 intake increased this slightly to 47 (Burnside et al. 2003: 38). The existence of the Scottish Parliament does provide a more accessible career structure for councillors if they wish. Therefore, adherence to 'party' can have long-term benefits.

One could argue that in twenty-first-century Scotland, the growth of participative devices such as citizens' juries and community forums poses a challenge to the dominance of parties. This is true, but perhaps we should not rush to proclaim the diminution of party power. The dominance of national voting patterns in local elections and the demands of party loyalty have remained fundamentally stable over the past two decades and more. In effect, party groups have 'slipped through the net' of local government modernisation, and their prominence in the working life of Scotland's councillors remains fundamentally unchanged (see Chapter 4 for further discussion).

Management Role

Councillors are heavily involved in 'managing', in the sense that they sit on a variety of committees (sometimes as convenor or deputy convenor) and take regular decisions on the formation and implementation of council policy. The workload of a councillor is considerable and amounts, in effect, to a full-time job. Martlew (1988: 51) in his study of Scottish councillors found that in 1983, they worked an average of 31 hours per week. A subsequent study for the Scottish Local Government Information Unit (1995: 20) found that councillors anticipated spending between 31 and 40 hours per week on council business. Further studies in 1999 found an average workload of 36 to 37 hours per week (Vestri and Fitzpatrick 2000: 71). There is as yet no study of workload for the 2003 intake but there is little reason to expect any significant difference from previous research. We should also be alert to variations depending on the type of council. For example, Bochel and Bochel (1998: 40–1) in their study of Scotland's councillors over the 1974–95 period found it not uncommon for councillors in small authorities to be on all committees. Where committee membership was limited, the median figure was four. In 2003, 52.1 per cent of councillors were in full- or part-time employment. Only 22.7 per cent were 'full time', although the demands of council work equate to those in a full-time job, and so a strong degree of employer flexibility is required (Vestri and Fitzpatrick 2000: 18). Councillors are more liable to come from the public and quasi-public sectors than anywhere else. In Scotland, about one quarter of all jobs are public and voluntary sector jobs, whereas 52.2 per cent of employed councillors in 2003 come from these sectors (Scottish Executive Social Research 2003: 20). This contrasts slightly with the situation in England and Wales, where 61 per cent of councillors in 2001 came from the private sector (IDeA and EO 2001: 2). A further difference with England may be in terms of workload. Although no recent figures are available, it is possible that the time demands of being a councillor in a unitary authority are greater than required under the county-district system which exists in most areas of England.

The biggest single issue in this context is whether councillors should be paid salaries commensurate with the workload and responsibilities involved. The system of councillors' allowances has taken various twists and turns over the years, but the current system came into operation in 1995 and is detailed in figure 5.2. Councillors without special responsibilities average about £6,000 per annum, whilst councillors with special responsibilities such as convenor and council leaders average just over £13,000 per annum (Report of the Renewing Local Democracy Working Group 2000: 40). Historically, remuneration has tended to be greater in Scotland than south of the border. There is no obvious reason for this, other than the fact that workloads have tended to be a bit higher in Scotland. In 2001–2, for example, the average annual allowance in England was £4,380 (Wilson and Game 2002: 255).

Figure 5.2   System of councillor remuneration in Scotland, 1995 onwards.

Basic Allowance: Payable to each councillor, depending on population size. Amount varies between £5,800 and £6,969 per annum.

Special Responsibility Allowance (SRA): Payable at the discretion of local authorities to councillors with additional responsibilities such as committee chair, leader of the council, and provost. In 1997, approximately two-thirds of councillors received SRA, averaging £7,510.

Travel and Subsistence Allowance: Payable by councils for expenditures incurred by councillors on council business. The maximum rate is decided by Scottish Executive ministers.

Attendance Allowance: An option, used by only some councils.

Source: Adapted from Scottish Parliament Information Centre (2002b: 1–2).

There are two main sets of arguments regarding councillors' allowances. One view we will call the Public Service Model. Its basic premise is that the financial rewards should be artificially low in order that those attracted to elected office in local government are not doing so for financial reward – they are doing so because of public duty. Indeed, it is argued, public confidence in councillors may slide as a result of councillors receiving full-time salaries. A focus group study by the Scottish Executive Central Research Unit (1999: 11) revealed a typical perception of councillors as having poor reputations, not commanding the trust of the electorate, and being motivated by self-interest. The Public Service Model also suggests that no matter how little the extra expense of funding full-time salary packages might be, even in a symbolic sense it would be difficult to justify additional Council Tax increases at a time when cutbacks in services are all too common.

A counter argument can be called the Fair Rewards Model. Its basic premise is that councillors should be paid an appropriate full-time salary for their full-time responsibilities. At the moment, councillor remuneration amounts to less than the minimum wage, but councillors control multimillion-pound budgets. Glasgow City Council (the largest employer operating in Scotland) has an annual expenditure of roughly £1.3b. The City of Edinburgh Council is close behind with £1.1b. Even smaller councils such as the Shetland Islands Council spend over £81m per year. Comparisons with large private sector companies in Scotland (figure 5.3) indicate that councillors are paid less than the typical graduate wage in Scotland and only a mere fraction of what is paid in the private sector. This model also suggests that a full-time salary would attract a wider range of people to stand as councillors, in contrast to the present system which is a barrier to entry. Full-time salaries would result in an influx of younger, fresher and more representative candidates, sweeping away the 'cobwebs' under the existing system. The increases would require finance, but this could be done by either a grant to councils from the Scottish Executive, or small increases in Council Tax. If Scotland's 1,222 councillors were paid at the same rate as MSPs (£49,315 in 2003), the total additional cost would be in the region of £45m per year. This would increase the average council tax for each household by between £22 and £28 per annum.

Figure 5.3 **Approximate annual salary/remuneration for posts in Scotland, 2003.**

Average basic councillor allowance	£6,000
Average graduate wage	£19,500
MSPs	£49,315
NHS Level 1 executive pay	£120,000
Chief Executive, Glasgow City Council	£133,000
Chief Executive, Royal Bank of Scotland	£2,213,000

A review of councillor remuneration was prompted by the McIntosh Commission in 1998 and the issue was dealt with in-depth by the 2000 Kerley Committee. The final report expressed some sympathy for higher remuneration, but the recommended rates still fell considerably short of other senior positions in the public sector. The proposed basic allowance was £12,000 per annum, with more for special responsibilities, the most demanding being leadership of Glasgow and Edinburgh councils. These individuals would receive the same allowance as MSPs. The Local Governance (Scotland) Bill was drafted by the Scottish Executive and published in February 2003 but not introduced into the Scottish Parliament. The outcome of the 2003 election included a Labour-Liberal Partnership Agreement and a commitment to introduce a Scottish Local Authorities Remuneration Committee to set salary levels for councillors. In August 2003, as a way of taking this forward, the Scottish Executive announced the setting up of the Councillors' Remuneration Progress Group, chaired by Lord Sewel, former Scottish Office minister and now Senior Vice-Principal at the University of Aberdeen. The investigation started badly with ministers suggesting, much to the anger of COSLA, that most councillors were 'part time'.

It will be mid 2004 before the Group reaches its conclusion and some time after this before a decision is taken by the Scottish Executive on a new system of councillor remuneration. Given these early signs, the outcome (for better or worse) is hardly liable to make elected office at the local level a financially viable career, except perhaps for council leaders. Interestingly, the case of Scottish councillors could be enhanced if Scotland went down the centrally prescribed route of local cabinets and elected mayors or provosts. Within an institutional framework prescribed by the Office of the

Deputy Prime Minister via the Local Government Act 2000, councils have freedom to decide allowances and many are beginning to pay accordingly for councillors and (mayors) with executive functions. For example, councils in Wales with a population range of 100,000 to 200,000 agreed jointly on a total remuneration for mayors (£41,820), council leaders (£35,437), and cabinet members (£22,762) (Stewart 2003: 113).

Elections and the Electoral System: Turnout, Voting Behaviour and FPTP v. PR

Elections lie at the heart of liberal, representative democracy. The received constitutional wisdom is that the electorate choose between competing candidates at periodic elections. Votes are cast and filtered through an electoral system which transforms winning candidates into elected representatives. The potential sanction of removal from office at the next election ensures that accountability flows back to the electorate. The outcome is a government based on the popular will, rather than some form of dictatorship where government is driven by a political leadership which either bans or emasculates elections by heavily restricting choices – usually to one candidate. In Scotland, just over 3.9m people were registered to vote in the 2003 local elections. From 1975 onwards, elections to the old regional and district councils took place on a four-yearly basis. In other words, an election took place every two years for one or other of these tiers of government. When the 32 new single tier councils came into being over the 1995–6 period, elections were initially scheduled to take place every three years, but the Scottish Local Government (Elections) Act 2002 brought elections into line with the four-yearly cycle of elections to the Scottish Parliament. The electoral system itself is known as First Past the Post (FPTP), or more colloquially as 'winner takes all'. Each local authority is divided into wards, and the electorate must make one choice from a range of competing candidates. The candidate with the most votes wins, irrespective of how large or small the number of votes he or she receives. The controversial deal struck between Labour and the Liberal Democrats as a consequence of the 2003 Scottish Parliament elections will lead to FPTP being replaced by a form of proportional representation (Single Transferable Vote) for the next local elections in 2007. We will return to this issue shortly.

Electoral systems worldwide generate intense debate because they involve issues of representativeness, fairness, voter interest, accountability and what constitutes 'strong' government. The system for local government elections in Scotland is no exception. There are three main issues which we can consider, pertaining not just to the electoral system itself, but also to Scottish local government elections in a wider sense.

Low Turnout

Voters tend to 'talk a good game' in terms of the worth of local elections, but are not so good at putting this into practice. Figures from the 2001–2 Scottish Household Survey reveal that 81 per cent of adults 'agreed' or 'strongly agreed' that it was important to vote in local elections (Scottish Executive 2003f: 162). However, table 5.1 reveals that after initial interest in the new councils for the 1974 elections when turnout was 51 per cent, average turnout in local elections ever since has been close to 45 per cent. Turnout increased only in 1999 and to a much lesser extent in 2003 when local elections were held on the same day as the Scottish Parliamentary elections. With the exception of the 1999 figure, turnout levels in Scotland are fairly consistent with municipal elections south of the border. Both contrast with general election turnout in the UK which has averaged

Table 5.1 Average turnout at local elections in Scotland, 1974–2003.

Year	Authority	Average turnout (%)
1974	Region	51
1974	District	51
1977	District	48
1978	Region	45
1980	District	46
1982	Region	43
1984	District	45
1986	Region	46
1988	District	46
1990	Region	46
1992	District	42
1994	Region	45
1995	Unitary	45
1999	Unitary	59
2003	Unitary	49

Sources: Miscellaneous.

about 75 per cent over the post-war period, the only exception being the 59.4 per cent recorded in 2001 – the lowest figure since 1918 (Morgan 2001: 8). Average turnout in Scottish Parliamentary elections to date is 59 per cent in 1999 and 49 per cent in 2003.

Why have voters tended not to turn out in their droves to vote in Scottish local elections? Several reasons can be put forward. First, voters may know little about local government and so are disinclined to vote. Even a cursory examination of the topics covered in this book make us aware that local government in Scotland is incredibly complex. It is also less accessible to students, academics and journalists, simply because of the English and Welsh bias in local government textbooks, articles and professional journals. A study commissioned by the Scottish Office focusing on people's knowledge and perceptions of local government did not reveal a particularly high level of knowledge (Scottish Office Central Research Unit 1995). Certainly, over 70 per cent of people sampled could correctly name the tier of local government responsible for particular services, but even a reasonable under-standing of the role of local government would require being able to answer more taxing questions. In the devolution era, there would almost certainly be a clear lack of knowledge displayed if people were asked (for example): Who sets business rate levels? What is the name of the body responsible for the auditing of local authorities? Who is responsible for the police service? What is Best Value? A focus group study commissioned by the Scottish Executive Central Research Unit (1999) found participants to have only a sketchy knowledge of local government, and little idea of the role of councillors and how council business was conducted. This is not to belittle those unable to show good understanding. Even academics struggle to come to terms with local government. It is simply to suggest that given the complexities of local government, we should not be surprised if people feel they have insufficient knowledge to make a judgement on polling day.

Second, a related reason may be voter apathy with local government. A major study by Miller (1988: 16), found that 64 per cent of his sample had little or no interest in local politics. Similarly, the Scottish Executive Central Research Unit (1999) study found that the main reason given for not voting was that nothing would change as a result. Lynch (2003) goes further and suggests that deeper, longer-term factors may be at work which are common to many advanced democracies. In particular, he suggests that there may be a growing sense of public alienation with politics and parties; a decline in party affiliations among the electorate; a decline in civic values of participation; and low levels of civic literacy.

Third, a belief may exist that local government powers are weak anyway, and so voting makes little difference. Miller (1988: 16) found that only 7 to 8 per cent of those surveyed felt issues of importance to be a matter for local councils. A later survey by System Three Scotland found that 49 per cent felt that central government had too much control over local authorities (Scottish Local Government Information Unit 1991: 2). Fourth, in areas where traditional voting patterns indicate a more or less inevitable electoral outcome, voters intent on voting for opposition candidates may simply not bother because they know their vote will in effect be 'wasted'. The FPTP system effectively facilities this type of thinking, and we will return to this issue further on in the chapter.

Fifth, and more controversially, is the suggestion that people may not vote because they are happy with local government. Arguments such as this have their contemporary roots in Dahl (1961) with *Who Governs?*, his classic study of local politics in New Haven, Connecticut, USA. One of his key assumptions was that people have an innate sense of democracy and justice (he called it the 'democratic creed') and whilst they may not know too much about local issues and may not always use their vote, they do know what is 'right' and 'wrong'. According to Dahl, politicians are aware of this and so are constrained in what they do because non-voters effectively act as democratic watchdogs: prepared to use their key political resource (the vote) if they are unhappy with the way local affairs are run. Perhaps Dahl went too far in accepting democratic failings as not particularly problematic, although it does not seem unreasonable to suggest that there is a grain of truth in his argument. If local elections in Scotland took place amidst a series of local policy failures such as mountains of uncollected rubbish, street lights rarely working and schools subject to widespread and unpredictable closures, we would surely expect electoral turnout to increase.

Sixth, there is the argument that the format of voting – the electorate having to attend a polling station on a certain day within specified hours – is anachronistic and unsuited to changing life-styles, voters with disabilities or infirmities, and the vagaries of the

Scottish weather. The modernisation agenda of New Labour and the Scottish Executive in particular has focused on such issues. The Scottish Local Government (Elections) Act 2002 allows councils to apply for ministerial approval to introduce various measures to make voting more accessible and increase turnout. Initially, this applies only to by-elections. Possible measures include:

- All postal votes.
- Voting spread across several days.
- Extending voting hours.
- Mobile polling stations.
- More voter-friendly locations such as supermarkets.
- Encrypted electronic voting.

Moves such as these may yield some success. For councils using them, all-postal ballots in England and Wales resulted in an average 14.78 per cent increase in turnout at the May 2000 local elections and a 10 per cent increase in May 2003 (Lynch 2003: 239; *Local Government Chronicle*, 8 May 2003). The very fact that local election turnout increased to 59 per cent (1999) and marginally to 49 per cent (2003) when local elections were held on the same day as elections to the Scottish Parliament tells us that ease of voting (in this case, while voters cast another vote) is an important factor in determining turnout. The negative implication, however, is that some people are only voting in local elections because they happen to be in the polling booth that day to vote in the Scottish Parliament elections. This does not bode well if we seek genuine local accountability.

Voting in Accordance with National Preferences

The constitutional wisdom of local democratic accountability is that local politicians present themselves at election time to be judged on their performance and/or their promise of what they will do if elected. In reality, however, the vast majority of people do not vote simply on the basis of local issues. Various studies down the years from Gregory, Rees and Hampton, Newton, the Widdecombe Report and others reveal a surprising consistency: roughly 80 to 90 per cent of people tend to vote the same way in local elections as they do in national elections. They may do so by voting purely and simply in accordance with their national preferences (paying no attention to local issues), or they may do so after genuinely weighing up the arguments and arriving at the same conclusion in terms of the party they wish to support.

Figure 5.4 A model of local election voting choice in Scotland.

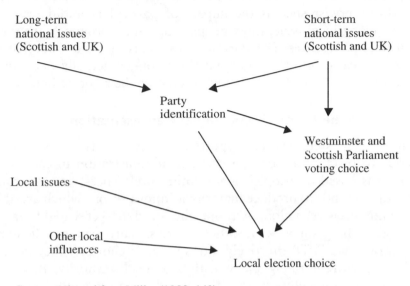

Source: Adapted from Miller (1988: 149).

In order to explore this matter further, figure 5.4 provides us with a model adapted from Miller (1988) of local election choice. It supports the idea that local issues are only one factor in shaping choices. The implications we draw from this model of voting choice are another matter. We could view from one angle and say that voters in Scotland are prepared to vote at times on local issues and so this is good for local accountability. In 1982, for example, the ruling Labour Party in Lothian Regional Council was voted out of office in the context of high rates rise and a high profile campaign against Scottish Office ministers, despite Labour improving its share of the vote in Scotland as a whole. Furthermore, a study by Denver and Bochel (2000) of the 1999 local elections, held on the same day as elections to the Scottish Parliament, found that in Aberdeen, at least 5.3 per cent of the electorate voted for different parties at ward and constituency level. Indeed, on a Scotland wide-basis, the Conservatives, Labour and Liberals performed relatively poorly in the local elections, with the benefits going to the SNP and independent candidates. Overall, therefore, we could argue that voting on local issues does take place, and in some marginal wards every vote is crucial. The counter interpretation is a much simpler one. The vast majority of voters vote in accordance with their national preferences. Therefore, unless there are compelling reasons to do otherwise such as the impact of particular candidates or a very strong local issue, most people vote in accordance with their national preferences. The stark implication is that it doesn't matter a great deal to most voters what their council actually does; they will not be sufficiently motivated to change their voting habits.

First Past the Post v. Proportional Representation

The FPTP system has its supporters and its merits. In essence, it tends to produce a local government administration in each area which is based on people's main voting preferences, and is strong because it tends to produce majority administrations which are able to take decisive action, without the need to get caught up in constant bargaining with other parties. Furthermore, at local election time, FPTP effectively offers voters a choice: if they do not like the current ruling party within a local authority, they can remove its councillors from office and vote in the candidates of a major opposition party. The vast majority of COSLA's membership strongly supports the FPTP system, arguing that maintaining the member–ward link and offering voters a clear choice is more important than achieving proportionality.

Table 5.2 Examples of the mismatch between voting patterns and council composition as a result of the 2003 local elections.

Council	Lab. votes (%)	Lab. seats (%)	SNP votes (%)	SNP seats (%)	Cons. votes (%)	Cons. seats (%)	Lib. Dem. votes (%)	Lib. Dem. Seats (%)
Glasgow	47.6	89.9	20.5	3.8	7.6	1.3	7.6	3.8
Edinburgh	31.2	54.5	14.7	0.0	23.4	22.4	25.5	25.8
Aberdeen	24.2	32.0	23.0	14.0	15.3	7.0	35.4	46.5
Midlothian	43.3	83.3	24.4	0.0	11.0	0.0	17.2	11.1

Note: Figures do not add up to 100% because of votes for smaller parties and independents.

By contrast, there are many opponents of the FPTP system, including the Scottish Liberal Democrats, Scottish National Party, Scottish Socialist Party and Scottish Green Party. Several accusations can be levelled at the current system. First, as illustrated in table 5.2, there is often a mismatch between people's voting preferences and the composition of their council. Second, and following on from this point, the broad make-up of councils throughout Scotland does not reflect voters' electoral choices. Table 5.3, based on the results of the 2003 elections, indicates that Labour is the main beneficiary, commanding less than third of the vote but obtaining 41.7 per cent of seats and only marginally less in terms of council control. The SNP is a major loser. Despite obtaining 24.0 per cent of the vote, it won only 14.8 per cent of the seats (many votes effectively wasted by the Party coming second and third) and control of one council (Angus). Votes cast for the Conservatives and the Liberal Democrats translate reasonably well into seats (especially in the case of the Liberal Democrats) but the real difficulty is the inability to win control of councils. The combined votes of the Conservatives and Liberal Democrats amount to almost 30 per cent of voters, winning 24.4 per cent of seats but controlling only 3.1 per cent of councils (Inverclyde).

Table 5.3 Voting patterns and seats won as a result of the 2003 local elections in Scotland.

Party	% votes	% seats	Seats won	% of councils controlled
Labour	32.6	41.7	509	40.6
SNP	24.0	14.8	181	3.1
Cons.	15.1	10.1	123	0.0
Lib. Dem.	14.6	14.3	175	3.1
SSP	3.3	0.2	2	0.0
Independent	10.2	18.9	231	18.8
Others	0.1	0.1	1	0.0

Note: Figures for votes and seats won do not add up to 100% because of rounding. Figures for % of councils do not add up to 100% because the remainder constitutes councils where the election result produced no party in overall control.

Source: Based on private information provided by David Denver.

Third, the system does not encourage high voting turnout because in councils dominated by one party there is little incentive for people to vote for opposing parties because they know it will make little or no difference to the final outcome. Fourth, and taking this point further, the argument is that the FPTP system helps create and perpetuate one-party 'fiefdoms'. Arguably, administrations remain largely unchecked because people either do not bother to vote, or if they do, they vote in accordance with their national preferences. In the extreme, this argument suggests that the FPTP is a catalyst for self-perpetuating, elitist and (on occasion) corrupt local government.

Arguments such as these have been well versed in recent years. The Report of the McIntosh Commission (Scottish Office 1999a) suggested that a new system should be able to:

- produce a more proportionate result;
- maintain a link between councillor and ward;
- provide a fair chance for independents to be elected;
- allow for geographical diversity among local authorities; and
- provide a close fit between council wards and natural communities.

The first of these is crucial. The McIntosh Report considered a form of proportional representation (PR) as an essential component of a local democratic system, arguing that the 'essence of the case for proportional representation is that it produces a result which more fairly represents the spectrum of opinion within the electorate' (Scottish Office 1999a: para. 82). McIntosh did not state a preference for a specific form of PR. The matter was taken further when the Kerley Committee was set up to look at a variety of issues pertaining to local democracy, the electoral system being one. It reported in June 2000 and favoured a Single Transferable Vote (STV) system, where wards are multi-member and voters rank candidates in order of preference. The intent is to virtually eliminate wasted votes because once a candidate has enough votes to ensure election (or, correspondingly, not enough to gain election), second and lower preference votes are utilised. In effect, the outcome is a complex, rolling calculation which produces (1) a highly proportional link between voting preferences and seats and (2) a new form of councillor–ward link, with constituents having several elected representatives (Report of the Renewing Local Democracy Working Group 2000).

The Scottish Executive initially vacillated on Kerley's recommendations, the reason being that the Scottish Labour Party was and is being pulled in two different directions. On the one hand, it is wedded to the FPTP system because this is the prime reason why Labour controls so many councils in Scotland. With only 32.6 per cent of the votes in 2003, it controls 13 out of the 32 councils. On the other hand, there is an element in New Labour thinking which seeks to eradicate some 'old Labour' councils, run in perpetuity (some would argue) by elitist, cronyist councillors who have the potential to bring the party into disrepute.

What has finally shifted the balance is political pragmatism. Scottish Labour prepared for this in the run-up to the 2003 elections. Under the broadly proportional outcomes produced by the dual electoral system for the Scottish Parliament, it was liable to need a coalition partner in order to form the Scottish Executive. Based on the previous result in 1999 it was likely to be the Liberal Democrats: strong and long-standing supporters of PR. Therefore, in the run-up to the 2003 Scottish Parliamentary elections, the Scottish Executive published the Local Governance (Scotland) Bill but did not introduce it into Parliament. Instead, it left it pending for the new Executive to consider, depending on the results of the May elections. The post-election outcome was a weakened Labour Party and a situation whereby FPTP supporters in the Scottish Parliament probably did not have votes to block a move by PR proponents to pass a Bill. Therefore, an important feature of the post-election Partnership Agreement between Labour and the Liberals became the introduction of the Local Governance (Scotland) Bill (Scottish Executive 2003e). Despite intense opposition from COSLA (with only a small minority of its members supporting PR) and rank and file Labour Party members, it will lead to the introduction of STV (based around three or four councillors per constituency) for the 2007 local elections. A Single Transferable Vote Working Group was established in August 2003, chaired by David Green of the Crofters' Commission and previously Convenor of Highland Council. A move to STV will dramatically alter the landscape of local electoral politics – working against Scottish Labour in particular. So far, local government in England and Wales has resisted the PR route for local government (with the exception of the Greater London Assembly [see Travers 2004: 59–60]). Generally speaking, it is easier to introduce PR in a new body (such as the GLA, Scottish Parliament or National Assembly for Wales) because there are no incumbents to protest. As testified by the reaction of most Scottish councils to the prospect of PR, reform dramatically upsets long-standing power bases of individuals and parties. If the Office of the Deputy Prime Minister does ever seek to introduce PR for mainstream local government in England and Wales, it is liable to be at a time when it feels that the benefits of PR will outweigh the political flak generated by electoral reform.

Overall, it can be argued that the 'theory' of democratic accountability via elections is one matter, the reality is another. Problems of low turnout, voting largely in accordance with national preferences and the vagaries of the electoral system can damage the validity and legitimacy of local elections. We should not assume, however, that alternatives are problem free. Issues surrounding elections are not those of an exact science, they are about politics and competing viewpoints. If voting were made compulsory, we could argue that this would infringe the democratic right not to vote. If voting were made too easy and accessible, we might argue that voting choices would be made in a disposable, uninformed way. The prospect of PR is horrific for most COSLA members and many councillors, who see it as (1) a distraction from real issues such as financial dependency on the Scottish Executive and (2) damaging democracy because it breaks the councillor–ward link. Added to this is the argument that voters under FPTP vote in the knowledge that if a party is elected to office, it will carry out its manifesto commitment. Under PR, 'wheeling and dealing' is done post-election, out of the direct control of the electorate, and depending on the overall profile of votes for each party. Indeed, PR may also give disproportionate power to a few councillors in minority (perhaps extremist) parties, whose votes hold the balance of power in an authority. No system is perfect. In a political world where the merits of election systems depend on our point of view, it cannot be anything else.

Conclusion – A Healthy Democratic Foundation?

Democracy is an elusive term. It means different things to different people. All forms of regime from dictatorships though to liberal democracies would claim to be 'democratic' (MacPherson 1966). Chapter 1 outlined marxist, elitist and pluralist interpretations of local government in Scotland and the arguments apply here.

A marxist interpretation of 'democracy' in Scottish local government would be less concerned about matters such as electoral systems and councillors' allowances: democracy can only be achieved with the absence of class exploitation. In a classless society, democracy concerns material rights: the right to a job, a home, a decent standard of living. Unless a society can guarantee these material benefits (and only a classless society can), then it is undemocratic. Therefore, a marxist view of the democratic failing of local government in Scotland would focus on problems such as homelessness, urban and rural deprivation, wage levels and child labour.

Elitist perspectives would tend to attack local democracy in Scotland from two different directions. Free-market ideologues such as the Adam Smith Institute would see real democracy as being one of rational market choices. At best, the role of elected local politicians should be a highly minimalist one, overseeing the awarding of contracts for local authority work. Indeed, the Adam Smith Institute (1989) has argued that local government in Scotland could be turned into a series of community companies, with local people being shareholders rather than voters. From this perspective therefore, local government in Scotland is to a large extent undemocratic because the self-seeking of councillors and officers is a barrier to efficient, effective (and hence democratic) local government. A more left-leaning elitist perspective would see the constitutional model of local democracy as something we must aspire to. Nevertheless, and sharing ground with the free-marketers, it would see the democratic problem as being the way in which councillors and officials are able to insulate themselves from popular pressures because of the vagaries of the electoral system, manipulation of consultation processes and so on.

A pluralist perspective on local government is the closest we come to a constitutional view and shares many values with the 'left' critique of elitism. In this tradition, Beetham (1996) usefully sets out four criteria we can use to measure the health of local democracy. We can briefly consider each in relation to local government in Scotland, recognising however, that there is no magical answer – much depends on our interpretation. Some of the analysis (below) will be developed in the next chapter.

First, democracy is founded on the principle of popular sovereignty, and hence government (in this case local government) needs popular authorisation through elections. In many respects, it is easy to be very positive in this regard about Scottish local government. Elections are conducted on the basis of universal adult suffrage and there is a constitutional recognition that the governance of local authorities is based on popular preferences as expressed through the vote. Many critics would exercise caution, however, focusing on the fact that the FPTP system distorts electoral preferences, exhibiting a bias in favour of majority parties within wards. A genuine 'popular authorisation' would be based on a proportional voting system that broadly reflects the diversity of voting patterns in the electorate. Thus, popular authorisation may be considered weak, depending on our viewpoint.

Second, elected representatives should be accountable to the people for the policies and actions they undertake when in office. In this regard, appropriate structures are certainly in place. A range of mechanisms exists to ensure that individuals holding political office at the local level are held to account for their activities. The people have at their disposal such devices as the right to vote and the right to complain about maladministration. In reality, however, the strength of these formal systems of accountability is less clear-cut. For example:

- The FPTP system is biased in favour of majority parties and exacerbated by low turnouts and voting largely in accordance with national preferences (as opposed to the record of councils).
- There is little evidence to suggest that the Scottish Public Services Ombudsman (and its predecessor the Commissioner for Local Administration) is particularly well understood or utilised by local people.
- A more fragmented system of local governance places aspects of local service formation and delivery (for example, through PFI contracts and fire authorities) beyond the direct control of local people. Whilst the activities of councillors in their local authority are once removed from the electorate, these wider areas of governance are twice removed.

Third, local government should be responsive, in the sense that it should take into account the full range of public opinion in its formulation and implementation of policies. Again, formal mechanisms are well entrenched – particularly the right of local people to be consulted as part of the Best Value and Community Planning regimes. In reality, however, consultation processes may at times be 'cosmetic', offering local authorities legitimacy for their decisions, but making little real difference to the content of policies. Indeed, local authorities are creatures of statute, and whilst they represent local people, they also represent the Scottish Parliament because they must implement national laws and policies. Furthermore, councillors are only one source of power in local authorities (party groups and officers being other notable sources) and so there are major constraints on their autonomy to be responsive.

Fourth, elected bodies (in this case local authorities) should be representative, in the sense that there are no barriers to any sections of society or opinion holding office. Once again, the 'theory' is straightforward: everyone is equal in terms of their right to stand for office, irrespective of class, employment status, age, race and gender. In practice, however, the overwhelmingly white, middle class, male bias in the profile of Scotland's councillors is a product of wider societal barriers to participation. It is heightened by the system of councillors' allowances which favours the middle class who have professional salaries to compensate the low financial reward for being a councillor. It should be noted that Beetham also adds a fifth criterion for assessing 'democracy', namely an alert and active citizen body. If local election turnout is a reasonable surrogate for this, historic low turnout figures (certainly compared with general elections) imply that the people of Scotland are less interested in local politics than national politics.

The 'health' of local democracy in Scotland is an issue that will always be a matter for debate. Constitutional liberal democratic structures are in place, based around principles of popular authorisation, accountability, responsiveness and representativeness. In reality, however, many would argue that local democracy in Scotland is weak, suffering from a range of ailments such as an unfair electoral system, national prejudices, apathy, under-funding for elected representativeness, fragmentation, often 'token' consultation, and dominance by the priorities of the Scottish Parliament. It is to be hoped that the three working groups set up in the summer of 2003 (councillors' remuneration, Single Transferable Vote and widening access to council membership) will go some way to tackling the many problems which exist.

? Key Questions ?

1. Does it really matter if the profile of councillors in Scotland is not typical of the profile of the electorate as a whole?
2. Are councillors unable to perform their roles effectively because they have too many competing expectations placed on them?
3. Should councillors be paid salaries which give them 'fair reward' for the hours they work and the importance of the decisions they take?
4. What are the main reasons for poor turnout in Scottish local elections and what can be done to improve the situation?
5. Will proportional representation make Scottish local government more accountable and democratic?

Further Reading

A study by Vestri and Fitzpatrick (2000) provides a detailed profile of the social characteristics and attitudes of the 1999 intake of Scotland's councillors. Figures for the 2003 intake can be found in a study by the Scottish Executive Social Research Unit (2003). A series of articles by Colin Copus (1999, 2001a, 2001b) provides a refreshing realism in its examination of the power of party groups in relation to councillors. The Report of the Renewing Local Democracy Working Group chaired by Richard Kerley (2000) examines the case for and against PR in Scottish local government, ultimately making a case in favour. It also examines the case for increasing the remuneration paid to councillors. A more recent overview of the case for and against PR in Scotland is given in a research paper by Stephen Herbert (2002) for the Scottish Parliament Information Centre. Long-term electoral trends in Scotland and throughout Britain are given unrivalled treatment in Rallings and Thrasher (1997), *Local Elections in Britain*. Developments over the next few years in Scotland can be monitored in the pages of *The Scotsman* and *The Herald* newspapers, the weekly *Local Government Chronicle*, and the academic journals *Local Government Studies*, *Local Governance* and *Scottish Affairs*.

Useful Websites

http://www.scotland.gov.uk/consultations/localgov/dlgsc.pdf
Scottish Executive Consultation on the Draft Local Governance (Scotland) Bill, including proposals for Single Transferable Vote.

www.cosla.gov.uk
The Convention of Scottish Local Authorities. Check press releases and the monthly publications *COSLA Connections* for updates on the main opposition to PR.

http://www.electoral-reform.org.uk
The Electoral Reform Society. A strong proponent of PR throughout the UK. It also publishes periodic studies on methods of boosting electoral turnout.

CHAPTER SIX

Beyond Elections: Non-Electoral Forms of Public Participation and Non-Elected Local Governance

In terms of British constitutional theory, elections are the bedrock of local democracy. There are, however, two sets of issues with democratic implications which exist 'beyond' elections. First, there are non-electoral forms of participation. In terms of the modernising agenda of the Scottish Executive, they include community consultation via Best Value and the Community Planning regime, as well as the development of specific forums such as people's panels and citizens' juries. Second, there is the growth of wider institutions of local governance such as police boards, further education colleges and Scottish Water, which to varying degrees are removed partly or wholly from the control of directly elected local authorities. This chapter will focus on each in turn and conclude with differing views on whether these trends contribute to a healthy local democracy in Scotland.

Non-Electoral Forms of Public Participation

Local communities are not restricted to four-yearly elections as the main means of exerting influence over council decision-making. One possible route is to join or even start an interest group. Using the categorisation provided by Stoker (1991) they include:

Producer/economic groups: Such as Edinburgh Chamber of Commerce, CBI Scotland, Fife Institute of Directors, Fire Brigades Union, Unison.

Community groups: For example, Glasgow Campaign Against Housing Stock Transfer, Campaign to Welcome Refugees.

Cause groups: Such as Scottish Coalition for Justice Not War, Friends of the Earth Scotland, Scottish Campaign for Nuclear Disarmament.

Voluntary sector groups: For example, Victim Support Scotland, Clackmannanshire Community Access Volunteers, Highland Sports Development Association.

In theory, the existence of such groups fits with pluralist assumptions about the benefits of power dispersal because groups provide a means of influence between elections (Judge 1995). Indeed, because they can form at will and lobby local councils, the pluralist argument is that no group will dominate in the longer term because countervailing groups will emerge to challenge. For example, employers' groups will never dominate in the long run because they will always be counterbalanced by trade unions. In reality, however, groups often have unequal access to power because of disparities in resources, varying roles in policy implementation, and unequal access to councillors (Wilson and Game 2002). A long tradition in political science exists, arguing that there is a state bias towards business as opposed to popular interests (Miliband 1969; Lindblom 1977). Harding (2000) in his study of urban regime formations, suggests that in the 1980s and 1990s, Edinburgh was governed by a narrow coalition of public-private, inter-agency and intergovernmental development interests. Kantor (2000) provides a similar examination of Glasgow, although he argues that business involvement in regeneration was dominated by the Scottish Office and its appointees in Scottish Enterprise.

The main focus of this section is less on interest groups as such and more on specific initiatives to encourage public participation. Some democratic theorists such as Schumpeter [1943] (1976) are unconvinced about the feasibility of widespread public participation, perceiving it to flounder on lack of public interest. Public participation also has the potential for instability by encouraging a 'free-for-all' on the part of sectional interests unrepresentative of society. Others such as Pateman (1970) and Barber (1984) argue that participation is vital, encouraging an ongoing sense of citizenship which benefits society as a whole.

What constitutes 'participation' is wide and varied. It may range from officials asking citizens basic information to assist with delivering services, through to consultation on policy proposals or active involvement in decision-making. It is the middle and latter end of the spectrum with which we are interested. Participation via public meetings, consultation on planning decisions and other methods is a fairly recent phenomenon in Scottish local government. The seeds of modern initiatives lie in the late 1960s and early 1970s, a time when new participatory devices such as Neighbourhood Councils and Joint Area Housing Committees were seen by Cockburn (1977) as a means of trying to quell unrest in the face of financial cutbacks and declining service provision. The report of the Royal Commission on Local Government in Scotland, otherwise known as the Wheatley Report (Cmnd. 4150 1969), was one of the first major investigations to recognise the need for a more localist approach, with local authorities benefiting from community input and advice where possible. However, in Scotland in the 1970s, participation exercises such as planning workshops between local people, officers and councillors were considered little more than the payment of 'lip service' to public participation (Young 1977: 78–9). Participation initiatives in Scotland only really started to develop in any meaningful sense in the 1980s and 1990s. Dual processes were at work. On the one hand, Conservative administrations were keen to try and encourage ways in which the power of (mostly Labour-controlled) Scottish local authorities could be held in check by 'popular' interests. Initiatives included school boards and housing co-operatives. On the other hand, many local authorities (faced with an array of financial cutbacks and new legislative commitments) were keen at times to consult local people in order to gain legitimacy for the case in defence of local service provision. In 1994, for example, Strathclyde Regional Council used a postal ballot to consult local people on whether water and sewerage should remain under local authority control. The response rate was a highly impressive 71 per cent, with 97.2 per cent of respondents favouring the status quo (*The Herald*, 23 March 1994).

As Lowndes et al. (2001: 205) note: 'Enhanced public participation lies at the heart of the Labour government's modernization for British local government.' This core thinking also applies to the Scottish Executive. The rationale for local public participation cuts across many areas, particularly: (1) social inclusion policies designed to integrate disadvantaged groups into public life; (2) the desire for joined-up, evidence-based policy-making; (3) promoting greater accountability and responsiveness on the part of local authorities; and (4) modernising and 'cleaning up' the image of local authorities. Early experiments in Scotland with citizens' juries occurred in 1997 in Fife Council (on the regeneration of Levenmouth) and South Lanarkshire Council (on tackling vandalism and graffiti). The Scottish Executive has since encouraged participation via four main means.

First, the Local Government in Scotland Act 2003 places a statutory duty on local authorities to make arrangements for Best Value. This means that local authorities must be committed to continuous service improvement, balance cost and quality, and consult with local people in doing so. Second, the Local Government in Scotland Act 2003 places a statutory duty of Community Planning on Scottish councils. As the Scottish Executive states in its Policy Memorandum accompanying the original Bill into the Scottish Parliament:

> Community planning is essentially a process to ensure greater engagement from communities in the planning and delivery of services and to secure effective joint working between agencies in promoting the well-being of communities. A shared vision with clear outcomes, allied to more effective partnership working, will result in better use of public money. The overall intention is to provide a basis for the delivery of better, more responsive services. (Scottish Executive 2002e: 2)

Third, and more generally, the Scottish Executive funds the Scottish Civic Forum (established in October 1999) which has a role in promoting and facilitating civic participation in public life (Lynch 2001). Fourth, through a combination of Best Value consultation imperatives and a genuine desire by many local authorities to modernise their approach, a number of other participative devices have been used. A summary is provided in figure 6.1. Councils in Scotland have developed a host of initiatives (Local Government Committee 2003a; 2003b; 2003c). Stirling Council has the Stirling Assembly, a forum involving citizens, community councils, local businesses and voluntary groups, regularly debating major issues

---

Figure 6.1   A summary of 'modern' participation methods in local government.

Seeking citizens' views

- *Citizens' Juries*: Representative groups of between 12 and 16 local people brought together over a three- or four-day period to consider an issue in depth, scrutinise evidence, examine witnesses and make recommendations.
- *Focus group/survey panels/citizen conferences*: Ad hoc groups of varying size, meeting frequently or infrequently to consider views on a particular local authority issue.
- *Deliberative opinion polls*: Large-scale and more statistically representative opinion polls, followed up by discussion of oral and written evidence.

Involving citizens directly in decision-making

- *Standing Citizens' Panels*: Statistically representative samples of residents used by a council as a 'sounding board'.
- *Community/user group forums*: To consider policies or proposals affecting a specific community, with the possibility of some delegated authority and a devolved budget.
- *Local referendums*: A single-issue ballot of residents. The outcome may be binding or advisory.

Developing the citizens' watchdog or scrutiny role

- *Panels of inquiry/public scrutiny committees*: Committees of residents with the right to ask for papers and hear evidence from councillors and officers.
- *Direct service scrutiny committees*: Similar to above, but with an exclusive focus on a particular service area.

Opening up the authority

- *Public question times at council meetings*: A slot of 20 to 30 minutes may be allocated for public questions, usually having been submitted in advance (in writing).
- *Co-option onto council committees*: This has a long history in Britain, with roughly one in four committee members being co-opted. The more modern variant of this tends to be proactive on the part of the council rather than responding (as is sometimes the case) to legislative requirements.
- *Experiments with alternative times and venues for council meetings*: For example, weekend meetings and meetings held in community halls rather than council chambers.
- *Devolution/localisation of council decision-making*: To local offices and local area committees.

Source: Amended and adapted from Wilson and Game (2002: 357–8).

---

and helping shape the Council's Community Plan. Renfrewshire Council has a Young Persons Housing Forum to involve representatives of the 16–25 age group in tenant participation processes. Angus Council has established the Angus Dialogue Youth Initiative and the Angus Youth Congress, both of which encourage greater youth involvement in the running and life of their communities. More widely, a Dialogue Youth initiative has been rolled out across all 32 local authorities in Scotland as a joint COSLA and Scottish Executive concern. One of its main aims is to empower young people by giving them a variety of forums in which they can express their views. Glasgow City Council has a Citizens' Panel, with approximately 700 members who are surveyed on a range of issues. North Lanarkshire Council and Aberdeenshire Council use external consultants to conduct residents' surveys. West Lothian Council has developed a system of Tenant Led Inspection whereby a group of tenants inspect council homes and make wider service recommendations. More generally, e-government is being developed by all councils in Scotland, and most councils operate on-line systems for registering complaints and making recommendations.

COSLA also supports the Demos project: an EU funded initiative launched in 2002 which links eight major city councils in Scotland, Finland, the Netherlands, Belgium, Poland, Greece and Germany. Two councils are directly involved in Scotland. The leader of the project is the City of Edinburgh Council. A particular consequence of Demos has been 11 pilot projects taken forward by its 6 Local Development Committees. These include local policy hearings, the Positive Images project involving non-verbal consultation with people with disabilities, and extensive community consultation with the local community on the environmental regeneration of Broughton Road. A wider audit of participation in Edinburgh revealed a vast range of devices for consultation with local people, including Local Community Forums, Equalities Forums, an Older People's Forum and a Parents' Consultative Committee (Demos 2002b). Aberdeen City Council is also involved and has developed:

- A Citizens' Panel of 1,500–2,000 local people, representative of the local community, to scrutinise existing policies and new policy proposals in the city.
- A Virtual Citizens' Panel to mirror the Citizens' Panel and allow an input from any individuals with access to the internet.
- A Young Persons' Website to consult with young people and make them aware of initiatives which will affect them. (Demos 2002a)

For all the benefits of participative exercises – particularly promoting a greater sense of citizenship and tailoring council policies more closely to the needs of local communities – there are a number of countervailing factors to consider. Arnstein (1969), in a seminal article, argued that 'participation' was less than straightforward. In reality, there exists a 'ladder of participation'. At the foot is manipulation masking as participation. As we progress up the ladder, we move through degrees of tokenism and finally reach the top: genuine citizen control. Figure 6.2 provides a summary of the main problems associated with public participation exercises in local government. Two in particular are worth highlighting in the Scottish context.

Figure 6.2 The potential inhibitors and drawbacks of public participation excercises in local government.

Potential inhibitors of participation

- Public apathy to involvement in particular, and political institutions in general.
- Goals of the authority may be unclear.

Drawbacks of participation

- Results can be subject to differing interpretations.
- Consultation may be 'cosmetic', making little or no difference to the final content of policy.
- Raising expectations which cannot be met (for legal, financial or political reasons), possibly leading to a loss of public confidence.
- Decision-making process can be become costly and protracted.
- Successful participants may not be representative of the wider community.
- Can produce an unhealthy focus on relatively trivial issues.
- Undermines the representative role of councillors.
- Consultation duplication and overload.

Source: Adapted from Demos (2002a) and various.

First, participation may be little more than a cosmetic exercise, driven by the need of councils to say they have consulted as part of the Best Value and Community Planning regimes but without having any significant influence on the making or implementation of local policies. A strong message emerging from focus group research conducted for the Scottish Executive Central Research Unit (1999) was a doubt that community representatives would be listened to. As one participant stated:

> Most people are not interested because most people aren't listened to. No matter what they say most people aren't listened to and the

car parking one is a prime example. Practically the whole of X was against car parking – no difference. None whatsoever. (Scottish Executive Central Research Unit 1999: 22)

Also, almost all the activists in a study for the Scottish Parliament's Local Government Committee were united in the view that their idea had little impact (Local Government Committee 2003b). Second, how should the results of public participation exercises by interpreted? In essence, the outcomes are 'political footballs' to be fought over by councillors, officials, party groups and local people. Each set of interests will tend to interpret and use results as they see fit. No group wants public participation to destabilise its own power base. In the aforementioned Local Government Committee study, over half of councillors stated that they should not be bound by the outcome of public participation exercises (Local Government Committee 2003b: 29). Indeed, the most favoured method for improving public participation was the provision of easier access to councillors themselves (Local Government Committee 2003b: 51). Overall, therefore, the growing trend promoting various non-electoral means of participation is to be lauded in democratic terms, but it is by no means as effective or straightforward as we might think. This issue will be developed in the conclusion to this chapter.

The Growth of Non-Elected Local Governance

As indicated in Chapters 1 and 2, not all local services in Scotland are delivered by directly elected local authorities. Indeed there never was such a 'golden age', although we are certainly moving further away from any such ideal. We are shifting from a system of local government towards a more fragmented system of non-elected local governance. An understanding of the issues is not a particularly easy task. In the first instance, no agreed definition exists of what constitutes a local service. In theory, any service delivered in a local area for the benefit of local people could be defined as 'local'. However, adopting such a definition would include central executive agencies such as the Passport Agency and the Benefits Agency, both of which are locally delivered for local benefit. We could also define 'local' services as those delivered by directly elected local authorities. However, this definition excludes community-based organisations such as housing associations, hospitals and further education colleges. Another alternative would be to define 'local' services as services where some sub-national autonomy is required in order to deliver different policies in different places. This definition has the advantage of being compatible with one of the major reasons why local authorities exist at all: to help manage differentiated social relations throughout the country (Duncan and Goodwin 1988). Unfortunately, however, there is no rational dividing line separating services where local autonomy is an imperative and local services where no real autonomy is required. In areas such as social work, education, water and sewerage, police, prisons and healthcare, the freedoms each of these service providers should have is very much a matter for political judgement, and will vary from country to country. The reality, therefore, is that what constitutes a 'local' service depends on our viewpoint.

Despite the haziness of our subject matter, one issue is clear: non-elected systems of local governance are not a new phenomenon in the public administration of Scotland. Whilst directly elected local authorities were being formed in the nineteenth and early part of the twentieth century, non-elected bodies were ubiquitous. Some were locally based such as School Boards, Police Commissioners, Fisheries Board, and Road Boards, whilst others were intermediate bodies such as the Board of Supervision for Poor Relief and the General Board of Commissioners in Lunacy for Scotland. Even after the advent of 'modern' local government structures via the Local Government (Scotland) Act 1929 and the rationalising of the Scottish Office in 1939, aspects of non-elected local governance continued over the next few decades. Examples include the Highlands and Islands Development Board, Scottish Development Board, Scottish Special Housing Association, Scottish Examination Board, Health Boards and New Town Development Corporations. The terminology often used to describe such bodies is quangos (quasi-autonomous non-governmental organisations), although the term itself is subject to much debate, and governments prefer the much narrower label of Non-Departmental Public Bodies (NDPBs) (see Ridley and Wilson 1995; Skelcher 1998; Flinders and Smith 1999). In simple terms, quangos are bodies appointed by ministers for public purpose. Stoker (1999: 42–3) identifies their benefits from the point of view of the centre. They provide:

- a mechanism for giving a greater profile to a type of activity;
- a capacity for concentrated and effective effort on a particular issue;
- a tool for involving non-partisans in decision-making on the basis of their expertise or involvement in relevant private or voluntary sector activities; and
- an expression of an 'above politics' approach to decision-making.

When the Conservative Party was in opposition during the 1974–9 period, it perceived quangos as a manifestation of bureaucratic, expensive, big government. When in office, however, such bodies proliferated, largely as a means of diminishing the powers of local government and attempting (so the Conservatives argued) to encourage a more business-like approach to the running of local affairs, drawing on the expertise of key figures in the business and civic communities. Throughout the UK, new bodies emerged such as Training and Enterprise Councils, NHS Trusts, Housing Action Trusts, and Urban Development Corporations. A major study by Weir and Hall (1994) estimated that quangos were 5,573 in number, run by between 57,000 and 63,000 individuals, and responsible for almost one third of all public expenditure. What John Stewart (1996) describes as this 'new magistracy' outnumbered councillors by almost 2:1.

Local government reorganisation in the mid 1990s heightened these trends, especially in Scotland, where the desire for unitary authorities and for all local services to be placed under 'one roof' failed to materialise, despite the rhetoric (see Chapter 3). The outcome was some services being wholly or partly removed from local authority control and a further proliferation of agencies and joint boards. In opposition pre-1997, Labour promised what Shadow Scottish Secretary George Robertson described as a 'bonfire' of the quangos when Labour came to power. In practice, the flames were nowhere to be seen. The Labour-dominated Scottish Executive found, like previous Scottish Office ministers, that NDPBs were much easier to give central direction to than elected and sometimes recalcitrant local authorities.

An important qualifying point is that non-elected local governance is more than simply NDPBs or even quangos. They are significant components, but they do not cover all non-elected bodies responsible for public money and public services at the local level. Local governance also includes the new wave of private companies involved in public-private partnerships. If we discounted these, we would miss an important trend in the further fragmentation of local service provision.

Overall, a number of bodies exist in Scotland, which, although not elected by local people, are involved in the formation of local policies and the delivery of local services. These cover areas such as housing, policing, further education, higher education, water and sewerage, and environmental protection. Obtaining precise figures, however, is not a particularly easy task. On a UK level, the House of Commons Public Administration Committee (2001) freely admitted in a report that it encountered considerable difficulty in producing precise categories of 'quangos' and definitive figures. Subject to some qualification, it did attempt to map out the 'local quango state' in the UK, and its final figure was some 5,338 bodies. We cannot give firm figures for Scotland because it will depend on our definitions of 'local governance' and 'quango'. As a rough guide, however, the system of non-elected local governance in Scotland would include:

- Executive NDPBs such as Scottish Water, Scottish Enterprise and the Scottish Environmental Protection Agency.
- Advisory NDPBs such as Local Government Boundary Commission for Scotland and Advisory Committee on Sites of Special Scientific Interest.
- Self-governing organisations such as further education colleges (46) and universities/higher education institutions (20).
- Registered housing associations (260 approximately).
- Local enterprise companies (25).
- Police boards and authorities (8).
- Fire joint boards (6).
- Health boards (15).
- Special health boards (8).
- Acute NHS trusts (14).
- Primary care trusts (13).
- Private companies operating local services under PPP.

It comes as little surprise that there is no agreement on how 'democratic' this fragmented system of local governance actually is. Supporters see several democratic merits. Perhaps the most fundamental is arrived at by a subtle redefining of the term 'democracy'. In essence, the message is that real democracy is not about electing local politicians who have little power anyway and who are insulated from genuine local accountability because of the vagaries of the voting system and national voting patterns. Real democracy is about delivering low-cost high-quality services (see Adam Smith Institute 1989). What could be more democratic (so the argument goes) than a system of boards and agencies with this clear focus, unimpeded by elections, party groups and the trappings of 'traditional' democracy? David Hunt, former Conservative Minister for Public Services and Science epitomises this view when talking of housing associations, local enterprise companies and other local bodies:

> There are many . . . areas where there has been as shift in power, and it has been towards local people . . . (T)hose working on such local bodies bring invaluable local knowledge to their work. They are members of the communities they serve. Accountability does not come much more direct than that. (Hunt 1995: 27)

Scottish Executive ministers have not been quite so stout in defending the local 'quango state' as a democratic gain. Their main focus has been to argue that greater transparency and openness of non-elected systems act as near surrogates for directly elected structures. Peter Peacock, the Deputy Minister for Finance and Public Services, spoke in support of the Public Appointments and Public Bodies Bill 2002, proposing a new office of Commissioner for Public Appointments:

> The bill will introduce changes that will modernise and improve our system of public appointments and ensure a further depoliticisation of the appointments process. The bill will guarantee openness, transparency and accountability and will underpin the existing commitment to appointments being made on merit. It will encourage more people to participate in public life and will have a positive impact on encouraging a more diverse range of people to serve on Scotland's public bodies. The bill will provide the basis for better and greater public confidence in our public bodies and the public appointment system. (Scottish Parliament Official Report, 31 October 2002: col. 14875)

Critics of non-elected local governance would certainly favour greater transparency and openness, but only as a second best option. Fundamentally, non-elected structures are seen as having many problems. Three are worthy of particular mention. First and foremost, they are removed from direct electoral control and so there is a democratic deficit. Citizens may have indirect means of complaint (for example through the Water Industry Commissioner for Scotland and the Scottish Public Services Ombudsman); some councillors will sit on police boards or health boards, but they are not directly elected to that position and so governance is twice removed from the electorate. Second, in cases of ministerial appointments, there is a history of ministerial bias in appointments, often dubbed 'cronyism'. Rosie (2002: 125) suggests: 'what government in its right mind is going to appoint its known political enemies to positions of power and influence where they can use that power and influence to thwart government policy.' It could be argued that the creation of the Commissioner for Public Appointments will not dispense with the problem because it is simply another ministerially appointed quango to oversee quango appointments. Third, the growth of PFI/PPP projects (particularly for schools) means that private companies deliver local services in accordance with contractual agreements. Contracts have been negotiated and agreed with directly elected local authorities, but nevertheless there is a further democratic 'distance' between the electorate and those who deliver local services.

Conclusion – Beyond Elections: Contributing to a Healthy Local Democracy?

Does non-electoral participation and the growth of non-elected local governance contribute to a healthy local democracy in Scotland? There is no conclusive answer to this question. We have just dealt with differing perspectives on the democratic worth of non-elected local governance. Similarly with regard to public participation, there is no straightforward agreement. Viewed from one angle, there is certainly little trouble in finding support for modern participation exercises. The political agenda has moved on from the 1950s and 1960s, not just in Scotland but also in developed industrial and post-industrial economies (OECD 2001). As Bishop and Davis explain:

> Why the new interest in participation? In essence, because of what Hindess (1997) labels a 'democratic deficit' as liberal democracies struggle to connect with, and satisfy the aspirations of, citizens. Declining trust in public institutions, the rise of social movements, public sector change and new expectations of service quality have made elected officials sensitive about legitimacy. Participation becomes an attractive strategy not just for policy improvement, but for drawing disaffected citizens back to the political mainstream. (Bishop and Davis 2002: 15)

The implication for Scotland is that non-electoral forms of public participation not only produce 'better' policy, but they also assist in producing a more stable Scottish civil society, in itself and its relations with political institutions. When we factor in that participation is linked to the 'modernisation' agenda of the Scottish Executive, the force of language is important. After all, who would argue against modernising aspects of public life? However, once we delve beneath the positive symbolism there is a counter perspective. Ironically, its seeds are contained in the previous statement by Bishop and Davis. Participation, it can be argued, is first and foremost an initiative of the centre with the primary role of ensuring stability and adding legitimacy to policy processes. When we add to this the arguments that the modernisation processes does not fundamentally alter the power of the Scottish Executive (Chapter 10) or party groups at the local level (Chapters 4 and 5), then there is a case for suggesting that modern methods of public consultation are to a large extent 'cosmetic'. Paradoxically, therefore, the tendency is not to disrupt existing power centres but to reinforce them. As we saw in the previous chapter, this means (for the moment at least) a fairly unhealthy local democracy, heavily constrained by the centre.

? Key Questions ?

1. Why does each phase in the desire for public participation need to be placed in its historical context?
2. Do modern methods of non-electoral participation genuinely shift the balance of power in favour of local communities?
3. Should structures of non-elected local governance in Scotland be brought under the control of the 32 democratically elected local authorities?

Further Reading

The works of Schumpeter [1943] (1976) and Pateman (1973) provide classic justifications of the arguments 'against' and 'for' public participation in government. A recent article by Lowndes et al. (2001) examines participation in the context of New Labour's modernisation programme. For Scotland, an essential read is the inquiry by the Local Government Committee (2003a, 2003b, 2003c) of the Scottish Parliament into Renewing Local Democracy: the main report; the research undertaken by McAteer, Orr and Bennett; and the report on civic participation events – all are invaluable reading. There is no definitive source on the structure of local governance in Scotland. Until such a document is produced, two useful documents are *How Government Works in Scotland* by Audit Scotland (2002a), and the report by the House of Commons Public Administration Committee (HC 367 2001) entitled *Mapping the Quango State*.

Useful Websites

http://www.demosproject.org
The Demos project. Funded by the EU and committed to improving citizen participation in EU states.

http://www.civicforum.org.uk
The Scottish Civic Forum. A body funded by the Scottish Executive to promote active citizenship.

http://www.cosla.gov.uk
The Convention of Scottish Local Authorities. Always useful to keep up-to-date with latest participation initiatives. The monthly *COSLA Connections* newsletter is a particularly useful source.

http://www.scotland.gov.uk
The Scottish Executive. Keep in touch with the creation and reform of non-elected structures.

CHAPTER SEVEN

Political Parties in Scottish Local Government

Political parties dominate local government in Scotland. The Scottish Executive may be the main 'driver' of local authorities but political parties are the 'engine'. As discussed in Chapters 4 and 5, the power of political parties in local councils manifests itself in party groups. Copus suggests:

> the party group has replaced the council chamber as the place in which majority councillors conduct representation, carry out political deliberation, make council decisions and set policy and where the minority group plan tactics, decide how to undermine the ruling group and conduct political debate. (Copus 2001a: 55)

The prominence of political parties in Scottish local government is a relatively recent phenomenon. Prior to the mid 1970s, local government in Scotland was a fairly uncontentious area of public life. It received annual increases in its funding and there were no dramatic attempts to curtail either its finances or powers. The numbers and involvement of independent councillors was high, and the level of party politics fairly low. From the mid 1970s onwards, however, council finances became squeezed on an annual basis and there were numerous central initiatives to reform, shape and curtail the powers, structures and finances of Scottish local authorities (McConnell 1995). Ever since this watershed, there have been initiatives such as grant clawback, rate-capping, Council Tax-capping, introduction of the Poll Tax, Compulsory Competitive

Tendering, removal of business rates from the control of local authorities, council house sales, severe limitations on capital expenditure and the ring-fencing of a growing proportion of central funding. It is unsurprising, therefore, that radical reforms have been met by a more radicalised Scottish local government, galvanising parties into action at local level and prompting them to contest more and more seats. Thus, most of Scotland's councillors are elected on a party ticket. In 1974, 67 per cent of councillors were elected as members of a political party (Bochel and Bochel 1998: 30). In 1995, 1999 and 2003, the figure increased to 86.3 per cent, 88.2 per cent and 81.0 per cent respectively (Denver and Bochel 2000: 123; private information provided by David Denver).

This chapter outlines and examines the profile in Scottish local government of the Scottish Labour Party, Scottish National Party, Scottish Conservative and Unionist Party, Scottish Liberal Democrats, Scottish Greens and Scottish Socialist Party. It also examines the tradition of independent councillors in Scotland. It concludes by assessing whether Scotland has its own distinctive tradition of political parties in local government.

Scottish Labour Party

Labour is the largest single party in Scottish local government and has used this local base as means of influencing public life north of the border (Hassan 2002). Its dominance has fluctuated over the years – always ahead of its nearest rivals the SNP – but its capture of the popular vote has declined in every local election since 1995. Table 7.1 contains detailed figures of the popular vote and seats won. In the 2003 elections, Labour obtained the support of 32.6 per cent of voters and took 41.7 per cent of council seats: 509 out of 1,222. Its control of councils is also less entrenched than we might think. As table 7.2 indicates, after the 1999 elections it held overall control in only 15 out of 32 councils. After the 2003 elections, it had an overall majority in only 13 councils and was the largest party in 4 others.

Labour's traditional electoral strength has been in the central belt (in councils such as West Dunbartsonhire, East Ayrshire, Midlothian and North Lanarkshire) and Scotland's four main cities, but this strength has been diminishing in recent years. In the 1995

Table 7.1 Performance of the main Scottish political parties in local government elections, 1974–2003.

Year	Authority	Labour		Conservative		SNP		Lib./ Lib. Dem.	
		Votes (%)	Seats	Votes (%)	Seats	Votes (%)	Seats	Votes (%)	Seats
1974	Region	38.5	72	28.6	112	12.6	18	5.1	11
1974	District	38.4	428	26.8	241	12.4	62	5.0	17
1977	District	31.6	299	27.2	277	24.2	170	4.0	31
1978	Region	39.6	177	30.3	136	20.9	18	2.3	6
1980	District	45.4	494	24.1	229	15.5	54	6.2	40
1982	Region	37.6	186	25.1	119	13.4	23	18.1	25
1984	District	45.7	545	21.4	189	11.7	59	12.8	78
1986	Region	43.9	223	16.9	65	18.2	36	15.1	40
1988	District	42.6	553	19.4	162	21.3	113	8.4	84
1990	Region	42.7	233	19.7	52	21.8	42	8.7	40
1992	District	34.0	468	23.2	204	24.3	150	9.5	94
1994	Region	41.8	220	13.7	31	26.8	73	11.9	60
1995	Unitary	43.8	614	11.3	82	26.2	181	9.7	121
1999	Unitary	36.6	545	13.7	108	28.9	201	13.6	148
2003	Unitary	32.6	509	15.1	123	24.0	181	14.6	175

Sources: Denver cited in Rallings and Thrasher (1997: 116); Denver and Bochel (2000: 120–3); *The Herald*, 'Election 2003', 3 May 2003; *The Scotsman*, 3 May 2003; private information provided by David Denver.

elections, Labour controlled the cities of Glasgow, Edinburgh, Aberdeen and Dundee. By 2003, it controlled only Glasgow and Edinburgh. It also managed victory in Stirling and held on to East Ayrshire, North Ayrshire, East Lothian and West Lothian, but lost outright control of South Ayrshire (gaining it subsequently only by a 'cut of the cards'). Labour's popular support in its power base is showing signs of being hit particularly by the Scottish Socialist Party (SSP). In Glasgow, for example, the SSP came second in 18 out of the 79 wards, a position normally expected of the SNP. A few more local elections are needed, however, before we are in the position to see if a longer-term trend is being established.

There are several issues to highlight in terms of our understanding of the Scottish Labour Party and local government. First, Labour is propped up by the FPTP system and it is unsurprising that its 2003 manifesto contained a commitment to FPTP (Scottish Labour Party 2003). After the 2003 elections, it held 89.9 per cent and 83.3 per cent of the seats in Glasgow and Midlothian respectively, despite obtaining only 47.61 per cent and 43.31 per cent of the vote. The situation is

Table 7.2   Political control of Scotland's 32 local authorities based on election results, 1999–2003.

Election year	Labour	Cons.	SNP	Lib. Dem.	Indep.	NOC
1999	15	0	1	0	6	10
2003	13	0	1	1	6	11

Note: Control of councils may change between elections, as a consequence mostly of by-election results, party defections and the breakdown of minority administrations. In NOC councils, no single party has an overall majority of seats and hence there is no overall control (NOC) based on election results alone. Control of such councils depends on political bargaining. Occasionally, however, the nature of the results means that bargaining is not feasible and control of the council is decided by a 'cut' of playing cards.

similar in other councils where Labour has an overall majority. In East Ayrshire, for example, it obtained 71.9 per cent per cent of the seats but only 49.3 per cent of the vote. It is also propped up by the fact that voters tend not to vote on the basis of local issues: they tend to vote in accordance with national preferences (see Chapter 4). This is not to suggest that Labour voters should 'get wise' to the reality of Labour councils; it is simply to suggest that Labour councils tend to benefit from in-built political allegiances within the working- and middle-class Scottish electorates, in terms of working-class identity and public sector sympathies (Bennie et al. 1997; Brown et al. 1999).

Second, when Labour was in opposition at Westminster, its rhetoric was much more 'localist' than the policies actually produced when in coalition with the Liberal Democrats in the first term of the Scottish Parliament 1999–2003. It did introduce a number of measures to give greater autonomy to local authorities such as the replacement of CCT with Best Value and the introduction of a power to promote 'well-being'. However, on major issues such as the return of business rates to local control, the abolition of capping powers or reducing financial dependence on the centre, the Scottish Executive has shied away from major enhancements of local freedoms. In essence, the realities of political office have come into play. In the same manner as governments in the post-war period, Scottish Labour has found that too many financial and political freedoms for local authorities have the potential to interfere with the financial and political priorities of the centre (see McConnell 1999).

Third, the main thrust of Labour's policies for local government is modernisation, including partnerships, joined-up working, community consultation, and social and environmental justice. The impact of such ideas is that they present a challenge to many of the traditional areas of Labour strength at the local level. In effect, Labour is attempting to modernise the Party by a 'trickle down' effect. Further pressures will come from this direction with the introduction of PR in 2007.

Scottish National Party

Over the past two decades, the SNP has become the main challenger to Labour in local government. Yet its difficulty is that it can command a reasonable percentage of the popular vote but cannot translate this into seats. In the three elections to unitary authorities from 1995 onwards, it polled 26.2 per cent, 28.9 per cent and 24.0 per cent of the vote. Unlike Labour, however, it is hindered by the FPTP system. Despite the fact that it obtained roughly one quarter of the vote over these three elections, it secured only 15.7 per cent, 16.5 per cent and 14.8 per cent of council seats, and control of only 9.3 per cent, 3.1 per cent and 3.1 per cent of councils. Its most solid base of support is north of the central belt. In 1995, it took control in Angus, Moray, and Perth and Kinross. In 1999, it retained outright control only in Angus. As a consequence of by-elections and defections, it then took control of Clackmannanshire and Falkirk, as well as sharing power in West Dunbartonshire and Dumfries and Galloway. In 2003, its only outright success was to retain Angus.

Several issues are worth highlighting in terms of the SNP and local government. It is a centre-left party with a long history wavering between a gradualist and fundamentalist 'big bang' approach to independence (Levy 1990: Lynch 2002a). Its manifesto for the 2003 Scottish Parliamentary elections clearly outlines its localist credentials:

> Local government is the building block of democracy . . . we need local governance legislation to define and protect our councils and to reform local government. We need legislation to allow communities to take their own decisions and set their own priorities in the areas for which local government is responsible. It means a hands off attitude from central government. (SNP 2003: 26)

Its policies include:

- Replacing Council Tax with Local Income Tax.
- Establishing an independent review of local finance with a view to allowing local authorities to take as much control as possible of their budgets and services.
- Replacing PFI schemes with Not For Profit Trusts.
- Reducing Scottish business rates to below the UK rate.
- Introducing a PR electoral system (Single Transferable Vote).

All opposition parties have an element of 'luxury' by the very fact that they are in opposition. In other words, they do not hold political office and so they are not in a position to put their policies into practice. Arguably, the SNP is no exception. It will certainly benefit from PR at a local level, but a major difficulty would arise if it achieved independence or was the majority partner in a devolved coalition and faced 32 councils of largely different political persuasions. Its strong demands for local autonomy whilst in opposition would be more difficult to realise in practice. No post-war government in the UK has ever been able to follow through in entirety its 'opposition' policies for local government. As we will see in Chapter 10, the demands of holding office are such that no government can afford to grant political and financial freedoms to local authorities to the extent that Executive policies are severely compromised.

Scottish Conservative and Unionist Party

Since the mid 1970s, the Conservative Party has experienced a slow death in Scottish local government. From the heights of 28.6 per cent of the vote in the first regional elections in 1974, it now commands roughly half that figure. In the 2003 elections, it obtained 15.1 per cent of the vote – a slight increase from the two previous elections. When we add the fact that roughly half the electorate don't vote in local elections, the reality is that only about 7 or 8 out of every 100 members of the electorate actually vote Conservative in local authority elections. The FPTP system also works against the Conservatives. Since 1995, the Party has failed to secure overall control of a single Scottish council. At the 2003 elections, its best result was to tie with Labour in South Ayrshire.

When in government at Westminster over the 1979–97 period, the Conservatives were unsympathetic to either a Scottish Parliament or local government. The Scottish Parliament was perceived as the 'thin end of a wedge' that would lead to the break-up of the UK. Local government was viewed largely as a bureaucratic and unresponsive power base for opposition parties. Thus, the electoral weakness of the Scottish Conservatives at the local level has been a product partly of what many voters perceive as its 'anti-Scottish' policies, and partly a rejection of new-found Conservative claims that local government needs to be revitalised. Current policies exhibit a strong element of continuity from the past. They propose to strengthen not local government as such, but the system of local governance by freeing communities from what the Party sees as wasteful and unaccountable councils. Policy proposals include:

- Substantially reducing the ring-fencing of Scottish Executive grants to councils.
- Management-led buyouts of Direct Labour Organisations and Direct Service Organisations.
- Facilitating a three-year real level freeze in Council Tax.
- Progressive transfer of all remaining council houses to community ownership and management.

Once again, the luxury of opposition is evident. Indeed, barring any fundamental electoral realignment, a marginal role in Scottish local government looms for the foreseeable future. It is a party deeply sceptical of local state provision, favouring a much more flexible system in which local authorities are simply one player in a system governed by local people, neighbourhoods and voluntary organisations. However, were the Party fortunate enough to achieve a majority in the Scottish Parliament, it would be difficult to actually carry through such apparently 'localist' policies, dispensing with central direction. It is easy, for example, to oppose the ring-fencing of central funds when they are being ring-fenced by a Labour-Liberal coalition. It would be less easy to oppose the withering away of ring-fencing if the purpose were to meet the priorities of a Scottish Conservative administration. Paradoxically, the only hope for a boost to Conservative fortunes at the local level is likely to be the introduction of PR, but the Party is opposed to such a move. The broadly proportional outcomes produced by the dual electoral system for the Scottish

Parliament have benefited the Conservatives but they did not introduce electoral reform themselves. Supporting PR for local elections would present the danger of having a knock-on effect and encouraging its use at Westminster. At the present time, this would be a step too far for an opposition that relies on FPTP to gain power at the UK level.

Scottish Liberal Democrats

Historically, Liberal parties have a strong tradition supportive of decentralising power and achieving local electoral successes that 'buck the trend' of national voting. Levels of support have varied considerably over the years, falling mostly within the 8–14 per cent range. The Scottish Liberal Democrats are clear losers from the FPTP system and have a historical commitment to PR in the form of the Single Transferable Vote. In the 1995 elections, they polled 9.7 per cent of the vote; they won 10.4 per cent of seats but did not secure control of a single council. In the 1999 elections, they polled 13.6 per cent of the vote, won 12.1 per cent of the seats and again failed to gain overall control of a single council. They did, however, manage to be the leading party in a coalition running Aberdeenshire, and the second largest party (in terms of the popular vote) in Aberdeen, Edinburgh, Inverclyde and East Dunbartonshire. At the 2003 elections, they polled 14.6 per cent of the vote, won 14.3 per cent of the seats, but controlled only 3.1 per cent of councils (one council, Inverclyde). They were also the largest party in East Dunbartonshire and Aberdeenshire.

Scottish Liberal Democrat policies for local government reveal a strong element of decentralisation and social democracy. They include:

- Replacing Council Tax with a Local Income Tax related to ability to pay, and allowing local authorities power over business rates.
- Seeking a consensus between the Scottish Executive and local authorities in relation to the freedom given to councils to spend money in areas of their choosing. This includes agreeing outcomes between the Scottish Executive and local authorities in order to achieve national public policy objectives.

- In distributing funding to councils, ensuring that account is taken of the variable costs incurred due to particular local circumstances.
- Encouraging councils to devolve responsibility where appropriate. This involves passing control of housing to community-based housing associations and tenants' co-operatives, community-controlled non-profit-distributing trusts providing one-stop services, and similar bodies owned and run by local people.
- Supporting the establishment of fairly-elected community councils and elected burgh councils in urban areas with limited power, using revenue to tackle community issues. (Scottish Liberal Democrats 2003)

The luxury of opposition is less evident than for other opposition parties, simply because the Scottish Liberal Democrats have been a coalition partner in the Scottish Executive since 1999. It is the opposition party best placed to implement some of its policies for local government, even though it is not a substantial force in local government itself (Lynch 2002b). Some policies are potentially attractive to a Labour-dominated Executive. For example, trying to achieve a consensus on priorities between the Scottish Executive and local authorities has already proved expedient for Labour. However, other policies are less appealing. As will be seen in Chapter 10, the history of central–local relations is riddled with conflict between two sets of democratically elected governments (central and local), each with democratic mandates but often different priorities and competing claims to 'represent'. Some Scottish Liberal Democrat policies are anathema to Labour. For all the theoretical merits of Local Income Tax in terms of fairness (and it has many supporters within the Labour Party), the introduction of new local taxes in the UK is particularly problematic where there is a reliance exclusively on one local tax, because governments inevitably face a severe backlash from the losers in the move to any new system (see McConnell 1999). For a Labour-dominated Scottish Executive, it would be politically very difficult at the present time to introduce a Local Income Tax or indeed any new tax as a replacement for the Council Tax. The introduction of PR in the form of Single Transferable Vote is another matter. In essence, it has been a key price Labour has paid for its weakened status in terms of the number of MSPs in the Scottish Parliament. Correspondingly, the prospect of PR for local elections in 2007 is a major victory for the Scottish Liberal Democrats.

Scottish Green Party and Scottish Socialist Party

The Scottish Green Party is left of centre and concentrates particularly on environmental matters, although strong themes of social justice permeate its policies (Bennie 2002). Proposals for local government include the introduction of Single Transferable Vote, phasing out of PPP and PFI projects, the introduction of Land Value Taxation, 'green' housing and planning policies, and the development of community recycling trusts (Scottish Green Party 2003). In the 2003 elections, it focused its attention on the Scottish Parliamentary elections and was very successful in obtaining seven MSPs. However, in the local elections it fielded only one candidate. Once again, FPTP works against smaller parties such as the Greens. In some respects, their influence is more akin to that of a pressure group, not holding political office but raising awareness of issues by helping push environmental matters onto the agenda of the Scottish Executive. The fact that Labour and the Liberal Democrats are committed to sustainable development means that to some extent, the Scottish Greens are pushing at a partially open door.

The Scottish Socialist Party (SSP) is currently led by MSP Tommy Sheridan, joined by a further five MSPs after the 2003 elections. His high public profile in Scotland makes him as well known as any other major political figure in Scotland. The policies of the SSP are clearly left of centre and focus on themes of redistribution, social justice and peace, within a wider commitment to an independent socialist Scotland (Bennie 2002). Its policies for local government include the introduction of a Scottish Service Tax based on ability to pay, free school meals for all schoolchildren, abolition of warrant sales, and ending of PFI projects to be replaced by public ownership and control (Scottish Socialist Party 2003). The 'list' vote for the Scottish Parliamentary elections allowed Tommy Sheridan to become an MSP in 1999 and be influential in raising awareness of issues surrounding warrant sales, school meals, private finance, the role of council housing and the 'unfairness' of the Council Tax. In the 2003 elections the SSP fielded 313 candidates in the local elections, obtained 3.3 per cent of the vote, but won only 2 council seats. Nevertheless, in many areas of traditional Labour strength, it pushed the SNP into third place. Whether the SSP will exercise sole control of a local authority is debatable. However, with the introduction of PR for local government elections, the influence of the SSP is liable to rise considerably.

Table 7.3 Independent councillors in Scottish local government, 1974–2003.

Year	Authority	Vote (%)	Seats
1974	Region	12.4	114
1974	District	14.1	345
1977	District	9.8	318
1978	Region	4.9	89
1980	District	6.7	289
1982	Region	5.1	87
1984	District	6.8	267
1986	Region	4.8	79
1988	District	6.4	231
1990	Region	4.5	73
1992	District	7.4	228
1994	Region	4.2	65
1995[1]	Unitary	7.7	155
1999[2]	Unitary	11.8	135
2003[3]	Unitary	10.2	231

Notes:

[1] Elections in 1995 took place only for the 29 mainland authorities. The figures for this year underestimate the support for independent candidates because they exclude substantial support in the islands. In 1994, although the Scottish average was only 4.2 per cent, the figure for the three island councils was 89.9 per cent.

[2] The only Scotland-wide voting figures available for 1999 (11.8 per cent) are for the 29 mainland councils. Separate figures for the three island councils indicate 79.9 per cent support for independent candidates and an additional 56 seats.

[3] The figures for 2003 are the first to cover all 32 councils.

Sources: Adapted from Lynch (2001: 214); Denver and Bochel (2000); information provided by David Denver.

Independents

In addition to political parties, there is a very strong tradition of independent councillors in Scottish local government. In other words, they stand for election as individuals – not on a party ticket. Some have never been members of parties and some have been party members but for one reason or another are not prepared to be constrained by the demands of party. Some are of long standing whilst others (such as Firefighters Against Cuts in 2003) are the result of short-term protests. Particularly in the islands, party politics at the local level has never been prevalent. As table 7.3 indicates, popular support has been reasonably stable (usually in the 5–10 per cent range), with the figure for 2003 being 10.2 per cent. The main areas of independent support are the Highlands and Islands, and to a lesser extent the Borders and Dumfries and Galloway. Many seats in the islands are uncontested and for those that are, independents dominate. In 2003, for example, all seats in Orkney were contested by independents. On most of the Scottish mainland, however, independents have diminished in the face of a more politicised local government generally, and the difficulty of competing against slicker party machines. Within specific geographical areas, nevertheless, the role of independent councillors is still considerable, even though their Scottish-wide vote is less than that for the Scottish Conservatives or the Scottish Liberal Democrats. After the 2003 elections, independents held majority control in Argyll and Bute, Moray, Highland, Orkney, Shetland and the Western Isles. Independents were also the largest group in the Scottish Borders and second largest grouping in Dumfries and Galloway. Thus, the tradition of independent councillors is very much alive in select rural and island areas. Independents in Scotland control more councils than any political party other than Scottish Labour.

Conclusion – A Scottish Distinctiveness in Party Trends?

Much has written about political parties in Scotland but little has been written about them at the local level (Kellas 1990; Midwinter et al. 1991; Brown et al. 1999; Lynch 2001; Hassan and Warhurst 2002a). However, we should not be discouraged by this lack of attention. The more general writings on the parties and how they operate (and have operated) at the Westminster and Scottish Parliament levels provide us with some pointers. We can identify three broad models which help us think about the distinctiveness or otherwise of party trends in Scottish local government.

First, there is the *homogeneity/union model*. A crude and dying argument can be found implicitly in writings such as Beer (1969) and explicitly in Birch (1973) which suggest that the Westminster Parliament and its sovereignty are the focal points for a relative homogeneity in society. Therefore, most political views can be accommodated within the Conservative and Labour Parties at Westminster, who run their affairs in a centralised manner, leaving little freedom for local parties. Following the logic of this argument, we would expect Scottish political parties at the local level to produce no discernible differences (compared with England and Wales) in either voting patterns or policies.

Second there is the *Scottish distinctiveness model*. This model can best be described as an exaggerated version of the argument of Kellas (1984) that there exists a 'Scottish political system'. It derives its distinctiveness from the historical, legal, educational, media and cultural, attitudinal, political, institutional, economic and organisational character of Scotland. Kellas himself is keen to emphasise the links with the British political system, but nevertheless his argument – by virtue of the considered defence of the term 'system' – contains the seeds of a view where the focus is essentially autonomous political interactions in the Scottish context. The implication of such an argument is that local electoral trends and party policies in Scotland would be virtually independent of trends south of the border.

Third there is the *politics of semi-autonomy model*. A good contemporary example can be found in the work of Hassan and Warhurst (2002b). They capture the dual dimension of party activity in two separate statements. On the one hand: 'Devolution . . . has changed the political environment and has forced the political parties to develop distinctive Scottish agendas and priorities' (Hassan and Warhurst 2002b: 13). On the other hand, the (1) continuing legislative role for Westminster because of the use of the Sewel Convention and (2) the Scottish Executive copying Westminster initiatives have meant that devolution has not been such a radical break from the past as might have been hoped. Therefore: 'we have . . . a limited conservative version of devolution, whereby the potential for change is being constrained' (Hassan and Warhurst 2000b: 15).

The broad implication for local party trends is that we would expect to find a combination of separate and shared trends in election results and political party activity. With regard to separateness first of all, there is no doubt that separate 'Scottish' trends exist. If voting behaviour is influenced by factors such as class, age, religion, race, gender, national identity, political values and family socialisation (Rose and McAllister 1990), we should expect the distinctive socio-economic profile of Scotland to produce an aspect of distinctiveness in voting behaviour and in the surrounding party systems. This is especially so in local elections where there may be micro-influences in terms of social profile, local issues, the personalities of local elites and local party interactions (Rallings and Thrasher 1997; Webb 2000). For example, although varying according to the locality, Scotland as a whole has a genuine four-party system in local government. The difference is made by the SNP. England of course has no such equivalent and operates essentially on the basis of a three-party system. Wales, by contrast, has Plaid Cymru although its local electoral strength cannot match the SNP's popular vote of roughly 24–9 per cent between 1992 and 2003. Since the first elections to the unitary authorities in the mid 1990s, Plaid Cymru obtained votes of 12.5 per cent (1995) and 18.2 per cent (1999) (Rallings and Thrasher 1997: 109; Morgan and Connelly 2001: 35). The Conservatives are also much weaker in Scotland. For example, in the three local elections in 1995, 1999 and 2003, they averaged 13.7 per cent of the vote but in England over the same period (excepting the Great London Authority and Mayoral elections), the average was 31.1 per cent (Rallings and Thrasher 1997: 112–13; Leeke 2003: 52; *Local Government Chronicle*, 8 May 2003).

Another aspect of Scottish distinctiveness is the strength of the Labour Party at the local level in Scotland. The distinctiveness is not in terms of Labour's share of the popular vote. Indeed, Labour is squeezed by the four-party system in Scotland, having to contend with a nationalist party (the SNP), especially in many areas of the central belt. The figures given in table 7.1 indicate that Labour averaged 37.7 per cent of the vote in Scottish local elections between 1995 and 2003, whilst figures for England over the same period are almost identical at 37 per cent (Rallings and Thrasher 1997: 112–13; Leeke 2003: 52; *Local Government Chronicle*, 8 May 2003). The difference is in terms of political control. Labour in Scotland has benefited particularly from the FPTP system because its support is heavily concentrated (especially in the central belt) and its votes are used quite efficiently. In England, however, Labour frequently has to engage in genuine two- or even three-party competition. In 1999 and 2003, for example, Labour in Scotland got 32.6 per cent and 36.6 per cent of the vote respectively, and obtained 41.7 per cent and 44.6 per cent the council seats. For the same years in England, it got 33.1 per cent and 30.0 per cent the vote, and 34.3 per cent and 25.8 per cent of the seats.

A degree of separateness also exists in party policies towards local government. For example, and unlike New Labour at

Westminster, Scottish Labour is not in favour of elected mayors and has rejected the idea of requiring councils to choose a form of executive leadership (see Chapter 4). Scottish Labour has also forged its own pathway by supporting PR, essentially for pragmatic reasons as a consequence of a post-election deal with the Scottish Liberal Democrats (see Chapter 5). More generally, the party machines of Scottish Labour, Scottish Conservatives and the Scottish Liberals all exhibit varying degrees of autonomy in policy-making (Hassan 2002; Seawright 2002; Lynch 2002b). Also, there is no equivalent of the SNP in England, and so there is no equivalent policy alternative of (for example) replacing PFI schemes with Not For Profit Trusts.

The party trends and policies mentioned above represent (at least in part) one side of the coin: the historical distinctiveness of Scotland, especially since devolution. The other side is the commonality stemming (in part) from the Union. Local electoral trends throughout the UK share many similarities. There are several main reasons for this. First, the majority of people vote on 'national' factors in local elections (see Chapter 5), and so their voting instincts (for example, 'for' or 'against' the government of the day at Westminster) will have much in common. Second, there are many broad similarities in the socio-economic profiles of the various nations of the UK. For example, figures from the National Statistics Office publication *Regional Trends* reveal that employment rates in 2002 were 79.7 per cent in England and 75.8 per cent in Scotland (Office of National Statistics 2003: table 5.1). Furthermore, average gross weekly income between 1998 and 2001 was £496 and £419 respectively (Office of National Statistics 2003: table 8.2). Figures from the 2001 census also reveal quite substantial north-south similarities in terms of race and gender. The basic point to be made, therefore, is that the similarities are more striking than the differences. Scotland is not so vastly different that it has (for example) the profile of a poor, underdeveloped Third World country. All the nations of the UK are (on average) fairly prosperous advanced industrial and post-industrial capitalist economies with liberal-democratic political structures.

In terms of party voting patterns, as a consequence, there is much in common throughout the UK. For example, as a product particularly of a reaction against successive Conservative Governments at Westminster, Conservative support in local elections fell by roughly half over the course of the 1980s and mid 1990s in both Scotland and England (Rallings and Thrasher 1997: 118).

Correspondingly there were Labour rises over the same period. Indeed, between 1995 and 2003, there has been the beginnings of a slight Conservative revival at the local level, north and south of the border. This may be due, in part, to a common anti-New Labour vote. Party policies for local government are also remarkably similar. For all that each party allows some autonomy for its sub-national variant, it generally shares more in common than it disagrees upon. To take Scottish Labour as an example, its rhetoric has been further 'left' of the British party than its actual policies (Hassan 2002). Therefore, core local government policies such as Best Value, support for Council Tax, central control of business rates, and the allowance of councils to promote 'well-being' are all common north and south of the border.

In the last analysis, it can be argued that the 'politics of semi-autonomy' best describes the activities of political parties in Scottish local government. They are different, but not quite as different as we might think. Over the next decade or so as devolution moves beyond its formative years, it will no doubt be accompanied by 'political' argument as to how much relative autonomy Scottish parties and institutions should have.

? Key Questions ?

1. To what extent is Labour's dominance of Scottish local government an accurate reflection of its popular support?
2. What is the likely impact of PR on the control of local councils in Scotland?
3. Why has Scotland retained a strong tradition of councillors who are not affiliated to any political party?
4. To what extent is party politics in Scottish local government different from party politics south of the border?

Further Reading

Tomorrow's Scotland, edited by Gerry Hassan and Chris Warhurst, is essential reading for an up-to-date analysis of Scottish political parties post-devolution. Peter Lynch's (2001) *Scottish Government and Politics* is much broader in scope and so political parties and electoral behaviour are situated within the structures, processes and politics of the Scottish Parliament. In *Local Elections in Britain* (1997), Rallings and Thrasher provide the most detailed examination yet of local elections. The book is now a few years old but there is substantial treatment given of Scotland and the analysis remains un-diminished. *The Modern British Party System* by Paul Webb (2000) is an exceptional book. It deals with political parties generally within the UK (including local government) with excellent treatment of Scotland, Wales and Northern Ireland. A particular strength is that it engages with political science perspectives on party orientation and electoral behaviour. Colin Copus (1999, 2001a, 2001b) has produced a very worthwhile series of articles on local parties. They deal with everything from national party control over local parties to the power of local party groups. More generally, the works of David Denver and Hugh Bochel have become the authoritative sources for elections and electoral behaviour in Scotland. Many of their articles appear in the journal *Scottish Affairs*, a very useful source more generally for keeping up to date with activities of Scotland's political parties.

Useful Websites

http://www.scottishlabour.org.uk
Scottish Labour Party.

http://www.snp.org.uk
Scottish National Party.

http://www.scottishtories.org.uk
Scottish Conservative and Unionist Party.

http://www.scotlibdems.org.uk
Scottish Liberal Democrats.

http://www.scottishgreens.org.uk
Scottish Green Party.

http://www.scottishsocialistparty.org
Scottish Socialist Party.

CHAPTER EIGHT

Reconstructing Accountability: Value for Money and the Rise of the Performance Culture in Scottish Councils

Until the late 1970s, local authorities in Scotland had substantial discretion in terms of how they provided local services. If they wished, they could contract out work to other bodies (private companies in particular) but there was no imperative to do so. Furthermore, even in the period immediately after the 1976 IMF-prompted public spending cuts, scrutiny of performance failings tended to be *post hoc*. In other words, if services were problematic in terms of policy, administration or delivery, 'traditional' systems of accountability came into play. Members of the public could complain to a local government official, raise the matter with their councillor, or take their case to the Commissioner for Local Administration (post-1975).

From the early 1980s onwards, a new system evolved. The underlying message was that local authorities could no longer be insulated from pressures to cut costs and improve services. In essence, traditional notions of public service delivery were being reconstructed. As a consequence, providing Value for Money (VFM) became the dominant assumption about the delivery of local services. Definitions of VFM put forward by the Accounts Commission (Scotland) and the Audit Commission (England and Wales) have become the norm in terms of public sector usage. VFM can be encapsulated as the 3Es:

- Economy: low cost.
- Efficiency: minimum wastage.
- Effectiveness: provision of high-quality services.

This chapter outlines and examines the main ways in which Value for Money requirements permeate the activities of modern Scottish local authorities. First, it provides a context by examining the system of Compulsory Competitive Tendering (CCT) which operated in Scotland under the Conservatives from the period 1980–97. Second, it focuses on the Scottish Executive's replacement: the Best Value (BV) regime. Third, it looks at the rise of the performance culture in Scottish councils, examining in particular the role of Performance Indicators as well as the roles of Audit Scotland and the Accounts Commission in 'policing' council performance. Finally, it takes a step back and explores the way in which VFM and performance imperatives have become an integral part of the new system of accountability in Scottish local government. Throughout, it makes comparisons, where appropriate, with England and Wales.

Background: The Old Regime of CCT

In order to understand the present BV regime in Scottish local government, it is useful to understand the preceding system of CCT. This gives us a sense, not just of the historical context of a central plank of contemporary Scottish Executive policy, but also the strengths and weakness of an alternative system designed to obtain value for money in Scottish local authorities.

CCT has its origins in the climate of the late 1970s and early 1980s. A series of public sector strikes took place in 1978–9 and became known as the 'Winter of Discontent' after the editor of the *Sun* used a quote from Shakespeare's Richard III to encapsulate the political strife in Britain. The argument from Conservative ministers was that never again would the country be held to ransom because of the power of trade unions, especially at the local level where councils were the sole providers of local services. At the same time, a view developed within much of British industry (articulated particularly by a pressure group called Aims of Industry) that the private sector should be given access to local authority work. A series of influential papers published by the Adam Smith Institute and the Conservative Political Centre, written by Michael Forsyth who would later become Secretary of State for Scotland, advocated precisely these views. The Conservatives were also under pressure from their natural base of support among domestic ratepayers. Groups such as the Federation of Scottish Ratepayers and the

National Association of Ratepayers' Action Groups lobbied ministers in an attempt to find ways of curtailing local expenditures (see McConnell 1995, 1999). Intellectual support for this shift in ideas came from the 'New Right'. In particular the writings of Downs (1957), Buchanan and Tullock (1962), Niskanen (1971) and others have been amalgamated into what is called 'public choice' theory. Midwinter usefully summarises its key propositions:

> the public choice approach has developed an economic model of politics which assumes that voters, politicians and bureaucrats engage in maximising behaviour in the pursuit of their own self interest. Voters seek to maximise their consumption of public goods at minimal costs, politicians to maximise votes, and bureaucrats to maximise budgets. (Midwinter 1989: 9)

The implication of this general thinking is that the discipline of competition will drive down costs and force a reassessment of service provision. Beyond the Conservative Party and some of its supporters, however, there was little sympathy for these views. Scotland had (and still has) a culture which was defensive of the public service ethos. It also had a plethora of Labour-controlled authorities which had no wish to tackle local trade unions. Nevertheless, in the pre-Scottish Parliament era a series of legislative initiatives came from Westminster and imposed CCT on reluctant Scottish councils. Further details are contained in figure 8.1.

The basis of CCT was that in specified areas of work, local authorities were required to invite bids from other contractors. The council itself could bid, but subject to the requirements of (1) establishing separate trading accounts for each service (therefore disallowing cross subsidy) and (2) making a 5 per cent rate of return over three successive years. Otherwise, the Secretary of State could use reserve powers to remove a service from the control of the relevant local authority. Whatever the source of bids, the contract should be awarded to the lowest bidder, subject to the bid meeting quality requirements. This entire process was by no means straightforward for councils. They had to assess their service requirements and draw up detailed tender documents. The work had to be advertised in appropriate national and international publications. The council itself had to submit a sealed bid (as did private companies), before reviewing the bids and awarding the contracts. Thereafter, monitoring was required to ensure contract

---

Figure 8.1   CCT legislation applying in Scotland, 1980–97.

Local Government Planning And Land Act 1980: Introduced CCT to Direct Labour Organisations (DLOs) covering aspects of building and engineering works, construction, and highways maintenance.[1]

Local Government Act 1988: Extended CCT to refuse collection, cleaning of buildings, street cleaning and litter collection, school and welfare catering, other catering, ground maintenance, repair and maintenance of vehicles, and management of sports and leisure facilities.[2]

Local Government Act 1992: Extended CCT to the 'white collar' work of Direct Service Organisations (DSOs) in the areas of legal services, construction-related services, information technology, financial services, housing management, corporate services, security services, and vehicle fleet management

Notes:

[1]In some of these areas there was a requirement for Scottish councils to put all work out to competitive tender, whilst in others only work valued above a specified level was subject to CCT requirements. In 1982 for example, the threshold level for general highways was £100,000 but by 1990 it had been reduced to £25,000. Correspondingly, the threshold for general maintenance work was £10,000 in 1982 but was reduced to zero in 1990.

[2]The management of sports and leisure facilities was added by an Order in December 1989.

---

compliance over the period of the contract, ranging from five to seven years depending on the particular area of work.

The experience of CCT in Scotland, based on a survey by the Local Government Management Board in 1994, was that an average of 4.9 contractors expressed an interest in bidding, 3.3 were actually invited to bid, and only 1.6 bids were finally lodged (Scottish Local Government Information Unit 1994: 1). A survey by COSLA in 1991 found that after the first three rounds of CCT, a total of 286 contracts were awarded with 252 (88.1 per cent) being won in-house. Of the remainder, 24 (8.4 per cent) were won by private contractors with a further 10 (3.5 per cent) being won by the DSO of other councils (Scottish Local Government Information Unit 1991: 2). Councils tended to win the higher-value contracts. In the 1991 survey they won 97.3 per cent of the value of the work, whilst in a slightly earlier survey they won 96.6 per cent of the work (Scottish Local Government Information Unit 1990: 1). Figures for the success of in-house bids tended to be higher north of the border. In England and Wales, a survey in 1993 by the Local Government Management Board found that DSOs won 67 per cent of contracts and 82 per cent based on value

(Greenwood and Wilson 1994: 410). Scottish Office ministers argued that the particular 'problem' north of the border was more powerful local trade unions acting as a deterrent to private bids, and the socialist sympathies of councils, doing everything they could to manipulate the 'rules of the game' and win contracts. By contrast, Scottish councils argued that they were simply more efficient than their counterparts down south.

Can CCT be described as a 'success'? Scottish Office ministers and their supporters argued that it did have weaknesses, but (following on from the point in the previous paragraph) that these were caused by local authorities engaging in anti-competitive behaviour. This included putting too much detail in specifications to deter contractors, and packaging contracts in such a way that they were too large for many companies to bid for without incurring excessive costs. A survey in 1994 found that 49.7 per cent of all contracts in Scotland were won with no competition for the local authority (Scottish Local Government Information Unit 1994: 1). Despite these problems, ministers felt that CCT was successful in VFM terms. It regularly cut costs because councils had to reassess (and reduce) their financial, personnel and material costs in the hope of winning the contract. A survey by the Labour Research Department in 1989 which encompassed Scotland, England and Wales found that in terms of contracts awarded:

- 53 per cent produced job losses;
- 12 per cent resulted in pay cuts;
- 17 per cent led to cuts in hours; and
- 6 per cent resulted in cuts in sick pay. (Scottish Local Government Information Unit 1990: 4)

For ministers, these cuts in costs were precisely the sorts of efficiency savings required. Furthermore, they suggested that effective service delivery was virtually guaranteed because quality requirements were written into legally binding documents with penalties for default. Beyond VFM benefits, supporters argued that it also had cultural benefits within councils. In order to ensure regularity and transparency in their financial affairs, authorities had to divide council administration (in terms of committees and within and between departments) along client-contractor lines. In other words, one aspect of council work involved being a client, drawing up specifications, awarding contracts and so on. Another entirely separate dimension was that of contractor, bidding 'blind' for work and (if successful) carrying out that work and being evaluated by the client. Therefore, CCT subjected councils to competition and shook-up any complacency they may have had. The fact that councils tended to win the vast bulk of contracts wasn't ideal, it was argued, but by experiencing competition with its VFM and cultural benefits, the process was still very much worthwhile.

Critics were scathing of CCT. Far from reducing costs, it actually increased them. Scottish Office ministers provided no additional funds for councils to administer the system on the assumption that savings would offset the costs of administration. In actual fact, administrative costs were considerable because of the host of new tasks involved (plus the costs of reorganising and running committees along client-contractor lines). Precise figures are difficult to ascertain, but what is available is research examining tangible costs to the Exchequer, specifically the payment of social security benefits and loss of Exchequer income through a reduction in Income Tax revenues, PAYE and indirect taxation. A study of 39 local authorities in England, Scotland and Wales by the Centre for Public Services found savings across four services of £16.4m. However, once these other costs were taken into account the costs were £41.2m (Escott and Whitfield 1995: 181–5). This amounts to a costs v. savings ratio of roughly 2.5 to 1. There are also the social costs of making people redundant, reducing wages, cutting sick pay entitlements and so on. It is impossible to quantify such costs but for the people affected they are very real. Furthermore, quality services were not guaranteed. The costs of re-tendering contracts for breaches of contract were considerable, and so clauses were written into contracts, allowing the local authority to deal with defaults. The position varied from council to council but included fines, delays in payment, warning notices and rectification notices. No figures are available for Scotland although there is little reason to suggest they were substantially different from those south of the border. A study by the Department of the Environment (1993: 113) found that 12 per cent of contracts in the shire counties and districts 'often' issued default notices, whilst the figure was 27 per cent for London boroughs. The implication is that quality can suffer, despite contractual commitments.

Not only did CCT have dubious claims to providing economy, efficiency and effectiveness, according to its critics, but it also damaged the ethos of local public service provision. It placed the 'contract' at the heart of service delivery and sidelined elected councillors in terms of influence. Indeed, it fragmented the authorities themselves (because of the client-contractor split), mitigating against an integrated approach to local service provision. More generally, CCT was widely condemned for its inflexibility by COSLA and most local authorities in Scotland. It was detested by the Labour Party north and south of the border and had few supporters except Conservative ministers. It is against this background that Best Value was born.

Best Value

Best Value developed differently north and south of the border. In England and Wales, the Department of the Environment launched a pilot scheme in 1997–8 involving 37 English and 23 Welsh local authorities. CCT was repealed and the Local Government Act 1999 introduced BV requirements for all local authorities for all services. In Scotland, a Best Value Task Force was established in 1997, comprising representatives from the Scottish Office, COSLA and Accounts Commission. Its role was to identify the key elements of BV. Shortly after the election, a moratorium on CCT (previously introduced because of reorganisation) was extended and a first report was produced in July 1997. BV was to apply to all services in all Scottish councils. The message from Donald Dewar and the Scottish Office team was that BV was 'not an easy option' and that CCT would be enforced if councils failed to comply. By February 1998, all councils had demonstrated sufficient commitment by drawing up BV plans. A second report was produced in July 1998, focusing on developing a coherent BV system. Shortly afterwards between September 1998 and March 1999, an appraisal round was undertaken. A third report in March 1999 helped refine the workings of BV and identified a series of issues that would need to be addressed for BV to be sustainable. A fourth and final report was produced in July 1999 and presented recommendations. BV finally became a legal requirement in the Local Government in Scotland Act 2003.

As Midwinter and McGarvey (1999: 93) suggest, 'There remains a certain woolliness' about BV. It is a complex concept, defined by ministers and Task Force reports in different ways and focusing on different principles. In order to make sense of BV, we can refer to figure 8.2 which details four core principles of BV as identified by the first Task Force Report. We can draw out the fact that BV differs from CCT in (at least) two notable respects. First, whilst BV

Figure 8.2   Core principles of Best Value in Scotland.

Accountability: In order for councils to be properly accountable to all stakeholders, robust performance information is needed. Customer input into services is also necessary for genuine accountability.

Transparency: Councils should be as open as possible in their actions and the decisions they take.

Continuous improvement: Councils should demonstrate, through reliable evidence, that they are committed to continuous improvement in the delivery of services. They need to regularly address the questions: What are we seeking to achieve? Why are we doing it? How are we doing it? Are we achieving our goals and can we get better?

Ownership: All relevant interests in the council and in the community should feel involved. Among other things, this requires processes to encourage participation.

Source: Best Value Task Force (1997: 4–5).

---

requires accountability and prudence for public funds, it recognises that stakeholders need to be consulted and so the cheapest option may not necessarily be the most socially desirable or provide 'Best Value' to the local authority area. Second, there is no compulsion for local authorities to seek bids from the private sector.

By the time BV became a legal requirement in the Local Government in Scotland Act 2003, the concept, although still vague in many respects, at least had a legal definition. The legal requirements for Best Value as defined in the Local Government in Scotland Act 2003 are as follows:

- It is the duty of a local authority to make arrangements which secure Best Value.
- Best Value is continuous improvement in the performance of the authority's functions.
- In securing Best Value, the local authority shall maintain an appropriate balance among the quality of its performance of its functions; the cost to the authority of that performance; and the cost to persons of any service provided by it for them on a wholly or partly rechargeable basis.
- In maintaining that balance, the local authority shall have regard to efficiency, effectiveness and economy; the need to meet the equal opportunity requirements, and doing so in such a way which contributes to the achievement of sustainable development.
- In measuring the improvement of the performance of a local authority's functions, regard shall be had to the extent to which the outcomes of that performance have improved. Source: Local Government in Scotland Act 2003 (chap. 1)

At the heart of councils implementing Best Value are service reviews, completed progressively for each service over a period of years. As can be seen from figure 8.3 which provides extracts from Glasgow City Council's Best Value Review of Museums, the volume of work and scope of reviews can be considerable. Initial introduction of BV placed considerable emphasis on Performance Management Plans, involving the setting of standards and targets, as well as reporting on performance and identifying areas for improvement. In order to carry out these tasks, Scottish councils have used a wide range of quality management tools such as the Balanced Scorecard, Business Excellence Model, and European Foundation for Quality Management. COSLA also facilitates the exchange of good practice between councils. A recent development which alters the 'rules of the game' comes via the Local Government Act 2003 which introduces BV audits. The Accounts Commission is now responsible for audits every three or four years. This follows two pilot studies in North Lanarkshire and Perth and Kinross (see Accounts Commission 2003b).

In many respects it is still too soon for a rounded assessment of BV in Scotland. Little academic research has been undertaken and the four BV Reports were much more about assessing progress than they were about the costs and benefits. We can, however, make some provisional and general comments. On the plus side, the general feeling among councillors is that nothing could be much worse than the inflexible and compulsory aspect of CCT. Allied to

---

Figure 8.3   Aspects of Glasgow City Council's Best Value review of museums, heritage and visual arts, 1998–2001.

The Setting

As part of its commitment to Best Value, Glasgow City Council in 1998 established Cultural and Leisure Services which brought together the former services for Performing Arts and Venues, Museums and Art Galleries, Libraries and Archives, and Sport, Recreation and Play. Glasgow City Council also gave a commitment to review all Council activities on a regular basis and it was agreed to review the Museums, Heritage and Visual Arts Services as part of its 1999–2000 Service Review Programme.

Research

Research was carried out by Cultural and Leisure Services during the period April–June 1999. It covered an audit of current resources, organisations, policies, strategies, visitor information and usage; trends and economic information across the range of museums, heritage and visual arts; resources, services and collections; an analysis of visitor surveys carried out at all City Council Museums during 1998; and 'benchmarking' comparisons of the Museums Service with other local authorities and national museums. Detailed

Figure 8.2 *continued overleaf*

Figure 8.3 *continued*

comparisons were also made regarding the allocation of funds by the National Museums of Scotland, National Gallery of Scotland, Tyne and Wear Museums, Dundee City Museums and Birmingham Museum and Art Gallery. Comparators were also drawn from data provided by the Group for Large Local Authority Museums (GLLAM) and Department for Culture, Media and Sport (DCMS) reports on excellence in national museums. A final report was prepared which brought together the information, issues and conclusions from the research.

Consultation

The review had at its heart an innovative and extensive process of consultation and involvement encompassing the public, staff, elected councillors, trade unions, national and local organisations and individual artists. First, a one-day Open Space event was held (17 June 1999) involving national, independent, commercial and community organisations in Museums, Heritage and the Visual Arts in Glasgow. The key priorities arising from the vote were then discussed at a programme of key issue workshops. Second, a Core Group of 23 members was established, comprising councillors, senior officers, staff representation, an academic from Glasgow Caledonian University and representatives of bodies such as the Scottish Museums Council and Centre for Contemporary Arts. Third, a Museums Service Staff Panel was established, involving staff from across the Museums Service and providing a forum for staff to discuss the key issues and priorities and feed their views directly into the Core Group. Fourth, a People's Panel was set up in the form of a second Open Space event (6 November 1999) to examine the public's perception of the Museums Service and how it could be improved. MoRI Scotland identified 75 people from the City Council's Citizens' Panel who were broadly representative of Glasgow's population in terms of age, sex and socio-economic profile and reflected the proportion of Glasgow's citizens who visited the city's museums. Panel members were encouraged to visit at least one museum before the Open Space event. The 52 citizens who participated discussed matters of concern to the public and to museum staff and voted on their priorities for action.

Consultation on the Draft Best Value Review Report

The draft Best Value Review Report of Glasgow Museums was approved by the Cultural and Leisure Services Committee on 20 June 2000 for wider consultation. A major consultation exercise involving the public, staff and a range of national, independent, commercial and community organisations was undertaken from July through to September 2000. By the end of this period, 170 responses had been received. A report summarising the responses received and recommending the actions required in addressing these responses was approved by the Review Core Group at its meeting on 5 November 2000.

Source: Extracted with minor amendments from Glasgow City Council (2001).

this, consultation with stakeholders and commitments to continuous improvement makes BV a more flexible policy, with built-in dimensions (particularly in terms of equal opportunities and sustainability) aligned with principles of social justice. Broadly speaking, it should also enhance local accountability because service reviews require consultation with a wide range of local interests.

Efficiency savings are also possible. For example, in North Lanarkshire Council, a review of three main departments identified £2m efficiency savings, amounting to 1.5 per cent of the total value of the services under review (Scottish Parliament Information Centre 2002c: 14).

Conversely, there are warning signs. First, the complexities of the BV process require extensive knowledge, expertise and time on the part of officers. There is a real danger that the vast majority of councillors become disengaged on the sidelines, leaving strategic decisions to a few key political and administrative elites. This does not bode well for local democracy. Second, there are immense difficulties in councils working and planning alongside partner organisations. This is particularly the case with health boards, where the differences compared with councils vary hugely in terms of culture, internal decision-making processes and external accountability. Third, the Accounts Commission will find it difficult to conduct Best Value Audits without reliance on the secondment of the very experts in local government who are responsible for improvement in councils (Yates 2003). Fourth, the expense of administering Best Value is considerable but councils have received no additional funds from the Scottish Executive. It is quite possible that a regime designed to ensure quality in local service provision is actually to the detriment of local services because of the 'opportunity cost' of administration. Fifth, varying aspects of community consultation may be 'cosmetic', in the sense that the final content of policy is largely unchanged as a consequence of consultation, but the local authority has the benefit of adding legitimacy to what it decides. Sixth, the 'value' dimension of Best Value should alert students of politics to the contestable nature of describing something as being of value. As John Stewart argues in his review of BV:

> it raises the issue of whose best value and who judges whether it has been achieved – the government, the inspectors or local councillors/and or local people. The possibility of disagreement on the meaning of value can easily be forgotten in the apparent certainty of procedures or the assumed rigour of inspections. The search for best value should encompass the exploration of meaning through debate, discussion and even political dispute, recognising that in the end there may not be agreement on best value . . . (Stewart 2003: 134–5)

Overall, BV is a complex initiative, often difficult to comprehend, and (as yet) with no overwhelming evidence which suggests that the benefits outweigh the costs. What it has done, however, is produce four discernible trends in local service provision (Martin 2000). First, it has shifted the focus away from external provision towards in-house provision. In so doing, it introduces a strong element of incrementalism by encouraging periodic commitments to improvements in service delivery. This contrasts with CCT under the Conservatives, where 'low cost' was the prime driving force. Second, and paradoxically, it has encouraged a market ethos by prompting councils seeking additional resources to look to the private sector. A good example is PFI for the building and refurbishing of schools. Councils such as Edinburgh, Glasgow, Highland and West Lothian have all undertaken PFI projects on the grounds of providing Best Value to their local communities. Third, and in contrast to the inter- and intra-agency fragmentation encouraged by CCT, BV is (at least in conception) much more integrative. It encourages the joining up of a range of services and issues (such as transportation, regeneration, sustainability, equal opportunities, housing) and also a range of stakeholder interests through community consultation. Finally, it integrates representatives of communities into the process of decision-making through devices such as citizens' panels and community forums. This equates with traditional practices of citizen consultation, rather than (in the case of CCT) assuming that consultation is unnecessary because their interests are embodied in mechanisms to achieve economy, efficiency and effectiveness. It could be argued, therefore, that BV is an attempt to supplement the three Es with a fourth – Equity. It is more tolerant of policies that may be justified on the grounds of social justice or 'value' to the community as a whole.

The Rise of the Performance Culture in Scottish Local Government

Cutting across CCT, BV and other aspects of local government in Scotland is the rise of a culture of performance measuring, monitoring and reporting. This pertains particularly to the advent of:

- Performance Indicators to promote the scrutiny of local services.
- Systems to 'police' the performance of local authorities.
- The politics of Performance Indicators.

Performance Indicators (PIs) are a logical complement to the Thatcherite reforms of the public sector, based loosely on the belief that markets are the best allocaters of resources, and that the public sector should be subjected to market or surrogate market competition (Midwinter 1995). The quest for economy, efficiency and effectiveness in local government led to the development of PIs because they 'appeared to offer the sharp edge equivalent to markets in the private sector' (Midwinter 1994: 37). The scene was set with the arrival of CCT in 1980. Whilst this did not lead directly to the development of PIs, it created a culture which challenged the traditional hierarchical organisational model of local authority self-sufficiency and replaced it with one based on fragmentation (the client-contractor split), contracts, and the formalising of relations in order to assure quality and minimise costs. Alongside the extension of CCT in 1988, the Accounts Commission in Scotland was given a new mandate to ensure that councils had made appropriate arrangements for VFM (the three Es). Progress in the first few years was slow. A study by Midwinter and Monaghan (1993: 117) found that 83.8 per cent of councils still did not make use of PIs for budget allocation and control purposes. Arguably, this is yet another example of a failed attempt to produce 'rational', goal-driven reforms. Instead, and supporting the 'bounded rationality' perspective of Simon (1958) and the incremental nature of policy change (Lindblom 1959), reform proceeded piecemeal because a supposedly rational process was impeded by lack of time, limited resources and political resistance on the part of both councillors and officers.

The process was given further momentum by John Major's Citizen's Charter (Cm 1599 1991) and its desire to empower citizens by giving them greater access to information about service performance and how it compares with other councils (Falconer 1996). Following this, the Local Government Act 1992 required the Accounts Commission to give direction to councils on standards of performance and provide them with indicators to measure performance. After consultation with COSLA, the Scottish Consumer Council and individual local authorities, a series of PIs was produced. The most recent figures published are for 2001–2 and reveal 76 indicators in total, covering councils, police forces and fire brigades. Indicators may focus on statistics pertaining to services, finances, success rates, response times and users (Midwinter 1995: 49). Figure 8.4 gives an example of the indicators which exist in the fields of education, cultural and community services, and the management of benefits, finance and corporate issues. The arrival of

BV added to an already complex system and there are no signs of a full-scale rationalisation of PIs. A consultation paper by the Accounts Commission (2003b: 9) allows local authorities to 'use whatever measures and evidence they feel are relevant and valid. Ideally, these would be drawn from existing performance and management systems'. The existence of what amounts to two different systems which are not mutually exclusive epitomises a classic dilemma at the heart of central–local relations. Exclusive top-down centralisation via statutory Performance Indicators conflicts with principles of local autonomy – in the present context, the freedom afforded to councils under the BV regime. Correspondingly, an exclusive reliance on local self-determination of Performance Indicators would undermine the right of the Scottish Executive to seek national standards for inter-authority comparisons. The present duality is a compromise which is not wholly satisfactory for either party.

As a test of local services, the use of PIs has been the subject of intense debate. The official view is typified by Professor Ian Percy, former Chairman of the Accounts Commission:

> Publication of the first report on comparative performance information about councils under the Citizen's Charter illustrated how the Commission can assist individual citizens with valuable information about how councils perform . . . 1995 was a milestone in giving citizens information about the performance of local authority services and in future years citizens will be able to look at comparative information which will allow them to gauge improvements being made by their council. (Accounts Commission 1995: 9)

By contrast, criticisms are considerable. PIs are typically subject to innumerable qualifications that are not easily identified by looking at headline data. For example, Accounts Commission data on the number of planning applications dealt with within two months needs to be seen in the context of the extent to which councillors speed up applications by delegating responsibility to officers; whether the application is subject to objections (such as neighbours); and whether applications require to be amended and resubmitted (Accounts Commission 2003c: 21–3). It is not possible to scientifically test the appropriateness of such indicators, simply because these additional factors are portrayed in Accounts Commission documentation as 'points to bear in mind'. This is not to suggest that PIs should be

Figure 8.4   Examples of Statutory Performance Indicators for Scottish councils, 2001–2.

Education

- The percentage of four-year-old children who received grant-aided pre-school education, and of these children, the proportion who received fewer than five education sessions per week.

- The average number of children per primary school class. The number of primary school classes of these types: single year, composite and classes containing P1 to P3 pupils.

- The proportion of classes that meet national class size standards.

- The total number of primary schools, and the percentage of schools where the ratio of pupils to places is 60% or less, 61% to 100%, and 101% or more.

- The total number of secondary schools, and the percentage of schools where the ratio of pupils to places is 60% or less, 61% to 100%, and 101% or more.

- The average time taken to complete an assessment of special educational needs, and the percentage of assessments completed within 26 weeks, and taking longer than a year.

Cultural and Community Services

- Borrowers from libraries as a percentage of the resident population and the average number of issues per borrower.

- Library stock turnover per 1,000 population.

- Average time taken to satisfy book requests.

- Proportion of museums that are registered under the Museums and Galleries Commission registration scheme.

- Number of attendances per head of population for swimming pools and other indoor sport and leisure facilities.

The Management of Benefits, Finance and Corporate Issues

- The time to process benefit applications in calendar days. The proportion of recoverable overpayments that were recovered in the year.

- The gross administration cost per case for housing and Council Tax benefit.

- The percentage of Council Tax due in the year (excluding reliefs and rebates) collected by the end of the year.

- The cost of collecting Council Tax per chargeable dwelling.

- The number of invoices paid within 30 days or other agreed time period.

- Proportion of working time lost due to sickness absence for chief officers; administrative, technical and clerical employees; craft and manual employees; and teachers.

- The proportion of employees within the council who are women.

Source: Accounts Commission (2003a).

modelled. Rather, it is to suggest that headline data is usually too crude for meaningful judgements to be made. Elements of this thinking seem to have filtered through to the Scottish Executive. In September 2003, for precisely these reasons, Minister for Education and Young People Peter Peacock announced his intention to scrap league tables for schools.

A further difficulty is that the Accounts Commission and Audit Scotland use the words economy, efficiency and effectiveness with much less rigour than we might think. PIs tend to be commented on in a fairly common sense way. There is nothing wrong with this of course, other than to suggest that the 'scientific' language of the three Es is not followed through in systematic assessments of each. A related limitation of PIs is the underlying assumption that service delivery is indeed a 'science', untainted by policy choices. For example, inter-authority variations in class size may not be caused by variations in efficiency. Instead, they may be a product of policy choices as local authorities and head teachers try to cope with the demands of financial cutbacks, curriculum changes, teacher shortages and so on. Furthermore, PIs are highly selective. Many issues are not covered, such as breaches of security at schools, numbers of tenants satisfied with council house transfers, parental satisfaction with head teachers, and the percentage of officials receiving training relevant to the needs of their post. Thus, a judgement has to be made in terms of which aspects of performance are suitable for performance measuring. Therefore, assessing performance is an art rather than an exact science. It involves making choices from a range of competing alternatives and so it is highly political.

The 'Policing' of Local Authority Performance

Local authorities are self-regulating to a certain extent because they have a variety of internal structures and processes to monitor their own performance. Yet they are also 'policed' externally. In 1975, the Accounts Commission for Scotland came into being. Its prime role was the 'traditional' audit of councils to ensure that their accounts procedures and practices were in accordance with standard accounting practice. During the Thatcher and then the Major years, however, the Accounts Commission took on board a strong VFM aspect to its role. In April 2000, as part of the Scottish Executive's wider rethink about a number of issues regarding public finance and accountability, a new body – Audit Scotland – was created. Figure 8.5 depicts the new audit arrangements. In statutory terms, the Accounts Commission is independent of the Scottish Executive and local authorities, but in practice the Scottish Executive (through legislation and guidance from ministers) can give direction to the Commission. Audit Scotland works on behalf of the Accounts Commission and is at the front line in terms of preparing reports regarding local government. Both bodies essentially 'police' Scottish local authorities in terms of Value for Money provision. The Accounts Commission does have power to take action against councils for breaking the law or losing money. In the main, however, its powers are recommendatory, but this does not imply that it is weak or ineffectual. Rather, the fact that it can hold public hearings, make recommendations to ministers and put reports into the public domain is of immense importance. Local authorities are invariably keen to avoid bad publicity and so if mutual agreement does not work (although it typically does), the threat of more high profile and media-attracting negative publicity is usually enough to elicit changes on the part of councils.

The Accounts Commission and Audit Scotland 'police' councils in five main ways. First, they undertake Value for Money studies of particular services delivered by councils. The development of this function has been a rather piecemeal process, lagging behind the situation south of the border where audit is the responsibility of the Audit Commission which was established in 1982 (Midwinter and Monaghan 1993). It was not until the Local Government Act 1988 that a duty was placed on the Auditor General in Scotland to ensure that Scottish councils had made proper arrangements for securing economy, efficiency and effectiveness. The first audits were conducted pre-emptively in 1986–7 of energy management, janitorial and cleaning provision in schools, and refuse collection. Since Audit Scotland came into being, it has conducted VFM studies which include managing rent arrears, refuse collection, home care services for older people, property management in schools, trading standards services, dealing with offending by young people, and local economic forums. Typical recommendations are for potential savings of between 3 and 8 per cent, as well as procedural reforms. Auditors conducted post-audit scrutiny to ensure that recommendations have been taken on board.

Second, the way in which councils operate Best Value has been subject to audit by Audit Scotland. From 1999 onwards, council procedures for BV were scrutinised by the Performance Management and Planning (PMP) audit. Under proposals published in the summer of 2003, this will change to an Audit of Best Value. As indicated earlier in the chapter, audits of individual local authorities will be conducted every three or four years. The audit will not only encompass BV arrangements themselves, but also Community Planning and Public Performance Reporting. Audit Scotland will report the findings of each audit to the Accounts Commission. Subsequent recommendations will result in improvement plans for each council, with the Commission able to take further action if the recommendations are not adopted.

Third, and overlapping not just with BV but also with the traditional audit, is the policing of local authorities' corporate governance arrangements. Based on joint work undertaken by CIPFA and SOLACE, this includes:

- Community focus, including procedures for consultation with stakeholders.
- Service delivery arrangements.
- Structures and processes, including audit committees and clear commitments to principles of corporate governance.
- Risk management and internal control which are embedded in strategic and operational planning activities.
- Standards of conduct of councillors and officers, as well as whistle blowing and anti-fraud policies. (Accounts Commission 2003a: 14–25)

Recent agreements in 2001–2 include:

- Fife Council agreeing to implement recommendations regarding weaknesses in its payroll processes.
- Falkirk Council agreeing to an action plan which would integrate the principles of audit committees into its general committee structures.
- Perth and Kinross Council agreeing to fill a gap in its procedures by developing a corporate risk management strategy.

Fourth, the Accounts Commission (based on work undertaken by Audit Scotland) publishes annual overviews of the performance of councils in different services areas, often highlighting the activities of individual councils. This equates with 'policing' in the sense that it monitors the activities of councils and ensures that examples of good and bad practice enter the public domain.

Figure 8.5 The auditing of Scottish public bodies (including local authorities).

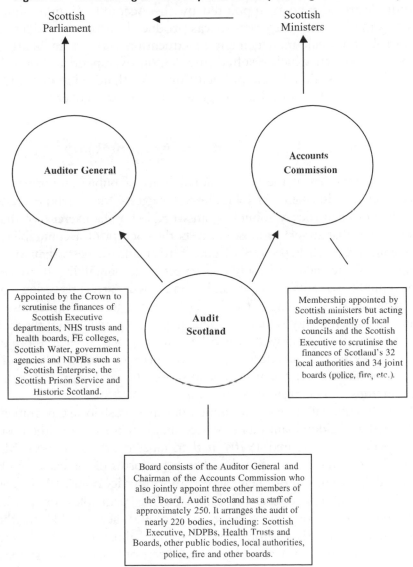

Source: Adapted from Audit Scotland (2002b).

Councils are typically keen to avoid negative publicity and so will usually alter their behaviour without any formal sanctions being deployed.

Fifth and finally, special reports (known as statutory reports) may be produced on the activities of individual councils when a specific problem is considered sufficiently serious by the Accounts

Commission and the Controller of Audit (a member of staff of Audit Scotland who is appointed by the Accounts Commission). For example, a statutory report was produced into poor budgetary control and weak management of education services in Scottish Borders Council which resulted in a £3.9m overspend in 2000–1. Amidst large-scale adverse publicity on a Scotland-wide basis, the council had little choice but to agree a three-year recovery plan.

Conclusion – VFM as the 'New' Accountability

Accountability lies at the constitutional heart of public authorities in Scotland and elsewhere. As John Stewart suggests: 'those who exercise public power in society should be answerable for the exercise of that power. On that simple proposition rests the concept of accountability' (Stewart 1993: 4). Pyper (1996) goes further and suggests that to be 'answerable' for actions is only one aspect of accountability. It implies that public servants (elected and non-elected) are 'answering' or 'explaining' their actions but doing little else. A more comprehensive view of accountability is that it also includes a preparedness on the part of public servants to amend their behaviour or practices when those to whom they are accountable feel aggrieved. This in turn implies that some forms of sanction (or threat of sanction) operate, otherwise there is no real incentive for changes to be made.

The 'traditional' system of accountability in Scottish local government operated as the dominant mode of accountability for most of the post-war period until the mid 1970s. It then tapered off as the post-IMF spending cuts took effect and the Thatcher reforms of the early 1980s marked the beginnings of a new phase (Bruce and McConnell 1995). The traditional system rested on long-standing principles of public administration. Councillors were elected and accountable to the electorate through the electoral system, with the threat of removal from office placing the power of citizens at the heart of a democratic system. Officers were impartial public servants, assisting councillors in their duties and accountable to them. If citizens were unhappy with the way in which local affairs were run, they could use 'traditional' devices in an attempt to seek redress. They could (1) use their vote at the next local election, (2) contact their councillor at his or her surgery, (3) contact local officials to complain and (4) from 1975 onwards, complain in more extreme circumstances of 'maladministration' to the Ombudsman (formally the Commissioner for Local Administration).

In essence, this system places 'politics' at the heart of local accountability. The people of Scotland are, at least in theory, sovereign and they use traditional democratic devices such as voting, lobbying and complaining when they are unhappy about the activities of those who exercise public power on their behalf. The systems which have developed in the decades since the mid 1970s are fundamentally different. Initiatives such as Compulsory Competitive Tendering, Best Value, Citizen's Charters, Performance Indicators and Value for Money audits involve a reconstituting of relationships. They place 'economics' at the heart of local accountability by constituting citizens as consumers of local services, whose interests are best served by regimes to ensure economy, efficiency and effectiveness. The traditional system remains as the constitutional wisdom, but it has been challenged by a policy practice which is imbued with different priorities.

It is important to qualify the foregoing and stress that the reality of local accountability is much more complex than either the traditional or newer models suggest. Councillors and officials in Scottish local government can be held to account by a number of actors including the people (as voters, citizens and consumers), Scottish Executive ministers, civil servants, Audit Scotland and the Accounts Commission, local businesses, political parties, media, police and the courts. To put it in simple terms, everyone wants to exercise some influence over the activities of local authorities. This further implies, of course, that accountability to one actor may conflict with accountability to another. The consequence is that local accountability in practice is riddled with tensions; none more so than the tension between the accountability of councils to the Scottish Executive and the accountability of councils to local people. For example, if voters in a local area wanted their local authority not to operate the Best Value regime, or give business rates back to local businesses, or bring water and sewerage back under local democratic control, they could not do so. As Chapters 1 and 10 indicate, the legal, financial and political power of the Scottish Executive is considerable. For councils to fight this, even in the name of local democracy, is an exceptionally difficult task; near impossible if it requires breaking the law. Therefore, we have a clash of democratic legitimacies between elected local authorities and an elected Scottish Parliament (headed by the Scottish Executive). The dominant legitimacy, and hence the dominant actor in terms of accountability, is the centre. Even although the BV regime involves consultation with local communities and stakeholders, the system is a creation of the centre.

To sum up, the traditional system was concerned with political channels of local accountability. Grafted onto it is the new system of 'economic' accountability with its emphasis on value for money. CCT lay at the heart of this for almost two decades under the Conservatives. Under the Labour-Liberal coalition in Scotland and the Labour Government south of the border, Best Value has reintroduced an element of 'politics' with the requirement for consultation with stakeholders. Whatever the benefits of this more recent shift, we should recognise that while BV, PIs and other such initiatives have made the accountability of Scottish councils increasingly complex, the dominance of the wishes of the centre is constant. The shift towards Value for Money initiatives and the rise of the performance culture are not, at heart, the initiative of local people or local councils. They are creations of the centre, originally the Scottish Office and now the Scottish Executive. In essence, Scotland's councils are allowed to be accountable, but only in the way the Scottish Executive wishes. Complex value for money reforms do not diminish this feature of Scottish politics – they simply make it more difficult to discern.

? Key Questions ?

1. Was Compulsory Competitive Tendering really as bad as its critics suggested?
2. To what extent does Best Value genuinely mean 'best value' for local communities?
3. Does Best Value marginalise the role of democratically elected councillors?
4. To what extent are Performance Indicators a sound basis for judging the performance of Scotland's councils?
5. Do Scottish local authorities really need extensive financial 'policing' by the Accounts Commission and Audit Scotland?
6. In what ways is the concept of public sector accountability changing to accommodate the views of successive governments that councils should deliver Value for Money?

Further Reading

The work of Arthur Midwinter is essential reading for anyone interested in the performance of Scottish councils. Particularly useful are *Local Government in Scotland* (1995) and *From Rates to the Poll Tax* (1993), the latter co-authored with Claire Monaghan. Other very worthwhile articles are Midwinter (1994) and Midwinter and McGarvey (1999). Back copies of the publication

Scottish Local Government (published by the Scottish Local Government Information Unit which in 2003 became incorporated within COSLA) are a worthwhile read for regular updates on the way in which CCT and BV developed. More generally, the literature on local government is replete with articles on CCT, BV, PIs and audit. Particularly useful journals are *Local Government Studies*, *Local Governance*, *Public Money and Management*, and *Financial Accountability and Management*. It is also important to access 'first hand' reports and investigations by the Accounts Commission, Audit Scotland and the Audit Commission. Publications by the Scottish Executive and COSLA should also be monitored for new initiatives and local authority responses to them.

Useful Websites

http://www.accounts-commission.gov.uk/accounts/index.htm
The Accounts Commission for Scotland.

http://www.accounts-commission.gov.uk/audit/index.htm
Audit Scotland.

http://www.audit-commission.gov.uk
Audit Commission.

http://www.scotland-legislation.hmso.gov.uk/legislation/scotland/acts2000/20000001.htm
The Public Finance and Accountability (Scotland) Act 2000.

http://www.scotland.gov.uk/bestvalue/perf_info.asp
Scottish Executive Best Value site.

http://www.scotland.gov.uk
Scottish Executive.

http://www.cosla.gov.uk
COSLA.

CHAPTER NINE

Financing Scottish Local Government

An inescapable fact is that local government in Scotland has to be paid for. In common with other systems of public revenues and expenditures throughout the world, the Scottish variant is exceptionally complex and generates intense political debate. Local government finance in Scotland is at heart a political issue because it raises serious questions about (1) who pays for local government, (2) how much they should pay, (3) the specific instruments used to raise revenue and (4) the degree of financial freedom that local authorities should have in relation to the Scottish Executive. The McIntosh Commission made a number of recommendations for a review of the system of local finance in Scotland (Scottish Office 1999a), many of which were accepted by the Scottish Executive (1999) although local authorities were left dissatisfied by many unresolved issues. These were taken up by the Local Government Committee of the Scottish Parliament when it agreed in June 2000 to a wide-ranging review of local government finance, and the final report was produced in March 2002. The Scottish Executive responded in June 2002, accepting some recommendations, rejecting many and agreeing to consult on others. In May 2003, the Partnership Agreement between Scottish Labour and the Scottish Liberal Democrats contained a commitment to yet another inquiry into local finance. As one might gather, review of local government finance is a never-ending process, tied in with political disputes between the Scottish Executive intent on exercising its powers over what it sees as the national interest and local authorities arguing that the national interest is best served by enhancing local autonomy.

This chapter will begin with a brief overview of local government finance in Scotland, before looking in detail at revenue and capital funding. It will concentrate on sources of funding, Scottish Executive restrictions and issues arising. It will conclude by exploring the various factors which constrain local authorities and their ability to incur expenditure. At appropriate points, key comparisons will be made with local government finance in England and Wales.

Local Government Finance in Scotland: An Overview

Scotland's 32 local authorities spent over £13.9b in 2001–02 and used up about 29 per cent of the total Scottish Budget. They engage in two main types of expenditure:

- *Revenue expenditure*: Consisting of day-to-day running costs such as wages, salaries, lighting, heating and telephone bills. It also includes the repayment of loan charges for capital expenditure borrowing. Revenue expenditure accounts for roughly 93 to 94 per cent of local authority expenditure in Scotland.
- *Capital expenditure*: Consisting of expenditure which creates, leads to the purchase of or the upgrading of long-term assets such as land and schools. Capital expenditure accounts for roughly 6 to 7 per cent of local authority expenditure in Scotland.

At times, the boundaries between capital and revenue expenditure are unclear and local authorities have used this lack of clarity in order to indulge in creative accountancy as a means of circumventing central controls (Midwinter 1984; Elcock et al. 1989). By and large, however, the distinction is now fairly well demarcated, with the main overlap being in terms of payback (capital funding being paid back through the revenue account), rather than what constitutes revenue and capital expenditure *per se*. The differences between these two categories of expenditure are important in any discussion of Scottish local government because they are financed in different ways and face different restrictions from the Scottish Executive. As figure 9.1 indicates, 68 per cent of local revenue funding for Scottish local authorities comes from the Scottish Executive in the form of what is termed Aggregate External Finance (AEF) (Scottish Executive 2003g: 15). There are three specific components to this: Revenue Support Grant (RSG), Specific Grants (sometimes known as ring-fenced grants), and Non-Domestic Rate Income (NDRI). The remainder comes mostly from Council Tax (about 12 per cent) and income from fees, rents, charges and miscellaneous (about 20 per cent). Capital expenditure comes from several sources. The main ones are capital grants from the centre, receipts from the sale of local authority assets, grants from the EU, and partnerships with the private sector. We can now explore each of the main sources of revenue and capital income, examining key areas of contention. It should be noted that there will be only minimal reference to housing finance. This is a largely separate issue from local government finance in general, with funds being contained and managed in a ring-fenced Housing Revenue Account (HRA) (see Scottish Parliament Information Centre 2002a; Scottish Executive 2002b).

Figure 9.1   Sources of revenue funding for Scottish local authorities 2001–2.

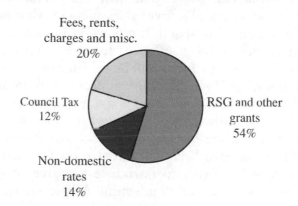

Fees, rents,
charges and misc.
20%

Council Tax
12%

RSG and other
grants
54%

Non-domestic
rates
14%

Source: Adapted from Scottish Executive (2003g: figure 2).

Revenue Finance: Sources, Restrictions and Issues

Revenue Support Grant

Until 1989, this was called Rate Support Grant and was reconfigured as Revenue Support Grant alongside the changes brought about by the introduction of the Poll Tax (Community Charge) and the National Non-Domestic Rate. The first step for the Scottish Executive in deciding how much to allocate each of Scotland's 32 councils is to calculate the Grant Aided Expenditure (GAE) figure for each council. This is not a grant as such, it is an assessment by the Scottish Executive of how much each local authority needs to provide comparable and consistent service levels, operating at the same level of efficiency. There are approximately 90 service-specific GAEs for each council, and the overall assessment is calculated by a method called the Client Group Approach. This determines a primary indicator of demand for each service or part of a service. Often, however, primary indicators need to be modified by secondary indicators in order to take account of demographic and geographic factors. Thus, for example, the number of children in day care is part of a primary indicator of the demand for nurseries under the remit of Social Work services. This is modified by a secondary indicator which takes into account the numbers of households under 'stress', thus giving an additional weight to the demands of providing day care for children with very difficult family circumstances. More generally, the overall impact is an attempt to produce an 'objective' assessment of what Scotland's 32 local authorities need to spend. It would be a mistake, however, to think that councils receive sufficient funds as a result. Ultimately, the formula decides how funds will be distributed between councils. The overall level of RSG is a political decision in the hands of the Scottish Executive (although there is annual statutory consultation with COSLA in advance of the Local Government Finance (Scotland) Order being laid before the Scottish Parliament). Since 2001, AEF levels have been calculated on a forward basis for a three-year period in order to introduce a degree of stability and certainty into local authority budgeting. AEF levels are determined by Scottish ministers, operating within a two-yearly Public Expenditure Review Process at Westminster. To use an analogy, the size of the Scottish 'cake' is decided through the Barnett Formula (Twigger 1988) which allocates funding to Scotland in proportion to changes made in English levels of public expenditure. The cake is cut by ministers into various slices (such as the health service and local government) with each local authority's share of this slice being determined largely by the Client Group Approach.

Throughout the years and continuing today, there have been a number of disputes regarding RSG. One is that levels have been insufficient to meet local spending needs. With the UK almost bankrupt in the mid 1970s and having to accept a loan from the International Monetary Fund (IMF), accompanied by a requirement to reduce public expenditure and borrowing, Rate Support Grant levels in Scotland were cut in the 1976–9 period. During the Conservative years 1979–97, there was a further squeezing of grant levels, prompted largely by a drive to keep down public expenditure levels, ease tax burdens on taxpayers (local and national) and reduce the financial power base of the Conservative's political opponents (principally the Labour Party in Scotland). Between 1979–80 and 1988-9, for example, government grants (as a percentage of Relevant Expenditure) fell from 68.5 per cent to 52.2 per cent (Midwinter and Monaghan 1993: 44). The advent of a Labour Government in 1997 and a Scottish Parliament in 1999 has seen annual settlements more sympathetic to councils, but COSLA sees this as only a marginal repairing of the damage done over many years. The Scottish Executive still has to operate within the constraints of the Chancellor's Public Spending Review, which is in itself constrained by many factors, particularly the need to (1) maintain UK public expenditure within the limits set by the Maastricht criteria for joining the single currency and (2) keep the British economy on a financially secure footing in order that it is able to survive if the UK decides not to join the single currency.

One of the difficulties in examining year-on-year figures for Government grants is that they mask a variety of issues such as new responsibilities on local authorities and the burden of having to finance national pay agreements. In recent years, for example, the Scottish Executive has continually suggested that local authorities have obtained real and substantial increases in RSG and other grants, but this is disputed by COSLA. A case in point was in December 2001 when local government settlement figures were announced for 2002–3. The minister announced a headline increase of 10.7 per cent but COSLA argued that this masked several important points:

- It included £137m for pre-school education previously outwith AEF but now brought into the mainstream. In other words, it was not 'new' money for local government.
- It included increased resources for new responsibilities (for example, £125m for care for the elderly).
- It included a transfer of £73m from the Department for Work and Pensions in order that councils could implement new responsibilities in residential and nursing home care.
- It included additional resources to fund the McCrone settlement on teachers' pay.

Thus, COSLA argued that once all these factors were taken into account, the underlying AEF increase was 3.6 per cent rather than 10.7 per cent (COSLA 2001a).

There is also a wider issue to consider. Much of the evidence submitted to the Scottish Parliament's 2000–2 investigation into local government finance (particularly from the 32 Directors of Finance) was critical not only of the complexity and lack of transparency of the system, but also of the way in which GAEs have been politicised and used by ministers as targets for councils. The Scottish Executive did not accept the latter point but did recognise that the system was in need of review. Several councils, particularly Glasgow City Council, have argued strongly that the system does not adequately take into account the level of deprivation in major cities and the level of expenditure which is needed to cope. This was a major factor behind the setting up in December 2000 of the Scottish Executive's Five Cities Review (Glasgow, Edinburgh, Aberdeen, Dundee and Inverness). It reported in January 2003 (by which time Stirling had also achieved city status) and introduced a number of measures such as a new City Growth Fund, aimed in effect at compensating for the wider deficiencies in the Client Group Approach (Scottish Executive 2003a). For COSLA, however, such measures are still not sufficient and its 2003 manifesto continues to make the case for additional funding (COSLA 2003).

Specific Grants

Funding for some services, notably the police and civil protection, has traditionally been the subject of a specific (ring-fenced or hypothecated) grant, where local authorities cannot use the funds for any other purpose. In recent years (as indicated in table 9.1), there has been an increasing use of specific grants in areas such the Public Transport Fund, Excellence Fund, Pre-School Provision for 3 and 4 Year Olds, Better Neighbourhood Services Fund, Strategic Waste Fund, Changing Children's Services Fund, Rough Sleepers Initiative and Social Inclusion Partnership Fund. Table 9.1 indicates that roughly 10 per cent of AEF is segregated in this way, with the figure increasing to over 18 per cent (for 2003–4) once non-AEF funding is taken into account. Furthermore, other funding for initiatives in areas such as social work, youth crime and drug rehabilitation come with 'strings' attached and a strong element of central direction. COSLA (2001b: part 4, para. 5) argues that the figure for both ring-fenced and

Table 9.1   Projected ring-fenced funding of local government in Scotland, 2001–2 to 2003–4.

	2001–2 (£m)	2002–3 (£m)	2003–4 (£m)	Total (£m)
Ring-fenced funding included within AEF	634.222	668.288	686.453	1,988.963
Outwith AEF	449.151	516.052	609.952	1,575.155
No detail of split over 3 years	–	–	–	491.700
Total ring-fenced funding	1,083.373	1,184.340	1,296.405	4,055.818
AEF	6,048.791	6,361.642	6,717.542	19,127.975
% ring-fenced	10.49	10.50	10.22	10.40
Total Scottish Exec. local authority expenditure	6,832.252	7,304.452	7,700.452	22,328.856
% Ring-fenced	15.86	16.21	16.84	18.16

Source: COSLA (2001b: part 4).

centrally directed funds is almost 30 per cent.

The advantages of this trend towards central direction and control are that the Scottish Executive is able to set priorities, introduce new initiatives and ensure that funds will be utilised accordingly. The disadvantage is that it is part of a further centralist drift which undermines local democracy and local initiative. For example, Argyll and Bute Council argued in its submission to the Scottish Parliament's Local Government Committee that:

> The view was that the ring-fenced moneys were acting against other initiatives and the on-going delivery of services. One example comes from our education department. We have made a succession of cuts in recent years in education. Teachers' posts were cut as part of the general need to cut expenditure. However, at the same time, classroom assistants were coming in. The belief within the education department is that if we had been given more flexibility, we could have concentrated on outcomes. (Local Government Committee 2002: vol. 1, para. 98)

The Scottish Executive's response to a recommendation from the Scottish Parliament's Local Government Committee to reduce and ultimately eliminate ring-fenced grants (with the exception of police grant) came from Local Government Minister Andy Kerr. He indicated in June 2002 that he would be prepared to consider each case on its own merits. A post-May 2003 independent review will undoubtedly examine this issue. Perhaps a sign of things to come can be found in a similar review by the Office of the Deputy Prime Minister in 2003–4 for England and Wales (in advance of the Scottish review). After initial enthusiasm for change, one commentator described the review as 'in danger of becoming a damp squib' (*Local Government Chronicle*, 2 October 2003). It is not too difficult to see why there is unlikely to be any fundamental shift in the existing balance, south of the border or in Scotland. The Scottish Executive will always want to exercise its prerogative to introduce new initiatives and set national priorities. To do otherwise may leave it vulnerable to policy failure. In a battle between national priorities and enhancing local democracy, the former tends to win because it has the legal, political and constitutional powers to do so (see Chapter 10 for further discussion).

Non-Domestic Rates

Taxation of properties for business purposes has a long history dating back to the sixteenth century (McConnell 1999). The tax was locally valued and levied, evolving over the years until reforms in 1929 laid the foundation for a modern non-domestic rating system in Scotland. Non-domestic properties (with some exceptions, notably agricultural land) were allocated a notional annual rental value for the property and revaluations took place (at least in theory) every five years. On an annual basis, every local authority set a standard rate poundage which was then applied to each property valuation in order to determine the bill levied on each property owner. In 1985 the system hit a crisis point in Scotland as a consequence of revaluation and this sparked an intense debate (alongside the debate about replacing domestic rates with a poll tax) on the fairness and accountability of the system (see McConnell 1995, 1997, 1999). The Conservative Government at the time argued that local authorities could not be trusted to set rate poundages (in effect, tax rates) which were 'good' for local businesses. Thus, the responsibility for setting the rate was removed to central government. With the arrival of a Scottish Parliament in 1999, setting the rate poundage became the responsibility of the Scottish Executive. Figure 9.2 gives further details about the

---

Figure 9.2   A general guide to non-domestic rates in Scotland.

- The current system has operated in Scotland since 1989.

- Business properties are valued and revalued every five years. The last revaluation was 2000 and the next is 2005. Some premises are exempt from rating such as agricultural land, police premises and public parks.

- Valuations are based largely on an estimate of how much each property can be rented for during a one-year period. This valuation takes into account factors such as rental evidence, location, age and condition. In effect, the more desirable the property, the higher the rateable value.

- Valuations are the responsibility of 10 Valuation Joint Boards and 4 councils that have valuation authority (Glasgow, Dumfries and Galloway, Fife and Borders) and appoint independent assessors for this purpose. The Scottish Assessors' Association is the umbrella body for assessors. Its major role is the co-ordination of assessor practices.

- A business does not pay the assessed value in rates. This has to be multiplied by a rate poundage which is set on a Scotland-wide basis by the Scottish Executive which has devolved responsibility for local government finance. Legally, the rate poundage cannot increase by more than the rate of inflation – except at revaluation.

- The rate poundage for 2003–4 is 47.8p in the £ and 48.8p (provisional) for 2004–5. For example, an assessment of £100,000 per annum in 2004–5 would result in a bill of £48,800.

- Various relief schemes operate in order to phase in changes brought about by revaluation. Businesses with a rateable value of more than £25,000 pay a £0.6p in the £ supplement (2003–4) to finance a relief scheme for businesses with a rateable value of £10,000 or lower. This supplement will fall to £0.3p in 2004–5. Also, properties with charitable status receive 80 per cent mandatory relief on their rates bill.

- Collection of non-domestic rates is the responsibility of each local authority but they do not keep the revenue they collect. Scottish revenues are pooled and then distributed back to local authorities on a per-head-of-population basis.

- The Scottish Rating and Valuation Council is a non-departmental public body. Its role is to advise the Scottish Executive on matters related to rating, valuation and the preparation of legislation.

- A Scottish Ratepayers Forum will be created in 2005. It will comprise representatives of the Scottish Assessors' Association and businesses. Its main purpose will be to facilitate the exchange of information and ideas, encouraging greater transparency in the non-domestic rates system.

Sources: Miscellaneous.

---

operation of the current system. Three main issues are particularly important in assessing the operation of non-domestic rates in Scotland.

First, the Scottish Executive's power to set the rate poundage means, almost inevitably, that the tax rate will differ north and south of the border. As a consequence of a variety of complex political, technical and financial factors, poundage levels (as shown in table 9.2) are higher in Scotland than in England. This has dismayed the Scottish Chambers of Commerce, Scottish CBI and others, who have argued that it places Scottish businesses at a competitive disadvantage and discourages inward investment. The likelihood of a return to a UK-wide Uniform Business Rate (UBR) is, however, virtually non-existent. It would mean a removal of a key tax-setting power of the Scottish Parliament, a move unthinkable in the present climate.

Table 9.2   Non-domestic rate poundages in Scotland and England, 1999–2000 to 2004–5.

Year	Scotland (pence)	England (pence)
1999–2000	48.9	48.9
2000–1	45.8	41.6
2001–2	47.0	43.0
2002–3	47.8	43.7
2003–4	47.8	44.4
2004–5	48.8	45.6

Note: 2000–1 was the first poundage set by ministers in the Scottish Parliament.

Sources: Miscellaneous.

Second, until 1989, non-domestic rates was a local tax, giving local authorities a degree of independent revenue-raising powers. Being able to set both the domestic and non-domestic rate pound-ages gave councils (the threat of capping aside) the power to raise approximately 50 per cent of revenue expenditure. Post-1989, non-domestic rates have in effect become a central allocation of funds and the Council Tax accounts for only about 12 per cent of revenues. The Scottish Parliament's Local Government Committee recommended that the balance be shifted back to as close to 50:50 as possible and that non-domestic rates be returned to local control. One of the main supporting arguments is that the present system blurs accountability, with uncertainty in the public mind about who (the Scottish Parliament or local authorities) is respon-sible for local services. This argument is supported by COSLA, CIPFA and the STUC. Unsurprisingly, it is rejected by the Association of Scottish Chambers of Commerce, CBI Scotland, Forum of Private Business in Scotland, and Federation of Small Businesses. They are concerned at businesses losing a system where the tax rate is the same throughout Scotland, is predictable, assists long-term planning and is well understood. The response from the Scottish Executive (similar to that of the Office of the Deputy Prime Minister) has been to side with business interests and reject calls for a return of business rates to local control. Perhaps the best that 'localists' can hope for at some time in the future is a modified system where local authorities have freedom to vary the poundage plus or minus a few percentage points. One possible version of this is Business Improvement Districts, already existing in England and Wales and subject to consultation by the Scottish Executive in the summer of 2003. They could lead to businesses and local authorities working in partnership and agreeing to levy an additional business rates levy in order to fund local services of mutual benefit (such as CCTV and environmental improvements) (Scottish Executive Finance and Central Services Department 2003).

Third, an issue of particular concern for city councils is the distribution method. Scotland's cities are faced with the situation where many people work within their boundaries but live outside where property prices are often cheaper. Hence, the city populations themselves are not a true reflection of the level of economic activity within city boundaries. For example, in Glasgow for the year 2001–2 (as indicated in table 9.3), the City generated roughly £265m in business rates but got back only £185m from the grant pool. For the City of Edinburgh Council, the situation was even worse. In 2001–2 it contributed £232m but received only £137m from the pool. The Scottish Executive (2003a) rejected calls to reform the system in favour of allowing councils to keep the NDRI generated in their areas. The difficulty with reform is that, politically and financially, it is a zero sum game. If Scotland's six cities were allowed to keep their non-domestic rate receipts, then the losers (in the absence of funding from the Scottish Executive) would be most of the other 26 authorities in Scotland. Developments south of the border are one indicator of the direction in which policy could go. In England, the Local Authority Business Growth Scheme will begin in April 2005, giving local authorities some freedom to retain a proportion of any increases in the revenue generated by business rates in their areas. Nevertheless, reforms such as this are liable to be incremental rather than fundamental. The desire of the centre to preserve its powers means that the current system of business rating in Scotland is liable to be with us for a very long time.

Table 9.3 Glasgow City Council non-domestic rate income, 1996–7 to 2001–2.

Year	Raised in the city (£)	Received from the national pool (£)	Net payment to national pool (£)
1996–7	219,410	159,507	59,903
1997–8	203,939	159,662	44,277
1998–9	231,326	167,718	63,608
1999–2000	239,193	172,008	67,185
2000–1	260,622	201,238	59,384
2001–2	266,242	185,602	80,640

Source: Glasgow City Council (2003: 10).

Council Tax

Property-based taxation has been the mainstay of local taxation in Scotland since at least the nineteenth century, and prior to that more loosely in a fragmented and primitive system of local taxation which took into account 'property' as a mean of assessing individuals for tax purposes (Midwinter 1990; McConnell 1999). This system – known as domestic rates, and where individuals were taxed according to the value of their property with rebates for those on low incomes – fell into disarray partly as a consequence of a Scottish revaluation crisis in 1985 (McConnell 1995, 1997) and was disrupted by the arrival of the Poll Tax in 1989 (formally called the Community Charge). This was in essence a per capita tax which spread the local tax burden from the middle classes to the working class. By making almost all over-18s (including students, the unemployed and pensioners) pay a minimum of 20 per cent, it was an attempt to ensure that everyone paid something towards local services and make them think twice about voting for high-spending authorities. The ideas fitted very much with radical New Right Conservative thinking which sought to reduce tax burdens and public expenditure in particular and the role of the state in general (Midwinter and Monaghan 1993; Midwinter 1995). Yet its introduction was a failure of disastrous proportions (Lavalette and Mooney 1989; Butler et al. 1994; McConnell 1997). In the first year 1989–90 in Scotland (one year prior to England and Wales), summary warrants for non-payment were taken out against 1,420,825 individuals: roughly 38 per cent of those registered (*Glasgow Herald*, 17 November 1990). In addition, there was a catalogue of administrative problems which in effect rendered the tax unsustainable. The final outcome in Scotland (and south of the border) was reversion in 1993 to a property tax called Council Tax. It is effectively a modified version of domestic rates because its core principle is that local taxation should be based on property ownership and occupation (unlike the Poll Tax which was premised on each individual benefiting from access to local services), with this being a broad indicator of 'ability to pay' and 'fairness'. Further details of how the tax operates are contained in figure 9.3. There are several matters of contention and some calls for its abolition. In this regard, four issues are worthy of mention.

First, as shown in table 9.4, recent Council Tax levels in Scotland have (with one exception) been above the rate of inflation, the increases being particularly high in the two years following the 1995–6 introduction of single tier authorities, real cuts in RSG, and the Government failing to fully fund the cost of reorganisation with the costs being passed onto Council Tax (see Midwinter and McGarvey 1997; Midwinter 1998). In many respects, this is indicative of the problem caused by the Scottish Executive (and previously the Scottish Office) providing the vast majority of revenue for councils. It means that changes elsewhere in the system impact disproportionately on Council Tax levels: in other words, local authorities' only real source of revenue-raising power. Thus, for example, if Scottish councils wish to recoup cuts in government grants which reduce their income by 1 per cent, they have to increase the Council Tax by just over 8 per cent. This is known as the 'gearing effect'. Working against large Council Tax increases, however, is the restriction that if individual councils set Council Tax levels above a threshold set by ministers, they are penalised by not receiving their full entitlement to the Council Tax Benefit Subsidy which they would normally receive to compensate for income they would lose through individuals receiving rebates or exemptions. In effect, this is very close to Scottish Executive 'capping' of local authority Council Tax levels. What it means in wider terms is that there is a limit to the extent that levels of Council Tax can accommodate reductions in Scottish Executive funding, with the result that the only real alternative left for councils is to cut service levels.

Second, there have been many calls for a review of Council Tax banding, although the Scottish Executive has to date been reluctant

Figure 9.3   A general guide to the Council Tax in Scotland.

- Council Tax is a property-based tax. It was introduced in Scotland on 1 April 1993 to replace the Poll Tax (Community Charge).

- Properties are assessed at market/capital value by 10 Valuation Joint Boards and 4 councils which have valuation authority (Glasgow, Dumfries and Galloway, Fife and Borders). They appoint independent assessors for this purpose. The last revaluation was 1991. There are no plans for a revaluation before the 2007 elections. Normally, a property will only be revalued when it is sold to a new owner.

- Assessors place properties into one of the following bands:

Assessed Market Value	Band	Proportions
Up to £27,000	A	100
Over £27,000 and up to £35,000	B	117
Over £35,000 and up to £45,000	C	133
Over £45,000 and up to £58,000	D	150
Over £58,000 and up to £80,000	E	183
Over £80,000 and up to £106,000	F	217
Over £106,000 and up to £212,000	G	250
Over £212,000	H	300

- Each of Scotland's 32 local authorities has the freedom to set the Council Tax level in each band. One important restriction on this is a legal requirement for each band to be a specified proportion of the other. For example, the Council Tax in Band H should be exactly double the level in Band D and three times the level of Band A.

- From 2001–2 onwards, councils have moved to a system of three-year budgeting and are required to publish Council Tax levels each year and indicative figures for the next two years.

- Where a house is someone's sole or main residence, the owner-occupier or tenant will usually be liable for the Council Tax bill. For other houses, including empty property, holiday homes, the tenant or owner will normally be liable.

- A variety of exemptions, rebates and discounts apply. Single-person households are entitled to a discount of 25 per cent. For the purposes of calculating Council Tax liability, individuals such as children, students, student nurses and apprentices do not count as residents. Council Tax Benefit of up to 100 per cent is available for people on low incomes or in receipt of social security benefit.

- Local authorities collect and keep the proceeds of Council Tax paid within their boundaries. Revenue Support Grant contains an 'equalisation' element in order to compensate councils for differentials in their Council Tax base.

- Collection rates in 2001–2 were an average of 90.6 per cent throughout Scotland although there were substantial variations. Orkney Islands Council was 97.3 per cent and Glasgow City Council was 81.5 per cent.

- The average cost of collection in 2001–2 was £12.92 per chargeable dwelling. The lowest figure was £5.74 in Falkirk and the highest was £23.01 in West Dunbartonshire.

Figure 9.3 *continued opposite*

Figure 9.3 *continued*

- Water and sewerage charges are levied separately by Scottish Water (prior to 2002 it was three separate water authorities). The charges are collected by local authorities on behalf of Scottish Water.

Sources: Adapted from Scottish Executive 2001; Accounts Commission 2003a; and miscellaneous sources.

to give any firm commitment on this issue. Some of the main arguments in favour of rebanding in Scotland are:

- Some bands are too wide, such as £106,000 to £212,000 which contains within it a vast range of properties from bungalows to mansion houses.
- There is a case for introducing a lower band for very low value properties (such as caravans). Equally, there is a case for introducing more bands at the top in order to be more progressive.
- Council Tax in the lowest band (A) must legally be three times that in the highest band (H), yet the difference in property values is roughly eight-fold. Thus, the range of tax burdens is much narrower than the range of property values.

Table 9.4 Council Tax increases in Scotland, 1993–4 to 2003–4.

Year	Band D equivalent (£)[1]	Increase from previous year (%)[2]
1993–4[3]	558	–
1994–5	602	7.9
1995–6	624	3.7
1996–7	708	13.4
1997–8	783	10.6
1998–9	827	5.6
1999–2000	849	2.7
2000–1	886	4.4
2001–2	929	4.9
2002–3	971	4.5
2003–4	1,009	3.9

Notes

[1] Figures exclude water and sewerage charges.

[2] The average inflation rate for the period 1994–5 to 2003–4 was approximately 2.5%. The average Council Tax increase over this same period was 6.2%.

[3] The first year of the Council Tax was 1993–4, and so there is no comparative figure for 1992–3.

Sources: Miscellaneous.

Third, and related, are calls for a full-scale property revaluation. Bands were set and properties allocated accordingly in 1991 yet there have been significant changes in property markets since then. Some areas have risen substantially, such as Edinburgh, Glasgow, Aberdeen and East Dunbartonshire. Correspondingly, others have fallen, such as Dundee and Renfrewshire. The Scottish Executive has stated that revaluation before the 2007 elections will not be possible for practical reasons and it has made no specific commitment beyond this period. This contrasts with the situation south of the border. The Office of the Deputy Prime Minister has committed England to a revaluation in 2007. Revaluation for Wales will come into effect earlier, in 2005. In essence, Scottish Executive reluctance reflects a classic dilemma for governments. On the one hand, property revaluations create winners and losers. Historically they have caused enormous disruption, misunderstandings, uncertainty and anxiety among local taxpayers, with politicians being on the receiving end of numerous backlashes (McConnell 1997, 1999). Thus, it is unsurprising that the Scottish Executive wants to avoid the political turmoil that will almost inevitably ensue in the event of a revaluation. On the other hand, not conducting a revaluation creates a different set of problems. It leads to a gradual build-up of pressures because it means widespread instances of unfairness – especially because properties have risen in value since 1991 but properties are still located in the same bands and so individuals are paying the same relative Council Tax rate. For Scottish Executive ministers, no revaluation meantime is politically by far the easier of the two options but it simply postpones the time when a revaluation will have to take place and leads to even greater disparities between the 'old' and the 'new' value when it does happen. All things being equal, the longer a revaluation is postponed, the greater will be the political backlash when it does occur.

Fourth, more fundamental criticism of the Council Tax comes from those who seek its abolition. The main alternatives are Local Income Tax (LIT) and Local Sales Tax (LST) (see McConnell 1999 for a full discussion). From a variety of very different political perspectives, there is remarkable convergence of opposition thinking. The commonality is a belief that local taxation should be based on ability to pay and that this is far better reflected (on grounds of fairness) in some form of locally based Income Tax than in a property tax. The Scottish National Party and the Scottish Liberal Democrats strongly support replacing the Council Tax with a form of Local Income Tax which would allow local authorities to levy a tax rate on individuals' incomes and wealth. Understandably, both have been reluctant to identify a typical tax rate because it gives ammunition to political opponents. The Scottish Socialist Party favours a Scottish Service Tax, which is a Local Income Tax in all but name. Supporting research undertaken by Danson and Whittam (2002) indicates that those on incomes in excess of £10,000 per annum would pay the tax. The initial marginal rate would be 4.5 per cent, rising to 15 per cent for those on incomes in excess of £30,000, 18 per cent for incomes in excess of £50,000, and 20 per cent in excess of £90,000. The cumulative effect is a progressive one, with tax paid (as a percentage of income) increasing as income increases (Danson and Whittam 2002: 24).

In England in 2003, Council Tax rises averaging 12.9 per cent provoked a high profile backlash against ministers. Local Government Minister Nick Raynsford stated that the Council Tax had reached the 'limit of acceptability', prompting a review of local government finance. A survey by Rita Hale Associates for the Local Government Information Unit suggested that the crisis was prompted by a combination of increased ring-fencing, under-funding from the centre and a fall in business rates burden (Local Government Information Unit 2003). Similar trends are evident in Scotland. For example, business rates contributed to 18.4 per cent of revenue income in 1996–7 and this dropped to 13.5 per cent in 2001–2 (Scottish Office 1999b: table 1; Scottish Executive 2003g: figure 2). Nevertheless, Scottish councils have managed to keep Council Tax rises reasonably low and stable (see table 9.4). For the meantime at least, therefore, Council Tax is a sustainable tax north of the border. It has sufficient political support, has not provoked demonstrations and is administratively quite efficient and effective.

Miscellaneous Fees and Charges

Fees, charges and other miscellaneous income account for about 20 per cent of revenue expenditure in Scotland's 32 local authorities. Just over half the revenue received is income from council house rents. Nevertheless, given that the vast majority of revenue income is beyond the control of councils, fees and charges are an increasingly important source of revenue. As indicated in figure 9.4, however, there are a variety of legal, political, citizen and service limitations on councils' ability to levy charges. One impact is a lack of a uniform approach across Scottish councils. A study by the Accounts Commission

Figure 9.4 Factors which affect local authority charges.

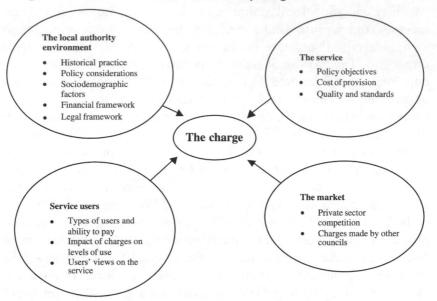

Source: Adapted from Accounts Commission (1998a: 12).

(1998a: 3) found that less than one quarter of councils adopted a corporate approach to charging for services. One of the advantages of such an approach is that it allows councils to adopt a standardised approach to concession, equality of opportunity and access across a range of council services. Many other councils are considering the benefits of a corporate approach, although a third have no plans to introduce a corporate approach to charging for local services. Figure 9.5 indicates the main areas liable to charging by councils.

Charging for local government services is the subject of a small but growing area of debate (Bailey et al. 1993; Bailey 1994; Chandler and Turner 1997). One message to emerge so far is that the decision to charge for local services is much more pragmatic than we might expect. It is not driven to any significant degree by party political philosophies. Charges are something of a 'safety valve' for local authority finances when there is nowhere else to turn. COSLA, supported by the Scottish Parliament's Local Government Committee, has argued for councils to be given a greater degree of freedom to set fees and charges for discretionary services. The Scottish Executive has accepted this recommendation and one possibility is the levying of congestion charges. The City of Edinburgh Council has been particularly active in attempting to pursue this option. In the longer

Figure 9.5 Services areas in Scottish local authorities typically subject to charging.

Central services

- Licensing (taxis, private hire cars, etc.)

Education services

- Adult education
- Musical instrument tuition
- Outdoor education
- School lets
- School meals
- School milk

Environmental services

- Burials and cremations
- Pest control
- Skip hire
- Special uplifts from domestic property

Miscellaneous property services

- Management of private property repairs
- Property enquiries

Planning and building control

- Building warrants
- Letters of comfort
- Planning permission

Roads and transport

- Bus stations
- Parking

Recreation, Leisure and Miscellaneous

- Community halls
- Library services
- Museums and galleries
- Sports and leisure
- Civil weddings

Source: Adapted from Accounts Commission (1998a).

term, given ongoing constraints on local government resources, usage of fees and charges is liable to expand in Scotland because it encourages local autonomy and does not involve any additional funding from the Scottish Executive. In England and Wales, the Local Government Act 2003 makes provision for local authorities to keep the revenue from penalty notices for dog fouling and littering. This may well create a precedent for the Scottish Executive.

Capital Finance: Sources, Restrictions and Issues

In 2001–2, capital expenditure in Scotland accounted for 6.7 per cent of all expenditure in Scotland's 32 councils (calculated from Scottish Executive 2003g: table 1). Capital expenditure is targeted at the construction and improving of physical assets such as buildings and roads. In Scotland, small amounts of funding comes from the Scottish Executive and the National Lottery although capital expenditure is financed largely from four main sources: borrowing subject to the restriction of capital consents; income from asset sales; EU grants; and Public-Private Partnership/Private

Finance Initiative (PPP/PFI). Capital financing is an immensely complex area and there are some differences in policy instruments north and south of the border although the main directions of policy are very similar. For purposes of clarity, we will focus simply on Scotland and look at each source of finance in turn, focusing on key issues.

Borrowing Subject to Capital Consents

Section 95 of the Local Government (Scotland) Act 1973 (as amended) is the mainstay of Scottish Executive control. Local authorities are issued annual capital allocations for non-housing investment, such as education, roads and transport, social work, general services, flood prevention and (non-council) housing. Councils receive a single allocation for the vast majority of capital expenditure and most of it is calculated on a formula basis comprising:

- a fixed element of £1m per council;
- a road lane lengths element and some special needs allowances;
- a simulated classroom numbers element, based on projected class numbers;
- a non-HRA housing element based on the average of the three years net allocations prior to local government reorganisation; and
- a population element. (Source: Scottish Executive 2002b)

A crucial point to note is that a capital allocation is not an allocation of money: it is simply a consent to borrow. Local authorities may borrow from a variety of sources (repayable from revenue expenditure over the life of the asset) such as the European Investment Bank, any authorised EU credit institution, and by issuing stocks. A particularly important source of borrowing is the Public Works Loan Board (PWLB), a statutory body financed by the Treasury which provides loans at favourable rates of interest. In 2002–3, Scottish local authorities borrowed just over £551m, with an accumulated debt of over £7.5b (Public Works Loan Board 2003: 2–3). Crucially, local authorities are not completely free to spend or borrow against the allocation as they wish. Capital expenditure for police and fire boards (which form part of the local authority non-housing allocation) is decided by the Scottish Executive, which also 'top slices' the allocation in accordance with national priorities in areas such as public transport, flood prevention, waste management and air quality. By the end of 2003–4, councils will have had access to only 62 per cent of their allocation (COSLA 2001b: part 20, section 10).

Since the early 1980s to the mid 1990s, capital allocations have been increasingly tight. In the Conservative years, not only was there an economic agenda to pursue of keeping down public expenditure, reducing public sector borrowing and reducing tax levels, but there was also a political one. In other words, Conservative Governments attempted to reduce the role of the state and marginalise those vested interests wedded to state provision. A prime target was Labour-dominated Scotland and in particular Strathclyde Regional Council, once described by Prime Minister John Major as a 'monstrosity'. The Conservatives could hardly allow local political opponents the freedom to engage in large-scale Keynesian-style capital programmes. From 1999 onwards, the Labour-Liberal coalition in the Scottish Executive has not exhibited the same political antagonism to capital projects, but the economic ones remain to a substantial degree. Local authority borrowing has an impact on UK fiscal policy because it adds to public sector borrowing. COSLA argues that even despite allocations being loosened slightly since 1979, the regime is still too restrictive for proper investment in public services. COSLA suggested in 2001 that it needed at least £2.8b to meet imminent needs (see table 9.5) and that:

> It is essential . . . that adequate and sustainable revenue funding is made available by central government to enable the necessary investment to be taken forward. Local government needs to be put in a position whereby it may also tackle years of under investment by addressing the crumbling infrastructure in schools, roads and other community facilities, take forward the modernisation agenda and invest in 'spend to save' initiatives. (COSLA 2001b: part 10, section 1.6)

In 2002, the Scottish Parliament's Local Government Committee recommended an overhaul of the capital finance system to give more flexibility to local authorities. The Scottish Executive has accepted this recommendation and capital consents will be replaced in April 2004 with a new system based on prudential rules, whereby borrowing is not limited by government but by a duty not to breach a prudential code. This

Table 9.5 COSLA 2001 estimate of future capital expenditure needs.

Area	Est. cost (£m)
Property repairs	1,300
ICT investment in schools	No figure
Flood prevention	60
Social work information systems	20
Public safety radio communications system	20
Roads maintenance	1,211
Waste management	200
Contaminated land regulations	10
Modernising agenda	No figure
Total	2,821

Source: COSLA 2001b: part 10, table A.

move will give local authorities a greater degree of financial flexibility, although prudential constraints and Scottish Executive guidance are likely to limit the possibility of a huge expansion in capital projects.

Income from Asset Sales

In 2001–2, 64.6 per cent of capital income came from local authorities disposing of assets such as council houses, land and buildings (Scottish Executive 2003g: figure 4). With one major exception, local authorities since 1998 have been free to use this revenue to fund new capital projects. The exception is revenue generated by council house sales, amounting to £309m in 2002–3 (Scottish Executive 2003h: table 16). Since 1996, as part of a move to (1) discourage new building and modernisation in the council house sector, (2) address the capital debt burden in Housing Revenue Accounts and (3) encourage stock transfer to non-council landlords, local authorities are required to use 75 per cent of the receipts to repay debt. This is payable through the revenue account. Thus, in 2002–3, almost £232m of receipts could not be used for investment in building or modernisation. COSLA has been extremely critical of the inflexibility brought about by this restrictive regime but as yet there are no signs of a fundamental reform.

EU Grants

Local authorities in Scotland have access to capital grants from EU structural funds which are part of a wider (and fragmented) EU regional policy, aimed at ensuring greater social and economic cohesion within the EU. The primary source of capital funding is the European Regional Development Fund (ERDF) which promotes infrastructure investment, local development and employment initiatives, and structures providing neighbourhood services. Gradual EU enlargements have meant an increased demand on limited resources for structural funds, particularly because many of the comparatively newer members (such as Greece, Spain and Portugal) contain regions with lower levels of growth and lower per capita incomes. The situation is liable to get worse in 2004 with the accession of 10 new members including Poland, Hungary and Slovenia. Thus the EU budget for the 2000–6 period produced a freeze in regional funding, as well as a redrawing of objectives and a greater targeting at the very 'poorest' regions. Figure 9.6 details the areas of Scotland which retain this special status, amounting to over £1,000m in the 2000–6 period (Scottish Parliament Information Centre 2001: 4). An important condition attached to

---

Figure 9.6 Objectives for EU Structural Funds, 2000–6, the Scottish dimension.

Objective 1: To assist in the development and structural adjustment of EU regions. Two thirds of all Structural Funds in the EU are devoted to those regions whose development is seen to be lagging behind. No area in Scotland is eligible.

Objective 2: To support the economic and social conversion of areas facing structural difficulties (particularly in areas of industrial decline, rural areas, urban areas and fishery dependent areas). In Scotland, Objective 2 areas are the South of Scotland, around the North East coast, and clusters in former industrial areas in central Scotland.

Objective 3: To support the adaptation and modernisation of education and training systems and employment policies. This is funding for projects outside the areas covered by Objective 1. Each member state of the EU receives a proportion of the total resources available on the basis of its share of eligible population. In Scotland, there are five priorities for action: raising employability, addressing social exclusion, lifelong learning, competitive economy, and addressing gender imbalance.

Note: In addition to these objectives, there are transitional support and special programmes for regions previously receiving assistance under one of the Structural Fund programmes but which do not meet the new eligibility criteria. The Highlands and Islands qualify for this, worth approximately £200m, which together with public and private co-funding amounts to £500m for the 2000–6 period.

Source: Adapted from Scottish Parliament Information Centre (2001).

obtaining EU funding is that it must be matched (usually up to 50 per cent) by national resources.

The Scottish Executive is the 'managing authority' for EU funds, but day-to-day co-ordination and implementation is carried out via the regional bodies of South of Scotland European Partnership, Western Scotland European Partnership, Eastern Scotland European Partnership, Highlands and Islands Partnership Programme, and Scottish ESF Objective 3. The very nature of EU Structural Funds (which not only require match funding but also usually require partnerships) is that local authorities are but one of a multiplicity of actors involved in bids for EU funds. Other bodies include Scottish Enterprise and Local Enterprise Companies (LECs), universities and further education colleges, enterprise trusts and local economic development initiatives, area tourist boards, voluntary bodies and charitable organisations. Local authorities have a variety of inputs into EU Structural Fund matters. On a wider EU level, COSLA is represented in Scotland Europa (a subsidiary of Scottish Enterprise, launched in 1992), a body promoting a variety of Scottish public, private and civil interests in Brussels. Also, the Scottish European Structural Funds Forum was established in October 2000 to take a strategic view of EU funds in Scotland. It comprises representatives from (among others) COSLA and several local authorities. Councils throughout Scotland have been successful in securing EU funding for a variety of capital projects. Examples include:

- New Stornoway ferry terminal, 1994–6, ERDF funding £4.5m.
- Glasgow Science Centre on the south side of the River Clyde, Glasgow, 1998–2000, ERDF funding £19m.
- The Millennium Link, a project to restore navigation to the Forth and Clyde Canal and Union Canal, 1999–2001, ERDF funding £8.59m.
- Redevelopment of Arbroath Harbour, 2002–7, ERDF funding £410,000.

Public Private Partnerships/Private Finance Initiative

Public Private Partnerships (PPPs) is a general term for a wide range of projects involving the public and private sectors. The most common, and controversial, is the Private Finance Initiative (PFI) launched by the Treasury and the Scottish Office in 1992 (Allen 2003). A Private Finance Unit exists within the Scottish Executive to promote and give advice on the private financing of capital projects. Unlike traditional capital investment, PFI funding means that public bodies do not typically own the asset: it is owned by the private sector, which also designs, finances, builds and operates the investment. Local authorities simply make regular payments (from the revenue account) to the relevant private company. Capital expenditure incurred under PFI is not subject to Scottish Executive capital consents. One reason is that in accounting terms, it does not count as public borrowing. Hence, as the Scottish Local Government Information Unit (2002: 1) suggests in its discussion of PFI projects and schools: 'councils chose PFI because it was the only investment option within the financial framework set by the Scottish Executive; i.e. it was PFI or nothing.'

As of 2003, the value of 'Done Deals' in Scotland was roughly £2.2b. High profile cases throughout the Scottish public sector include the Skye Bridge, the Royal Infirmary in Edinburgh and the replacement for Law and Hairmyres Hospital in East Kilbride. Local authorities account for about 48 per cent of known PFI projects (Scottish Executive Private Finance Unit 2003). There are 47 local authority projects completed or underway by late 2003 (two notable examples are given in figure 9.7) but this figure will increase considerably when schools and waste management projects move beyond the initial development phase.

Supporters of PFI argue that it has many advantages. It provides much needed capital investment when there is no other realistic

---

Figure 9.7 Examples of major local authority PFI projects in Scotland.

Glasgow Schools Project 1997–2003: Glasgow City Council, for the replacement or modernisation of 29 secondary schools and one primary school, and the introduction of an ICT programme. This is the largest PFI education project in the UK. Contract awarded to 3ED Consortium, a private company. Contract length 30 years and capital cost £225m. 3ED undertakes responsibility for functions such as janitation, security and cleaning, and a programme of planned maintenance for each building, costing approximately £200m over this period.

Baldovie Waste to Energy Plant 1993–9: Dundee City Council, for the building of a waste to energy facility at Baldovie, Dundee. Contract awarded to Dundee Energy Recycling Ltd (DERL), a special-purpose company formed between BICC plc, Kvaerner Investments and Dundee City Council. DERL developed, owns and operates the plant, obtaining revenue from fees for waste disposal, sale of power generated by the plant, and sale of recovered metals. The contract length is 20 years and the capital value is £43m.

alternative. It benefits from private sector management expertise. It requires careful objective setting and planning, thus contributing to long-term coherence and value for money, as well as allocating appropriate responsibility for risk management. A major UK survey by Arthur Andersen and Enterprise LSE (2000: para. 5.5) found that in 29 projects reviewed with an estimated procurement cost of £6.1b, the estimated savings of PFI were almost £1.1b. A report by Audit Scotland in 2002 into PFI in Scotland's schools was also largely positive:

> The evidence of outcomes so far is that the PFI providers are delivering the required new/refurbished schools rapidly, largely on time and without significant cost changes for the client. Bearing in mind the scale of the construction works this is an important achievement. Users also appear to welcome the improved accommodation and level of service that has come on line. (Audit Scotland 2002b: 8)

In contrast there are a series of criticisms, coming from bodies such as Unison Scotland, the Association of Direct Labour Organisations and the Centre for Public Services. They argue that PFI does not produce value for money in the way often assumed. There are hidden costs such as local authority staff developing PFI projects, and the true costs will not be known for 25 to 30 years. The SNP argues that for Scotland's schools alone, the cost could be an extra £747m (*The Herald*, 7 June 2002). Separate studies of Scottish local authorities by Hood and McGarvey (2002) and Asenova and Beck (2003) found that councils were generally ill-prepared for the risk transfer process, and at a severe disadvantage compared with commercial operators who have substantial expertise in this area. The latter of these studies found there to be a particularly steep learning curve for councils engaged in school projects. More generally, unless there is something approaching parity between public and private sector expertise, the outcome is liable to be a lack of value for money in the long term. A further argument is that projects are not viable unless supported by the Scottish Executive. In the case of Glasgow schools, the Scottish Executive is providing £13.8m per annum over the first seven years, rising to £16.1m per annum for the remainder of the contract (Centre for Public Services 2001: section 6.7). Furthermore, public sector comparisons are flawed because PFI project teams may seek to prove the worth of their projects, leading to an exaggeration of the benefits and an underestimation of the costs. There is also a lack of democratic accountability, and the nature of service provision under PFI is further removed from local people.

In 2002, the Scottish Parliament's Local Government Committee suggested that councils may be pushed into inflexible PFI schemes (which may prove costly in the long term) because there is no other realistic option available, whereas what is needed is greater flexibility. For precisely these reasons, West Dunbartonshire Council and Falkirk Council both backed away from full use of PFI to fund school refurbishment. The SNP has been particularly vocal in its opposition to PPPs and PFIs, proposing an alternative of local Not For Profit Trusts. For the foreseeable future, however, PPPs and PFIs are here to stay. For better or worse, PFI offers local authorities the only major escape route from a situation where their power to fund large-scale building and refurbishment projects is exceptionally limited because of restrictive capital allocations. The replacement of capital allocations in 2004 by a prudential code is liable to reinforce the use of PFI rather than undermine its use.

Scotland's 32 Local Authorities: Free to Spend?

In 2001–2, local authorities spent roughly £2,750 per annum on each man, woman and child in Scotland. As table 9.6 indicates, the biggest revenue spends are education and social work, which in combination accounted for 56.3 per cent of net revenue expenditure in 2001–2. We have already seen how the vast majority of local authorities' revenue income comes from the Scottish Executive rather than being raised locally by councils. Whatever the source, are councils free to engage in revenue expenditure as they see fit? It is difficult to give a definitive answer, other than to say that a series of constraints exist which impinge on local autonomy (see McConnell 1999). Five constraints are particularly important.

First, ministers no longer publish expenditure guidelines for councils, but retain reserve capping powers over local authority budgets if they consider spending plans to be 'excessive'. This is a subtle but important restraint on councils because it means that their budgetary plans may be adjusted in order to pre-empt intervention from ministers. Second, a large proportion of council expenditure is incurred because of statutory requirement to provide certain services such as education, social work, fire and police.

Table 9.6 Net current expenditure by service, general fund, 1996–7 to 2001–2.

| Service | Net expenditure financed from grants, non-domestic rates, council tax and balances (£m)[1] | | | | | |
	1996–7	1997–8	1998–9	1999–2000	2000–1	2001–2
Education	2,415	2,393	2,499	2,661	2,788	3,001
Social work	1,069	1,087	1,135	1,200	1,261	1,352
Police, fire and emergency planning	796	860	882	916	950	1,008
Roads and transport[2]	492[3]	376	378	383	391	373
Environmental services	280	287	288	312	329	369
Culture and related services	430	416	417	435	446	457
Planning and economic development	79	78	100	122	115	126
Other services[4]	338	338	309	296	228	310
Loan charges	657	652	710	702	709	739
Total[5]	6,556	6,487	6,720	7,029	7,217	7,735

Notes:

[1] All figures exclude general fund contributions to housing, trading services and interest on revenue balances.

[2] These figures include general fund contributions to transport (local authority and non-local authority).

[3] This figure differs substantially from later years because of a change in the recording of grant-in-aid of expenditure on rail passenger services.

[4] This figure includes housing expenditure which is not part of the Housing Revenue Account.

[5] As a consequence of prior rounding, most column totals in the original source do not add up. Totals have been amended slightly, as appropriate, to ensure they reflect the figures given in each row.

Source: Adapted from Scottish Executive (2003g: table S1).

Indeed, there are also non-statutory agreements such as pupil-teacher ratios which constrain local spending decisions. Third, there is a growing trend towards ring-fencing (hypothecation) of central funding, and therefore monies allocated must be spent in accordance with central requirements in areas such as pre-school provision, neighbourhood services, strategic waste and social inclusion. Furthermore, some funding in areas such as social work, youth crime and drug rehabilitation comes with conditions attached. Fourth, local authorities have to achieve Best Value in their service plans (see Chapter 8) and all expenditures have to take into account the constraints imposed. Best Value is supported and reinforced by the auditing regime of the Accounts Commission and

Audit Scotland. They 'police' local authorities and their Best Value Plans, undertake Value for Money studies in specific policy areas, and generally ensure that councils have in place the necessary arrangements for economy, efficiency and effectiveness in local government services. Finally, local authorities are constrained by what local communities will accept. This is reinforced by the Local Government in Scotland Act 2003 which places a statutory duty on councils to plan and provide for local services, after consultation with a wide range of public and community bodies.

One possible means of partially reconciling central priorities and local freedom is through Local Outcome Agreements (LOAs). A Scottish Executive/COSLA pilot was launched in July 2001, covering children's services, educational attainment and neighbour-hood services. LOAs continue to evolve for a number of services such as community care and the Rough Sleepers Initiative. LOAs are outcome based and involve local authorities agreeing to formal objectives which reflect a combination of national and local priorities. They have the potential to increase local freedoms although much will depend on a freeing up of 'inputs' (such as ring-fenced grants) and other Scottish Executive financial restrictions. We would suggest that marginal changes are possible but that it is difficult to see how it will lead to any fundamental change in local financial freedom. It is likely to 'cement' the existing balance of power rather than alter it in favour of councils.

Conclusion

Local government finance in Scotland is immensely complex. We should not forget, however, that at the heart of it is 'politics'. Over the years, the legislation, regulations, instruments, funds and names may change, but the core issues remain. In other words, who pays for local government? Domestic taxpayers? Non-domestic taxpayers? National taxpayers? How much should each of them contribute? What specific instruments should be used to raise revenue – a property-based tax, a Local Income Tax? How much financial freedom should Scottish local authorities have to raise finance locally? How much freedom should they have to spend money allocated from the centre? We can be sure the future developments in the financing of Scottish local authorities will continue to wrestle with these perennial questions.

?	Key Questions	?

1. Is it reasonable that a substantial portion of Scottish Executive funding for councils is 'ring-fenced'?
2. Should local authorities be allowed to keep the business rates generated in their area?
3. Should business rates be returned to local authority control?
4. Is the Council Tax sustainable in Scotland?
5. Is PFI the best way forward for councils seeking to engage in capital expenditure programmes?

📖	Further Reading	📖

The best source of statistics on local government finance in Scotland is the annual *Scottish Local Government Financial Statistics*, published by the Scottish Executive. It is usually over a year behind actual financial years and so subsequent figures on aspects of local government finance can often be obtained from COSLA, the Accounts Commission and Audit Scotland. Debates about the 'politics' of local finance are spread around various books and texts. The numerous works of Arthur Midwinter (cited in the Bibliography) are easily the most authoritative commentaries over the past two decades and more in Scotland. The report of the Layfield Committee (Cmnd. 6453 1976) is well worth a look for its careful and detailed deliberations. The Local Government Committee (2002) of the Scottish Parliament produced a report with evidence which is well worth reading as the most recent investigation into local finance Scotland. My own book *The Politics and Policy of Local Taxation in Britain* (1999) covers the cases for and against local property, sales and consumption taxes. As a further 'plug' for my own work, a book called *State Policy Formation and the Origins of the Poll Tax* (1995) details how the Poll Tax came about in Scotland. A focus on the British-wide origins and disastrous implementation of the Poll Tax can be found in *Failure in British Government: The Politics of the Poll Tax* by David Butler, Andrew Adonis and Tony Travers (1994). A very useful overview of PFI can be found in a House of Commons Research Paper entitled *The Private Finance Initiative* (PFI) by Allen (2003).

Useful Websites

http://www.cosla.gov.uk
Convention of Scottish Local Authorities.

http://www.scotland.gov.uk
Scottish Executive.

http://www.scotland.gov.uk/about/FCSD/FIN-EXP-POL/
00018232/intro.aspx
Scottish Executive site on PPPs and PFI.

http://www.scotland.gov.uk/library5/finance/spfm/spf-00.asp
Scottish Public Finance Manual.

CHAPTER TEN

The Bigger Picture: Central–Local Relations, Multi-Level Governance and Globalisation

Scottish local government exists in a wider context, a bigger picture which helps us develop a deeper and more rounded understanding of its activities. This chapter will examine three areas of crucial importance. First, it will explore the relationship between the Scottish Executive and local authorities, situating this within wider models of central–local relations. Second, it will consider issues of multi-level governance, examining ways in which the system of local governance in Scotland is a product of politics and policies at the local, Scottish, Westminster and EU levels. Third and finally, it will offer the beginnings of an approach which situates Scottish local government within the context and constraints of an increasingly globalised world.

Central–Local Relations

Main Control Mechanisms

Scotland's local authorities and the Scottish Executive need each other. The Scottish Executive needs local authorities to:

- Deliver local services in accordance with national political and financial priorities.

- Tailor services to local needs and circumstances as efficiently as possible.
- Conduct themselves in a manner which is compatible with the financial, political and social parameters set by the centre.
- Espouse values of local democracy in order to legitimise the democratic nature of Scottish society within which the Scottish Executive operates.

Correspondingly, local authorities need the Scottish Executive to:

- Provide the legal and policy basis for councils to undertake their activities.
- Provide significant financial resources in the form of Revenue Support Grant and Non-Domestic Rates, as well as financial autonomy in areas such capital finance and charges for individual services.
- Engage in policy consultation in order to ensure the practicality of policies.
- Give councils as much legal, financial and political autonomy as possible in order to represent local communities.

We can see that their fortunes are entwined but not entirely compatible. Local government is elected in order to represent local communities in policy areas such as education, housing, transport and social work. Equally, the Scottish Executive is formed from an elected Scottish Parliament in order to set national policies in these same areas and more. What we have, therefore, is the potential for a clash between competing democratic legitimacies: the democratic legitimacy of Scotland's 32 local authorities versus the democratic legitimacy of the Scottish Parliament and the Scottish Executive. How is this potential for conflict resolved? The simple answer is that the centre uses a number of key mechanisms to control local authorities. We can adapt the work of Wilson and Game (2002) and identify five main mechanisms in all.

First, the Scottish Executive initiates the vast bulk of the primary legislation (passed through the Scottish Parliament) to which local authorities must adhere. As Chapter 1 indicates, Scottish local authorities must not act *ultra vires*: beyond the powers bestowed on them. When they perform their roles of providing services, regulating local activities, representing local communities, planning, promoting and advocating and innovating, they only do so as long as national legislation exists to require or permit their actions. Even the power to promote 'well-being' as contained in the Local Government in Scotland Act 2003 is set by the centre and has its legal limits. Overall, therefore, the Scottish Parliament (and in effect the Scottish Executive) is the legal master of local government. Over 25 Acts affecting local government were passed in the first term of the Scottish Parliament 1999–2003.

Second, Statutory Instruments (known sometimes as subordinate, delegated or secondary legislation) are often used to flesh out the implementation of legislation. A significant number of Acts emerging from the Scottish and Westminster Parliaments contain 'enabling' clauses, allowing for ministerial discretion at a later stage. They may appear in the form of Orders, Rules or Regulations. For example, the Local Government Act 1992 requires an annual grant to be paid to Scottish local authorities, but sensibly leaving room for grant settlements to be decided on an annual basis. Every year as a consequence, the Scottish Parliament debates a Local Government Finance (Scotland) Order as the basis for the Scottish Executive's proposals for Aggregate External Finance. Table 10.1 indicates that there were almost 100 Scottish Statutory Instruments affecting local government over the 1999–2003 period. They are still subject to Parliamentary scrutiny but this secondary scrutiny (usually in committee and sometimes in the chamber) involves only the right to accept or reject. The core content is determined by Scottish ministers.

Table 10.1 Local government subordinate legislation considered by the Local Government Committee of the Scottish Parliament, 1999–2003.

Year	Affirmative	Negative	Total
1999–2000	9	16	25
2000–1	4	15	19
2001–2	7	17	24
2002–3	8	21	29
Total statutory instruments	28	69	97

Note: Affirmative subordinate legislation requires Scottish Parliamentary approval. Negative subordinate legislation is assumed to be effective, unless specifically rejected by the Scottish Parliament.

Source: Local Government Committee (2003d: table 3).

Third, ministers can give policy direction to local authorities without the need (at least in the short term) for legislation. The Best

Value regime operated on this basis for the 1997–2002 period, initially with the threat of a return to CCT for a failure to comply. Policy direction only became law with the Local Government in Scotland Act 2003.

Fourth, Scottish Executive departments issue circulars to local authorities, usually when clarification or further guidance is required. They have no legal force, as such, but most are directive to some degree. In 2003, for example, the Scottish Executive issued guidance on child protection, the power of 'well-being', performance information and assessment in relation to the Joint Futures initiative, making direct payments for adult community care and children's services, Environmental Impact Assessments, and securing Best Value.

Fifth, as detailed in Chapter 9, the Scottish Executive has enormous power over local authority finances. It provides and determines about 68 per cent of revenue income by setting Revenue Support Grant and business rate levels, as well as restricting capital expenditure through capital consents. It also has the power to decide mandatory and permissive expenditures, cap budgets and ring-fence grants. Furthermore, it has the ability in effect to constrain and 'police' local authority expenditures through the Best Value regime and the inspection and audit functions carried out by Audit Scotland and the Accounts Commission for Scotland.

Pressure Points

The political autonomy afforded to local authorities is a crucial area of contest between local authorities and the Scottish Executive. Local authorities are democratically elected and have a major role in representing the interests of local communities. Correspondingly, the Scottish Executive is derived from a democratically elected Scottish Parliament that exists to represent these same local communities. The Scottish Executive (like any other national administration) does not want its political priorities to be thwarted by the political autonomy it gives to councils, especially if these councils are under the control of opposition parties. In the days of the Scottish Office, for example, the policy of the Conservative Government was to require local authorities to offer council houses for sale to tenants, whilst using capital expenditure controls to all but eradicate new house building. This was part of a wider political philosophy that encompassed the promotion of private ownership and the discouraging of state provision and dependence on the state. We were assured by Mrs Thatcher that 'there was no alternative' to these ideas. From the Conservative standpoint, therefore, it would have been politically suicidal if it had espoused such ideas but left it optional for local authorities to sell housing stock and build new council houses. Twenty years and more afterwards, little has changed in the logic of central political priorities versus local political autonomy. Modernisation is at the core of the Scottish Executive's policies for local government. But would the Scottish Executive be prepared to leave councils 'unmodernised' if they so wished (indeed, if local communities so wished)? The answer is no. Unless forced to do so, the Scottish Executive has no desire to see its political priorities undermined by giving 'excessive' political freedoms to councils. Indeed, Midwinter (2002) suggests that under devolution, the Scottish Executive has shifted the focus slightly from expenditure controls to setting the priorities of councils. Certainly, there seems to be a counterbalance via the Local Government in Scotland Act 2003 which is one of the few pieces of legislation since the 1970s to enhance the political freedoms of local authorities. However, the reality is that it enhances policy freedoms within such restricted parameters (ranging from Best Value requirements to explicit limitations on the power to promote 'well-being') that the centre is 'safe'. If councils find a loophole to enhance their political autonomy in such a way as to antagonise the Scottish Executive, we can be almost certain that moves will be made to close the loophole.

The financial autonomy afforded to councils is a related area of contest. Local government received over £7b from the Scottish Executive in 2003–4. This equates to just under one third of the Scottish Budget. Unless it is forced to do so, the Labour–Liberal Democrat coalition in the Scottish Executive has no wish to compromise the Scottish Budget (or the macro-economic policies of the Chancellor at Westminster – especially under a Labour Government). What this means is that the main areas of conflict are the amount given by the centre to local councils and the degree of freedom they should have to spend. As detailed in the previous chapter, local authorities have a high dependence on central funding and there is little sign of a major change. The opportunity to return business rates to local authority control has been dismissed by Scottish Executive ministers and high levels of central dependence show little signs of changing, save for the commitment to look on a case-by-case basis at the number of ring-fenced grants. In essence, the Scottish

Executive is stuck either way. If it gives too much financial independence to local authorities, a number of risks will be created:

- *Councils' income-generating powers will have negative economic effects.* For example, high, locally set non-domestic rates will affect business profitability in Scotland, and freely set Council Tax levels will distort the housing market. Both of these would affect disposable incomes, demand in the economy, and attract the attention of the Chancellor, were they considered to interfere with UK macro-economic priorities.
- *Councils' income-generating powers will have negative political effects.* For example, the Scottish Executive will undoubtedly feel the political backlash from high local tax levels free of central constraint, given a system where there has been a historical confusion (at least in the public mind) about who is responsible for local finance.
- *Councils' expenditure powers will have negative economic effects.* For example, complete freedom to incur capital expenditure will affect employment levels, economic demand and local inflation levels. This may also attract unwelcome attention from Westminster where control of the macro-economy is 'reserved'.
- *Councils' expenditure powers will have negative political effects.* For example, locally determined wage agreements for public sector workers (such as teachers and fire fighters) could undermine the political credibility of a national policy on public sector pay.

Correspondingly, a policy of strong central control over local revenue raising and expenditure powers leaves the Scottish Executive in a difficult position because it can be accused of unnecessary interference in the right of democratically elected authorities to manage their own affairs. This, however, is by far the least risky option. Ministers are well versed in manipulating the political agenda and exploiting the hazy, constitutional overlap between centre and locality in order to deflect criticism of its approach. In the game of Scottish central–local finance, all the key cards are held tightly by the Scottish Executive.

Outcomes: The 'Village Life' of Scottish Central–Local Relations

If Scottish local authorities are unhappy with the general drift of central–local relations or the nature of individual policies, they have three main 'ideal type' options at their disposal (Moore 1991). The first is to engage in high-profile resistance, possibly involving a breaking of the law. However, this strategy is almost non-existent in Scotland. The nearest was in the early 1980s when Scottish Secretary George Younger attempted to stop what he described as the 'runaway train' of local expenditure and there was a prolonged and very public battle (particularly with councils in Edinburgh, Stirling, Lothian and Strathclyde) about the impact that cuts would have (see Midwinter 1984). But councils were keen to avoid illegality (such as refusing to set a domestic rate) and the Scottish Office was keen to avoid being overly prescriptive in the running of local affairs. Even in the 1989–93 period when almost every council in Scotland was opposed to the Poll Tax, they still attempted to collect it rather than refusing to do so. The needs to generate income and avoid councillor surcharge for acting *ultra vires* were no doubt key explanatory factors.

A second option is to engage in pragmatic and lower-profile resistance. Such a tactic may have different elements. At one extreme it involves creative accountancy (Elcock et al. 1989: 108–11) and generally finding a low-key way of exploiting existing freedoms to circumvent central intentions. At the other, it involves challenging ministers and officials – sometimes quietly and other times in public. The Scottish Executive commitment in May 2003 to PR in 2007, as well as calling councillors 'part time', has stirred COSLA and the bulk of local authorities into fierce criticism of the Executive (see Chapter 5). A third option is pragmatic acceptance of central direction – a 'muddling through' to use the words of Lindblom (1959). These latter two options are the norm of Scottish central–local relations.

Relations in Scotland have tended to be more consensual than the situation south of the border, particularly in the mid 1980s when ministerial capping powers were used extensively and some councillors were surcharged and disqualified from office (see Stoker 1991). McGarvey (2002) suggests that the reasons for relative harmony in Scotland networks include the small number of councils, physical proximity and interpersonal relations between COSLA and Scottish ministers and civil servants. The outcome is something akin to the portrayal by Heclo and Wildavsky of 'village life' in UK public expenditure networks (Midwinter and McGarvey 2001). We have a fairly small policy community with a considerable degree of consensus on priorities. As McGarvey notes:

> Post-devolution Scottish local councils are pivotal institutions for the Scottish Executive delivering on its commitment to make a difference to the . . . lives of ordinary Scottish people. Local government is a key partner in the Scottish Executive's desire to deliver on the social justice agenda that forms the framework of the programme for government. Councils are critical to the executive delivering its key pledges and objectives such as strong communities, and enterprising workforce and sustainable development. On a broad level, councils are also important for delivering on devolution's objectives of strengthened democratic control and political accountability in Scotland. (McGarvey 2002: 30)

Scottish councils may disagree with the Scottish Executive as to how this rhetoric translates into practical policies, but at least in terms of strategic language, there is substantial commonality between the two sets of interests in the close world of Scottish central–local relations.

Models of Central–Local Relations, Scottish Style

How do we conceptualise the relationship between Scottish local authorities and the Scottish Executive? In order to think about this issue, we can turn to models of central–local relations. They are many in number and include the agency model, partnership model, stewardship model, power-dependence model, policy network theory, dual state thesis, regime theory, uneven development model, and marxist model. We will focus on three in particular, in order to get a basic sense of where key differences arise, each attempting to theorise relations between centre and locality.

The *agency model* came to prominence in the 1980s among those reacting against the centralism of the Thatcher Government. Some of its proponents hark back to a pre mid 1970s mythical 'golden age' of local government. The basic premise of the agency model is straightforward. It suggests that local government is effectively an agent of central government. Its independent powers are insignificant and it exists simply to carry out the wishes of the centre. In some senses this argument seems quite plausible. All activities of Scottish local authorities take place within the context of legislation inherited from Westminster or set by the Scottish Parliament. Local government, therefore, is a 'creature of statute' and it carries out the wishes of the Scottish Executive. If we ask the question 'What determines the nature of local government service delivery in Scotland?' the answer would be Scottish Executive policy and legislation in specific areas such as Education and Social Work, as well as cross-cutting initiatives such as Best Value and Community Planning. However, whilst the dominance of the centre is difficult to dispute, this is not incompatible with the existence of some local freedoms. If local authorities were agents of the centre, they would have no freedom to produce differentiated responses. Glasgow City Council, for example, has opted for PFI projects for schools in a substantial way, whilst several other councils such as West Dunbartonshire (when controlled by the SNP) very publicly rejected this option. Local authorities have also adopted different approaches to public consultation. Stirling Council has a Stirling Assembly, Glasgow City Council has a Citizens' Panel, whilst others utilise consultation (sometimes conducted by external consultants) on a service-by-service basis. This variability points to local autonomy, influenced by factors such as party politics, councillor–officer relations, community needs/wants and budgetary settlements. The agency model focuses on the undeniable issue of central dominance but exaggerates it to the exclusion of everything else.

The *power-dependence model* is a sophisticated version of an older partnership model that perceived central government and local government as more or less equal partners. The power-dependence model stems from Rhodes (1981, 1986, 1988, 1999) who drew originally on US intergovernmental theory and who has revisited the model on several occasions. The power-dependence model rejects the idea that intergovernmental relations can be explained by either 'rational' decision-making or a clearly demarcated power relationship. Relationships between centre and locality are akin to a 'game': each participant possesses resources (constitutional-legal, hierarchical, financial, political and informational) which it uses to manoeuvre, bargain and negotiate with and confront the other. Figure 10.1 outlines the main resources used by each side.

The power-dependence model has been heavily criticised for a rosy view of central–local relations and an underplaying of the superiority of the centre (Marsh et al. 2003; Wilson 2003). In many respects, it can be argued that Rhodes is correct in his portrayal of a less than omnipotent centre. The resistance of many local authorities in the mid 1980s to rate-capping is a good example of the fact that local authorities (1) do not all act the same way and

---

Figure 10.1 Central and local resources in the power-dependence model.

Central government

- Control over legislation and delegated powers.

- Provides a large part of local finance.

- Controls capital expenditure.

- Sets standards for and inspects some services.

- National electoral mandate.

Local government

- Employs all personnel in local services.

- Local knowledge and expertise.

- Control of policy implementation and key knowledge about how to administer policy.

- Independent tax-raising powers to fund local services.

- Local electoral mandate.

Source: Adapted from Rhodes (1988: 42).

---

(2) do not always act at the behest of the centre. Rhodes' model is an indictment of the agency model because it illustrates the point that diffusion, complexity, variability and mutual dependence are the order of the day in intergovernmental relations. Indeed, according to Rhodes, there is a contradiction between central power and its interdependence with local government. But does the power-dependence model help us conceptualise central–local relations in Scotland? The answer is yes and no. It does help us understand that the relationship between Scotland's councils and the Scottish Executive is neither as simple nor as structurally determined as we might think. Local authorities cannot be considered one single 'bloc' (the differing attitudes to membership of COSLA and the benefits of PR illustrate this) and neither can the Scottish Executive, where the local government portfolio is spread over six Scottish Executive Departments. Outcomes of central–local relations are also neither predictable nor based unrelentingly on 'top-down' assumptions. For example, in March 2003, Education Minister Cathy Jamieson announced what effectively amounted to a climb down, having been persuaded by COSLA that an additional £80m for 2003–6 was needed to fund the final stages of the McCrone agreement on the teaching profession.

Despite its benefits, the power-dependence model also has limitations. First, local government 'victories' can be seen from the vantage point of the Scottish Executive as a way of securing the successful implementation of national policy. For example, Scottish local authorities argued for many years in favour of 'general competence powers' to do anything which central legislation did not explicitly prohibit. They got something reasonably close in 2003 via the power to promote 'well-being'. We *could* view this as a success for COSLA in securing a piece of legislation to enhance local autonomy. However, the relevant Local Government in Scotland Act 2003 stopped short of 'general competence' and is viewed by many authorities as liable to make little difference because of the various constraints imposed on the use of this power. From the point of view of the Scottish Executive, nevertheless, the move can be presented as a means of bolstering its 'modernising' and 'listening' credentials. Second, policy outcomes may not be completely predictable and we can always find divisions within and between local authorities and the Scottish Executive. Nevertheless, the basic trend is well established – the view of the Scottish Executive prevails over Scottish local authorities because it sets the basic legislative and financial parameters for councils. Of course, there are always exceptions, but that is no reason to generalise from them. It reminds us of the argument many years ago (perhaps apocryphal) by Margaret Thatcher who argued that the North–South divide was a myth because Porsches could be found in Glasgow and poverty found in London. True, but this did not detract from differentials in average incomes and wealth. Likewise, Scottish Executive (or indeed Westminster dominance) should not be dismissed, just because the outcomes are complex, differentiated or produce periodic 'victories' for councils (Wilson 2003).

The *uneven development* model has one particular attribute that the power-dependence model does not: it has a theory of the state within a wider social system. Duncan and Goodwin (1988) are the main proponents of this model. They argue from a neo-marxist perspective and locate the role of the state as one that upholds dominant/subordinate class relations. Hence:

> State institutions are invaluable in the organization and management of the increasingly large-scale, differentiated and changing societies typical of capitalism. But this very differentiation complicates such management, and one response is to use specifically local state

institutions to deal with specifically local situations. In other words, without the uneven development of societies there would be no need for local – that is subnational – institutions in the first place . . . [Furthermore] national representation cannot always deal adequately with local differentiation, and so local electoral politics was clearly a necessary part of representative democracy. But adding a democratic or popular element to some local state institutions also strengthens and legitimises the role of representing local interests to the centre. (Duncan and Goodwin 1988: 45–6)

They argue that the need for local institutions is particularly pressing in the context of the mid 1960s onwards and more differentiated political, social and economic systems within the UK. A contradiction is evident, however, because local authorities act in some respects as agents of centre (determining laws and finances in order to manage the diversity of social relations which exist), yet they also have policy freedoms that can disrupt the centre. As Miliband (1969: 49) argues, sub-central governments are 'instruments of central control and obstacles to it'.

How far does this uneven development model help us with an understanding of central–local relations in Scotland? It can be suggested, although not without qualification, that it has much to offer. The role of local government in managing uneven relations is well made. The prospect, for example, of Scotland without local authorities and managed by a national civil service would result in exceptional difficulty in catering for urban/rural, mainland/island divisions. The very fact that local government exists allows different communities to make their own choices. The low level of party politics in the islands has led to a dominance of 'independent' councillors, whilst most of mainland Scotland chooses councillors standing on a party ticket. Similarly, policies vary from place to place. Edinburgh City Council's ongoing moves towards congestion charges are hardly likely to apply in Orkney. Equally, the Western Isles Council and its role in completing the Eriskay Causeway is peculiar to the geography of that area. A causeway would not be needed between Kilmarnock and Irvine! The uneven development model also allows us to recognise that local authorities can be controlled by the Scottish Executive but also be barriers to that dominance. As Finance Minister Andy Kerr said to a conference in late 2002: 'I sit around a table with other ministers, and not everybody loves local government' (*Local Government Chronicle*, 5 December 2002). However, one does not need to support Duncan and Goodwin's argument to make sense of contradictions. Most pluralist or neo-pluralist arguments (and the power-dependence model falls loosely into the latter camp) could arrive at a similar conclusion. In other words, the dispersal of power is such that for every interest, a counter interest will emerge to challenge it.

Where pluralists and neo-pluralists part company with the uneven development model is the perception that we have a local state system (as part of a wider state system) whose primary role is to uphold capitalist relations and the dominance of a ruling class – doing so in a contradictory way. Duncan and Goodwin's concrete elaboration of this is limited, but it is certainly possible to develop the point. As mentioned in Chapter 1, we could argue that through the provision of education, housing, social work and other such services, Scottish local authorities assist the vast array of indigenous and multinational interests by ensuring a workforce 'fit to work'. In parallel, systems of local democracy and accountability institution-alise class contest in the 'safe' structures and procedures of the state, ensuring the stability of capitalist relations. They are supported in this role by the 'hard' policing of the eight police forces and the 'soft' policing of families by roughly 50,000 social work staff. The outcome is not purely an agency model but a combination of central domination and local autonomy – often impeding the former.

Overall, there is no magical answer to how we conceive of the relations between the Scottish Executive and Scotland's 32 local authorities. Models of central–local relations vary in the autonomy they attribute to councils, the degree of central dominance and the role of the state more generally. Each has something to offer although like all areas of politics, our sympathies will depend to a large extent on our own values.

Scottish Local Government and Multi-Level Governance

The making of 'local' policies in Scotland is not just a matter for local government or even the Scottish Executive. They are two layers within a multi-layered system of governance, comprising local authorities, Scottish quangos, Scottish Parliament, UK quangos, Westminster Parliament and the European Union (see Sloat 2002; Scottish Parliament European Committee 2002). Local authorities are the first layer. They make bye-laws in certain areas of activity, provided that statute enables them to do so. They are also responsible for budgetary matters, setting priorities and delivering services – again provided that statute allows them to do so. Post-1999, primary legislation for local government in Scotland is made by the Scottish Parliament but it does not operate in a vacuum. Many years of legal obligations on local authorities were inherited from the Westminster Parliament which is still responsible for 'reserved' matters able to impact on local government such as weights and measures, trading standards, transport safety, social security benefits and employment. The Westminster Parliament itself also does not operate in a vacuum. More than half of all new laws in the UK originate at the EU level. Legislation emanating from the Westminster Parliament simply translates them into specific UK legislative instruments. Not all 'local' policy areas involve all layers of governance, but some examples of broad influences indicate the multi-level dimension of local policy areas.

There is no area of local government activity that involves simply authority bye-laws or local authority discretion. An illustration will suffice. We might assume that dealing with the very narrow issue of dog fouling is purely a matter of local discretion. At this 'lowest' level, local authorities do have some discretion in terms of how to deal with this not inconsiderable issue, given that roughly 80 tonnes of dog excrement are produced every day in Scotland. Councils in Edinburgh, Renfrewshire and Moray have been particularly active in initiating local schemes such as Environmental Wardens and public awareness campaigns (Payne 2002). They can only do so, however, because they have statutory freedom in this area. The Environmental Protection Act 1990 gives councils a duty to keep certain types of land free of litter and refuse, subsequently clarified via the Litter (Animal Droppings) Order 1991 to make clear that it applied to dog faeces. The Civic Government (Scotland) Act 1982 also makes dog fouling an offence in public places. These are all Westminster laws although the policy area is now within the remit of the Scottish Parliament. Indeed, the Dog Fouling (Scotland) Act was passed in 2003: a move intended to aid enforcement and widen the types of physical locations to which it applies. In essence, therefore, this apparently 'local' policy area involves local, Scottish and UK levels of governance.

This multi-layered dimension to local policy is quite typical. Indeed, some areas such as education, housing and social work are even more multi-layered. Education is a particularly good illustration because of the host of quangos and NDPBs which add another layer.

For example: school qualifications are awarded by the Scottish Qualifications Authority; schools are regulated by HM Inspectors of Schools; teachers must be registered with the General Teaching Council for Scotland; and guidance and review of the curriculum is the responsibility of Learning and Teaching Scotland. A further level of governance is added in some local policy areas that are affected by Westminster legislation. One example is the Human Rights Act 1998 which confers a variety of rights on individuals. For local authorities, this has many implications for the decisions they take in areas such as excluding children from schools, detention of individuals on mental health grounds, taking children into care, granting planning permission for mobile phone masts, closure of residential care homes, banning of marches, and awarding licenses. Indeed, every area of local government activity is open to challenge if someone feels that it contravenes ECHR legislation.

Some policy areas are even more multi-dimensional because of the European Union. A good example stems from the EU's growing involvement in producing Regulations and Directives in the field of the environment. One aspect of this is waste disposal and management. Scotland's councils are responsible for commercial and household waste disposal and collection. They do so in the context of the Scottish Environment Protection Agency (SEPA) which sets recycling targets for councils. SEPA itself is a public body sponsored by the Scottish Executive Environment and Rural Affairs Department (SEERAD). This follows on logically from environmental matters being devolved to the Scottish Parliament. The Minister for the Environment and Rural Development chairs a Scottish Waste Strategy Advisory Group and the Scottish Executive also gives advice to councils on making the transition from disposal of waste to a more integrated waste management system. The Local Government in Scotland Act 2003 also builds sustainable development requirement into Best Value. Another layer of governance is then added when the UK dimension is introduced with the Landfill Tax: a levy charged by HM Customs and Excise to landfill operators for each tonne of waste disposed. A further layer is added with the EU dimension. The Landfill Tax itself is a product of the EU Landfill Directive 1999, which is part of the Commission's 6th Environmental Action Programme.

Multi-level governance also involves the funding of local affairs. As indicated in Chapter 9, local authority income comes from different levels of governance. Council Tax and fees and charges are raised locally, whilst non-domestic rates, the Revenue Support

Grant and other grants come from the Scottish Executive, which is in itself financed largely from the Block Grant received from Westminster under the Barnett Formula. Furthermore, local authority capital expenditure is frequently funded (in part) by the EU, through the European Regional Development Fund.

Multi-level governance is also more than local authorities being involved in the implementation of legislation and decisions (or in

---

Figure 10.2 Scottish local authorities and their means of information exchange and influence in the context of multi-level governance.

Level of activity	Local authority activities
EU	Lobbying and information exchange via Scotland Europa, Scottish Executive European Office, Committee of the Regions, COSLA office in Scotland House (Brussels), Highlands and Islands European Partnership office in Scotland House, European Local Authority Network (ELAN), Council of European Municipalities and Regions (CEMR). Individual local authorities often maintain their own transnational networks. For example, Glasgow City Council has developed partnerships with the West of Scotland European Consortium, Eurocities and Atlantic Arc. The City of Edinburgh Council and Aberdeen City Council are both involved, along with other European cities, in the EU-funded Demos project to enhance citizen participation.
UK	Lobbying the Westminster Parliament (ministers, civil servants, MPs as appropriate) on UK legislation of importance to local authorities in Scotland and maintaining links with English and Welsh local authority associations such as the Local Government Association (LGA), Welsh Local Government Association (WLGA) and Employers Organisation for Local Government (EO).
Scottish	Lobbying and information exchange with Scottish Executive ministers and civil servants, MSPs, Scottish Parliamentary committees, agencies such as Communities Scotland and Scottish Enterprise; non-departmental bodies such as Audit Scotland, Accounts Commission for Scotland and the Scottish Environment Protection Agency; relations with European Partnership bodies such as West of Scotland European Partnership and also the strategic Scottish European Structural Funds Forum.
Local	Self-support through organisations such as the Convention of Scottish Local Authorities (COSLA), the Society of Local Authority Chief Executives and Senior Managers (SOLACE), the Association of Directors of Education in Scotland (ADES), the Association of Local Authority Chief Housing Officers (ALACHO) and the Scottish Local Authority Economic Development Group (SLAED).

receipt of funding) emanating from different levels of local, Scottish, UK and EU political systems. Scottish local authorities are also involved in exchanging information, lobbying and attempting to influence at these levels of governance. Figure 10.2 gives examples of some of the main activities at these various levels. At times, the overlap between them is not as clear-cut as we might think. For example, the European partnership bodies that play the central role in the implementation of EU structural funds are both 'Scottish' and 'EU' in nature. More generally, the lesson for students of Scottish local government is that we should not think about it in narrow 'Scottish' or even 'UK' terms. Like other local governments in Western Europe, Scottish local government operates in a multi-layered and increasingly European context, generating considerable debate about the autonomy afforded to different levels of governance (see Rhodes 1997; Atkinson and Wilks-Heeg 2000; John 2001; Sloat 2002).

Globalisation and Scottish Local Government

The wider context of local government in Scotland (and indeed the wider systems of multi-level governance) exists in an increasingly globalised world. There is no common agreement on the term 'globalisation'. But this should not distract from identifying the broad thrust of the changes that have taken place. Globalisation is not a new phenomenon. Early modern globalisation took place from approximately 1500 to 1850, with the development of global empires – principally European expansionism into the Americas and Oceania (Held et al. 1999). This was a time of the large trading companies, the slave trade and developing colonial power. From the mid nineteenth century through to the end of the Second World War, largely European-led networks (particularly British, Dutch and French) expanded into North Africa and South East Asia, leading to entrenched networks of capital flows, transportation, political rule and military power. Post-1945, globalisation has accelerated, and there is an increasing multinational presence for companies such as Coca-Cola, McDonald's, Sony, Fox, Adidas, IBM, Shell, Ford, General Electric, Unilever, Mitsubishi and Deutsche Bank. Accompanying this global 'economics' has been a global 'politics' in the sense of global institutions for decision-making, such as the United Nations, World Trade Organisation,

International Monetary Fund and World Bank. Held and McGrew capture the extent of this accelerating interconnectedness:

> Globalization has an undeniably material aspect in so far as it is possible to identify, for instance, flows of trade, capital and people across the globe. These are facilitated by different kinds of infrastructure – physical (such as transport of banking systems), normative (such as trade rules) and symbolic (such as a lingua franca) – which establish the preconditions for regularized and relatively enduring forms of global interconnectedness. . . . [It] . . . suggests a growing magnitude or intensity of global flows that such states and societies become increasingly enmeshed in worldwide systems and networks of interaction. (Held and McGrew 2000: 3).

In the same vein as there is no agreement on the power of nation states within the EU, there is no agreement on the power of nation states in a wider globalised world. Hay (2002) argues that the extent of globalisation has been grossly exaggerated and has little impact on major areas of UK public policy. Others such as Ohmae (1995) argue that the global power and free movement of investment, industry, information technology and consumerism have made nation states obsolete. Somewhere in between these polar views in the British context is Rhodes (1997) and his 'hollowing out of the state' thesis. He argues (controversially for many such as Marsh et al. [2003]) that its role has been hollowed out: downwards to special-purpose bodies, outward to agencies, and upwards to the European Union. He expands on this latter (external) hollowing out by suggesting that although the state remains 'pivotal', globalisation provides a context for and delimits (among other things) governance structures, networks and policies.

If we use Rhodes' argument as a 'mid point', it can be suggested in a very basic sense that nation states are partially autonomous and partially constrained by global interactions. It can be argued that powerful global interests are agenda-setters, producing a 'mobilization of bias' (Schattschneider 1960) in terms of values and preferred policy routes which constrain British Government and its devolved bodies. At times these constraints may be 'hard' in the sense that certain policy options are virtually impossible, or they may be 'soft': encouraging policy transfer and learning across nation states. Global agendas cascade downwards to national and sub-national levels with varying degrees of strength. What does this mean for local government in Scotland? A full analysis would make a very interesting research programme, but in the meantime it can be argued that globalisation sets the agenda for Scottish local government in a multitude of complex ways. Two broad examples will suffice.

First, Scottish local government finance is heavily constrained. The annual Revenue Support Grant settlement is itself severely limited because funding for the Scottish Parliament is allocated to the Scottish Parliament on the basis of the Barnett Formula (Twigger 1998). In turn, the Chancellor's Public Spending Review is constrained by what international markets will expect. Should he (or she) give any signs of 'excessive' public expenditures which will inject inflation into the British economy, the result is liable to be large-scale selling of sterling and shares. This would also mean that the British economy would breach the economic conditions for joining the single currency. Indeed, if the decision were taken not to join, public expenditure would still need to be contained in order to maintain international confidence in sterling (in particular) and the British economy (more generally). A similar argument could be deployed to suggest at least one reason why the international agenda mitigates against the return of business rates to the control of Scottish local authorities. Scottish Executive ministers would not wish to incur the wrath of the Treasury by leaving Scotland vulnerable to pockets of inflationary pressures, caused by councils levying higher-than-inflation poundages in order to fund additional expenditures. Indeed, high business rates could be a disincentive for multinationals to invest in Scotland. Equally, of course, one could argue that councils (with freedom to set rate poundages) might offer lower rates to attract inward investment to their areas. In both instances, globalisation would have an impact on Scottish councils and their finances.

Second, globalisation has an impact on the structures and processes of local government and governance. Liberal-democratic systems of elections and mechanisms for public accountability (such as the Scottish Public Services Ombudsman, Audit Scotland and the Standards Commission for Scotland) are not only prerequisites for EU membership but are also part of systems of 'good governance' as promoted by everyone from the USA to the World Bank and IMF. The development of non-elected local governance (such as Scottish Water, Scottish Environment Protection Agency and so on) is shaped by global forces. For the Scottish Executive which has to operate within public expenditure constraints (as mentioned above), it is much easier to control the expenditure of such bodies (through legislation, appointments and funding) rather than hand over all powers to elected local authorities with independent tax-raising powers. Also, the emergence of various methods of revitalising local democracy (see Chapters 4, 5 and 6) are part of a wider trend within liberal democracies of trying to cope with 'democratic deficits' and a declining public trust in politicians and public institutions (OECD 2001; Bishop and Davis 2002).

It is important to qualify the above and note that globalisation doesn't influence Scottish local government in a linear, deterministic and 'total' way. The various policy networks surrounding Scottish local government (see Chapter 2) have their own agendas, which co-exist in a combination of supportive and conflicting ways with the wider values trickling down from the global agenda. For example, in annual statutory consultation with COSLA for the annual Revenue Support Grant, the agenda of Scotland's 32 councils (usually arguing for increased funding and increased local autonomy) meets the agenda of the Scottish Executive (usually for tight financial controls and limited local autonomy), which in itself is constrained by the UK's financial and political position in a globalised world. A 'mobilisation of bias' in terms of the powers and values of the Scottish Executive allows the interests of COSLA to be largely filtered out of the system in a classic instance of what Bachrach and Baratz (1970) describe as 'non-decision making'. Thus, we have a system of asymmetric power within British Politics: a series of structured inequalities which ultimately favours the prime minister and the core executive at the expense of other interests in the country (Marsh et al. 2003). Ironically, it can be argued that similar inequalities are part of a globalised 'mobilisation of bias' which heavily restricts the autonomy of the prime minister and the core executive. In this context, Scotland's 32 local authorities are quiet voices struggling to be heard in the gale of a globalised world. Local government's multi-level presence is not the same thing as genuine multi-level participation (Wilson 2003).

Conclusion

Developing a detailed understanding of local government in Scotland involves more than simply knowing how it works or even an awareness of specific issues. It is also about awareness of the 'big picture'. This chapter has sketched out basic themes in terms of central–local relations, multi-level governance and globalisation. There is a paucity of academic study in each of these areas with regard specifically to Scotland. It is to be hoped, however, that future research will be able to take forward some of these themes.

?   **Key Questions**   **?**

1. Is there a particular model of central–local relations which best explains the relationship between the Scottish Executive and Scotland's 32 local authorities?
2. Does Scottish local government's participation in multi-level governance networks equate with multi-level influence?
3. How significant is globalisation in shaping and constraining the affairs of Scottish local government?

Further Reading

The best analysis of relations between the Scottish Executive and Scottish local authorities can be found in articles by Neil McGarvey (2002), Arthur Midwinter (2002), and research for the Joseph Rowntree Foundation by Bennett, Fairley and McAteer (2002). A special issue of *Local Government Studies* (volume 28, number 3) provides a wider examination of central–local relations in the UK and elsewhere in Europe. The work of Rhodes (1981, 1986, 1988, 1999) is essential reading for central–local relations and wider governance networks in the UK. Critiques are provided by Marsh et al. (1993) and Wilson (2003). The latter is particularly useful for its treatment of local government in the context of multi-level governance. More radical views of central–local relations can be found in Cockburn (1977) and Duncan and Goodwin (1988). A book entitled *Scotland in Europe* by Amanda Sloat (2002) provides an excellent overview of Scottish governance in the context of the EU. An older article focusing specifically on Scottish local government and the EU is Sutcliffe (1997). *Local Governance in Western Europe* by Peter John (2001) provides a very incisive analysis of UK trends in local governance and the commonalities they share with other Western European states.

Useful Websites

http://www.scotland.gov.uk
Scottish Executive site for keeping up to date with new, central initiatives.

http://www.scottish.parliament.uk
Scottish Parliament. Particularly useful are the research papers for overviews of particular policy areas.

http://www.cosla.gov.uk
Convention of Scottish Local Authorities. New releases and the online publication *COSLA Connections* are particularly useful for keeping up with COSLA campaigns.

http://www.tagish.co.uk/tagish/links/localgov.htm
Tagish's directory of local government websites. A useful gateway to the website of every local authority in Scotland and the vast majority in the UK.

Conclusion: Has Devolution Made a Difference to Local Government in Scotland?

A 'difference' in this context refers to the pre-1999 situation, and more generally in comparison with local government in England and Wales. Both aspects are connected and comprehending them needs to begin with the nature of Scottish local government pre-1999.

Prior to devolution, Scottish local authorities were governed by the Scottish Office: a territorial department of Westminster government. A certain type of devolution existed – administrative devolution – which was much more about tailoring policies to the Scottish context that doing something different compared with England and Wales (Midwinter et al. 1991; Smith 2001; Mitchell 2003). Mitchell (1996, 2003) describes this as a 'Union state', essentially Unionist in character but offering some autonomy in the Scottish context.

Local government during the Conservative era exhibited a substantial amount of 'Unionist' commonality north and south of the border. Structures were based largely on upper and lower tiers, both being rationalised in the mid 1990s (see Chapter 3). Political management structures were also largely similar, with the corporate approach coming under pressure from the New Public Management, accompanied by attempts to 'depoliticise' decision-making structures post-Widdecombe (see Chapter 4). Finances were also largely similar – even if the specific financial instruments had different names and if the timings were slightly different. In essence, local government north and south of the border was subject to similar policies: squeezing of central grants, removal of business rates from local authority control, introduction and then abolition of the Poll Tax (Community Charge) and tight restrictions on capital expenditure (see Chapter 9). Coupled with core policies such as Compulsory Competitive Tendering and the 'right to buy', there is little doubt that local authorities in Scotland were subject to very similar pressures as their counterparts in England and Wales. This gave rise to other commonalities – a shared sense of being under attack from the centre. Central–local relations generally became much more adversarial and local government struggled to stop the onslaught of new and often unwelcome initiatives. Therefore, as Paul Carmichael concludes in an article entitled 'Is Scotland Different? Local Government Policy under Mrs Thatcher':

> This examination of policy developments in Scotland in the Thatcher years accepts that differences in structure and process largely stem from the need to overcome the particular geographical, legal, political and administrative constraints within which national UK policy operates in Scotland. Notwithstanding the special position obtaining in Scotland, Scottish differences are overwhelmingly a reflection of the way things are done, not of what is done. The need for policy uniformity in the British cabinet system assumes just that. . . . Special arrangements do exist in the conduct of Scottish affairs within the parameters of the overall British system of government as evidenced by the use of separate Acts of Parliament. To argue, however, that this constitutes policy 'differentialism' is wholly fatuous. (Carmichael 1992: 30)

Despite these commonalities, the nature of the 'Union state' pre-1999 was that it also contained elements of decentralisation and diversity. The Scottish Office would not have existed were there not territorial differences to cater for in terms of law, education, media, culture, politics, economics and so on (Kellas 1984). Hence, there were often Scottish variations in policy. For example, the two tier system in Scotland was supplemented by non-statutory community councils, whereas in England and Wales, parish and community councils (respectively) had minor statutory powers and so constituted a third tier of local government. The mid 1990s restructuring also produced slightly different outcomes: a single tier system in Scotland but a hybrid system in England (two tiers in some areas and single tiers in others). Local government in Scotland also tended to be more sceptical of the corporate approach to management and decision-making (Midwinter 1978, 1982) as well as (arguably) being less influenced by the client–contractor split implications of CCT. It also tended to be subject to more draconian financial reforms such as an earlier introduction of rate-capping and the Poll Tax, as well as tighter controls on capital expenditure (Midwinter 1984; McConnell 1995; Midwinter 1998). However, the smaller number of Scottish local authorities, their physical proximity to the Scottish Office and the nature of the political networks meant that relations never reached the 'depths' of those south of the border (McGarvey 2002). Paradoxically, a further difference was Scotland has only a very small and diminishing Conservative Party base in Scottish councils, yet the Party was governing Scottish local government through the British Cabinet and the Scottish Office. For supporters of devolution and independence, this typified the Scottish 'problem': a country governed by a party of marginal significance in either local or parliamentary elections. The outcome for Scottish local politics and democracy was considered to be stifling and counterproductive to the democratic will of the Scottish people.

This tension between 'Union' commonality and limited Scottish autonomy was one that many pro-devolutionists thought would dissipate with the advent of a Scottish Parliament. The McIntosh Commission (Scottish Office 1999a) was fairly typical of this view. It recognised the potential for conflict between the democratically elected Scottish Executive and democratically elected local authorities but felt that mutual trust and mutual respect were the building blocks of a partnership that would produce local policies that fitted with Scottish needs and aspirations.

Has devolution produced such a sea change for local government? In some senses, the answer is 'yes'. Scottish authorities no longer have to make the geographical or political journey to Westminster in an attempt to shape legislation. They have much better access to the legislature and elected representatives who sit on committees which scrutinise and are consulted on legislative initiatives and general policy areas. In many respects, this brings the governance of Scotland much closer to the people: an illustration of pluralism and democracy in action. As one would expect, therefore, there have been instances where Scotland has carved out its pathway for local government, independent of local government south of the border. For example, it has:

- Taken on board electoral reform, and the prospect of proportional representation (Single Transferable Vote) is likely in 2007.

- Introduced free personal care for the elderly.
- Watered down councils' ability to recover debts via poundings and warrant sales.
- Not been required by law to adopt executive forms of leadership.

As suggested in previous chapters, Scottish differences can be explained partly by the increased autonomy afforded to Scotland since the advent of the Scottish Parliament. In essence, a form of 'political devolution' has been added to the old 'administrative devolution'. The flexibility of the Union state has been increased to a certain degree, resulting in a closer link between government, the people and civil society.

The flip side, however, is that enormous similarities remain. As has been evident throughout this book, the vast majority of key policies for local government are virtually identical north and south of the border: powers of well-being, Best Value, retention of business rates at the centre; ring-fencing of grants in accordance with central priorities; support for citizen participation and encouragement of various means to boost electoral turnout. In essence, the 'Union' element still dominates – if not in legislative terms, in agenda-setting for the Scottish Parliament. Taking a step back even further, the wider context of local government is a system of multi-level governance. It extends 'upwards' to the EU and beyond in terms of the fiscal and political values trickling down to national governments via global interests: limiting Westminster as a result. Therefore, as Mair (2000) argues in his review of the first year of the Scottish Parliament's relationship with local government, the inheritance from Westminster has led to continuity in attitudes and (at least on one level) the possibility that little has changed. Hassan and Warhurst (2002b) take the argument further and suggest that the new social democratic consensus is only 'new' in relation to Thatcherism. In actual fact, they argue, it is 'Back to the Future' in the sense that it is a return to the values of Scotland in the 1950s and 1960s.

The implication for local government is that its evolution under the Scottish Parliament has been conservative rather than radical. The post-devolution debates reinforce this view. 'Classic' issues which confront local government have been present since the arrival of the Scottish Parliament. These include issues such as:

- How much financial freedom should local government have from the centre?

- Should local government be given more political freedoms to respond to the wishes of local people?
- Is local government genuinely democratic, given the low interest in local elections and the power of party groups?
- What is the best way for local authorities to organise their decision-making structures?

Has devolution made a difference for local government in Scotland in terms of its ability to break free from the pre-1999 situation and the experiences of councils in England and Wales? The answer is 'yes', but not nearly as much as we might think. As argued in Chapter 10, the constraints of globalisation heavily delimit the UK national agenda, which in turn dominates the financial and political agendas of the Scottish Parliament. The semi-autonomy afforded to Scottish local government post-1999 is welcomed by most, and certainly has many of its own characteristics, but we should not inflate its scale or distinctiveness to an unrealistic level.

Bibliography

Note: I have given web links where, to my knowledge, they are available. I have tried as far as possible to cite links to PDF versions where original documents are simply posted on-line. It should be noted, however, that some publications are available on-line only or with the on-line version being different from the paper version. When I have accessed materials in either of these ways, no place of publication is cited.

Accounts Commission (1995), *Performance Information for Scottish Councils 1993/94*, Edinburgh: Accounts Commission.

Accounts Commission (1998a), *The Challenge of Charging*, Edinburgh: Accounts Commission.

Accounts Commission (1998b), *Performance Information for Scottish Councils 1996/97*, Edinburgh: Accounts Commission.

Accounts Commission (2001), *Making Progress with Best Value: A National Overview of the Performance Management and Planning (PMP) Audit 2001/02*, Edinburgh: Accounts Commission, http://www.audit-scotland.gov.uk/publications/pdf/01pf07ac.pdf

Accounts Commission (2002), *Taking the Initiative: Using PFI to Renew Council Schools*, Edinburgh: Accounts Commission, http://www.audit-scotland.gov.uk/publications/pdf/02ar03ac.pdf

Accounts Commission (2003a), *Performance Indicators 2001/02*, Edinburgh: Accounts Commission, http://www.audit-scotland.gov.uk/performance/index.htm

Accounts Commission (2003b), *The New Audit of Best Value: Consultation Paper – July 2003*, Edinburgh: Accounts Commission, http://www.audit-scotland.gov.uk/publications/pdf/2003/03bv04ac.pdf

Accounts Commission (2003c), *Performance Indicators 2001/02: Environmental and Regulatory Services*, Edinburgh: Accounts

Commission, http://www.audit-scotland.gov.uk/performance/documents/pamphlets/03pi06ac.pdf

Adam Smith Institute (1989), *Shedding a Tier: Reforming Scotland's Local Government*, London: Adam Smith Institute.

Allen, G. (2003), *The Private Finance Initiative (PFI)*, House of Commons Research Paper 03/79, London: House of Commons, http://www.parliament.uk/commons/lib/research/rp2003/rp03-079.pdf

Arnstein, S. (1969), 'A Ladder of Participation', *Journal of the American Institute of Planners*, vol. xxxv, pp. 214–16.

Arthur Andersen and Enterprise LSE (2000), *Value for Money Drivers in the Private Finance Initiative*, http://www.ogc.gov.uk/sdtoolkit/library/PFI/series_1/andersen/7tech_contents.html

Asenova, D. and Beck, M. (2003), 'Scottish Local Authorities and the Procurement of Private Finance Initiative Projects: A Pattern of Developing Risk Management Expertise?', *Public Works Management and Policy*, vol. 8, no. 1, July, pp. 11–27.

Atkinson, H. and Wilks-Heeg, S. (2000), *Local Government From Thatcher to Blair: The Politics of Creative Autonomy*, Cambridge: Polity Press.

Audit Scotland (2002a), *How Government Works in Scotland*, Edinburgh: Audit Scotland, http://www.accounts-commission. gov.uk /publications/pdf/2002/02ar04ag.pdf

Audit Scotland (2002b), *Providing Assurance, Promoting Excellence*, Edinburgh: Audit Scotland, http://www.audit-scotland.gov.uk/publications/pdf/2002/02qg01as.pdf

Bachrach, P. and Baratz, M. S. (1970), *Power and Poverty: Theory and Practice*, Oxford: Oxford University Press.

Bailey, S. J. (1994), 'Charging for Local Government Services: A Coherent Philosophy', *Public Administration*, vol. 72, no. 3, pp. 365–84.

Bailey, S. J., Falconer, P. and McChlery, S. (1993), *Local Government Charges: Policy and Practice*, Harlow: Longman.

Bains Report (1972), *The New Local Authorities: Management and Structure*, London: HMSO.

Ball, R. (1998), *Performance Review in Local Government*, Ashgate: Aldershot.

Barber, B. (1984), *Strong Democracy: Participatory Politics for a New Age*, Berkeley: University of California Press.

Beer, S. H. (1969), *Modern British Politics: A Study of Parties and Pressure Groups*, London: Faber and Faber.

Beetham, D. (1996), 'Theorising Democracy and Local Government', in D. King and G. Stoker (eds), *Rethinking Local Democracy*, Basingstoke: Macmillan.

Bell, J. and Paton, J. (1896), *Glasgow: Its Municipal Organization and Administration*, Glasgow: James Maclehose and Sons.

Bennett, M., Fairley, J. and McAteer, M. (2002), *Devolution in Scotland: The Impact on Local Government*, York: Joseph Rowntree Foundation.

Bennie, L., Brand, J. and Mitchell, J. (1997), *How Scotland Votes*, Manchester: Manchester University Press.

Bennie, L. G. (2002), 'Exploiting New Electoral Opportunities: The Small Parties in Scotland', in G. Hassan and C. Warhurst (eds) (2002), *Tomorrow's Scotland*, London: Lawrence and Wishart.

Best Value Task Force (1997), *Report 1*, Edinburgh: Scottish Office Development Department.

Birch, A. H. (1973), *The British System of Government*, 3rd edition, London: Allen and Unwin.

Bishop, P. and Davis, G. (2002), 'Mapping Public Participation in Policy Choices', *Australian Journal of Public Administration*, vol. 61, no. 1, March, pp. 14–29.

Bochel, C. and Bochel, H. M. (1998), 'Scotland's Councillors 1974–1995', *Scottish Affairs*, no. 24, pp. 29–44.

Brown, A., McCrone, D., Paterson, L. and Surridge, P. (1999), *The Scottish Electorate*, Basingstoke: Macmillan.

Bruce, A. and McConnell, A. (1995), 'Local Government and the NHS: Accountability in the Hollowed Out State', *Public Policy and Administration*, vol. 10, no. 3, Autumn, pp. 15–28.

Buchanan, J. M. and Tullock, G. (1962), *The Calculus of Consent*, Michigan: University of Michigan Press.

Burnside, R., Herbert, S. and Curtis, S. (2003), *Election 2003*, Edinburgh: Scottish Parliament Information Centre, http://www.scottish.parliament.uk/research/briefings-03/SB%2003-25%20Election%202003.pdf

Butcher, H., Law, I. G., Leach, R. and Mullard, M. (1990), *Local Government and Thatcherism*, London: Routledge.

Butler, D., Adonis, A. and Travers, T. (1994), *Failure in British Government: The Politics of the Poll Tax*, Oxford: Oxford University Press.

Byrne, T. (2000), *Local Government in Britain*, 7th edition, London: Penguin.

Carmichael, P. (1992), 'Is Scotland Different? Local Government Policy under Mrs Thatcher', *Local Government Policy Making*, vol. 18, no. 5, May, pp. 25–32.

Carmichael, P. (1995), *Central-Local Government Relations in the 1980s: Glasgow and Liverpool Compared*, Aldershot: Avebury.

Carmichael, P. and Knox, C. (1999), 'Towards "a New Era"? Some Developments in Governance of Northern Ireland', *International Review of Administrative Sciences*, vol. 65, no. 1, pp. 103–16.

Castells, M. (1978), *City, Class and Power*, London: Edward Arnold.

Castells, M. (1983), *The City and Grassroots*, London: Edward Arnold.

Centre for Public Services (2001), *Private Finance Initiative and Public Private Partnerships: What Future for Public Services?*, Sheffield: Centre for Public Services, http://www.centre.public.org.uk/briefings/pfi_and_ppp.html

Chandler, J. A. and Turner, R. (1997), 'Pricing and Local Authorities', *Public Money and Management*, vol. 17, no. 2, pp 37–42.

Chisholm, M. (2002), 'The Cost of Local Government Structural Reorganisation in Great Britain During the 1990s', *Environment and Planning C: Government and Policy*, vol. 20, no. 2, April, pp. 251–62.

Clancy, T. O. and Crawford, B. E. (2001), 'The Formation of the Scottish Kingdom', in R. A. Houston and W. W. J. Knox (eds), *The New Penguin History of Scotland*, London: Allen Lane.

Cm 1599 (1991), *The Citizen's Charter: Raising the Standard?*, London: HMSO.

Cm 4014 (1998), *Modern Local Government: In Touch With the People*, London: The Stationery Office, http://www.odpm.gov.uk/stellent/groups/odpm_localgov/documents/pdf/odpm_locgov_pdf_605468.pdf

Cm 4310 (1999), *Modernising Government*, London: The Stationery Office, http://www.archive.official-documents.co.uk/document/cm43/4310/4310.htm

Cm 5511 (2002), *Your Region, Your Choice: Revitalising the English Regions*, London: The Stationery Office, http://www.odpm.gov.uk/stellent/groups/odpm_regions/documents/pdf/odpm_region_pdf_607900.pdf

Cmnd. 4040 (1969), *Royal Commission on Local Government in England and Wales: Report* (Redcliffe-Maud Report), London: HMSO.

Cmnd. 4150 (1969), *Royal Commission on Local Government in Scotland: Report* (Wheatley Report), Edinburgh: HMSO.

Cmnd. 6453 (1976), *Local Government Finance: Report of the Committee of Inquiry* (Layfield Report), London: HMSO.

Cmnd. 8115 (1981), *Report of the Committee of Inquiry into Local Government in Scotland* (Stodart Report), Edinburgh: HMSO.

Cmnd. 9216 (1983), *Committee of Enquiry into the Functions and Powers of Island Councils of Scotland* (Montgomery Report), Edinburgh: HMSO.

Cmnd. 9797 (1986), *The Conduct of Local Authority Business: Report of the Committee of Enquiry into the Conduct of Local Authority Business* (Widdecombe Report), London: HMSO.

Cmnd. 9800 (1986), *The Conduct of Local Authority Business: Report of the Committee of Enquiry into the Conduct of Local Authority Business, Volume III, 'The Local Government Elector'*, London: HMSO.

Cochrane, A. (1993), *Whatever Happened to Local Government?*, Buckingham: Open University Press.

Cockburn, C. (1977), *The Local State*, London: Pluto Press.

Cohen, M., March, J. and Olsen, J. (1972), 'A Garbage Can Model of

Organisational Choice', *Administrative Science Quarterly*, no. 17, pp. 1–25.

Controller of Audit to the Accounts Commission (1998), *Overview Report on the 1995/96 Audits of the Former Local Authorities*, Edinburgh: Accounts Commission.

Copus, C. (1999), 'The Political Party Group: Model Standing Orders and a Disciplined Approach to Local Representation', *Local Government Studies*, vol. 25, no. 1, pp. 17–34.

Copus, C. (2001a), 'New Political Management Arrangements and the Party Group: New Models of Political Behaviour', *Local Governance*, vol. 27, no. 1, pp. 53–63.

Copus, C. (2001b), 'Citizen Participation in Local Government: The Influence of the Political Party Group', *Local Governance*, vol. 27, no. 3, pp. 151–63.

COSLA (2001a), *LGF Settlement 2002/03: Briefing on 6 December 2001 Announcement*, Edinburgh: COSLA, http://www.cosla.gov. uk/attachments/briefings/briefing038.pdf

COSLA (2001b), *Submission to Inquiry by Local Government Committee of the Scottish Parliament into Local Government Finance in Scotland*, reproduced in SP 551, Local Government Committee: Report of Inquiry into Local Government Finance, vol. 3, Edinburgh: Scottish Parliament, 2002, http://www.scottish.parliament.uk/S1/official_report/cttee/local-02/lgr02-06-vol03-06.htm#50

COSLA (2003), *COSLA Manifesto 2003*, Edinburgh: COSLA, http://www.cosla.gov.uk/attachments/publications/coslamanifesto.pdf

Dahl, R. A. (1961), *Who Governs? Democracy and Power in an American City*, New Haven: Yale University Press.

Danson, M. and Whittam, G. (2002), *Paying for Local Government, Water and Sewerage Services Fairly: The Case for a Scottish Service Tax and a Scottish Water Charge*, Paisley: University of Paisley.

Dearlove, J. (1973), *The Politics of Policy in Local Government*, Cambridge: Cambridge University Press.

Dearlove, J. (1979), *The Reorganisation of British Local Government: Old Orthodoxies and a Political Perspective*, Cambridge: Cambridge University Press.

Dehousse, R. (1998), *The European Court of Justice*, Basingstoke: Macmillan.

Demos (2002a), *A Comparative Audit of the City of Aberdeen*, Edinburgh: Demos, http://www.demosproject.org/admin/files/audit_aberdeen.pdf

Demos (2002b), *A Comparative Audit of the City of Edinburgh*, Edinburgh: Demos, http://www.demosproject.org/admin/files/audit_edinburgh.pdf

Demos (2002c), *Demos Research Findings: Literature Review*, Edinburgh: Demos, http://www.demosproject.org/admin/files/demos_literature_review.pdf

Denver, D. and Bochel, H. (2000), 'The Forgotten Elections: The Scottish Council Elections of 1999', *Scottish Affairs*, no. 30, Winter, pp. 115–23.

Department of the Environment (1993), *Competition and Service: The Impact of the Local Government Act 1998*, London: Department of the Environment.

Devine, T. M. (1995), *Exploring the Scottish Past*, East Linton: Tuckwell.

Devine, T. M. (2000), *The Scottish Nation 1700–2000*, London: Penguin.

Dicks, B. (1983), 'The Scottish Medieval Town: A Search for Origins', in G. Gordon and B. Dicks (eds), *Scottish Urban History*, Aberdeen: Aberdeen University Press.

Downs, A. (1957), *An Economic Theory of Democracy*, New York: Harper and Row.

Duncan, A. A. M. (1975), *Scotland: The Making of the Kingdom*, Volume One, Edinburgh: Oliver and Boyd.

Duncan, S. and Goodwin, M. (1988), *The Local State and Uneven Development*, Cambridge: Polity Press.

Dunleavy, P. (1980), *Urban Political Analysis*, Basingstoke: Macmillan.

Dunleavy, P. (1991), *Democracy, Bureaucracy and Public Choice*, London: Harvester Wheatsheaf.

Dunleavy, P. and O'Leary, B. (1987), *Theories of the State: The Politics of Liberal Democracy*, Basingstoke: Macmillan.

Elcock, H. (1982), *Local Government: Politicians, Professionals and the Public in Local Authorities*, 2nd edition, London: Methuen.

Elcock, H., Jordan, G. and Midwinter, A. (1989), *Budgeting in Local Government: Managing the Margins*, London: Longman.

Ellwood, S. (1999), 'Parish and Town Councils: Left Out in the Cold but Invited to the Party', *Public Money and Management*, vol. 19, no. 3, July–September, pp. 7–9.

Escott, K. and Whitfield, D. (1995), *The Gender Impact of CCT in Local Government*, Manchester: Equal Opportunities Commission.

Evans, M. (1995), 'Elitism', in D. Marsh and G. Stoker (eds), *Theories and Methods in Political Science*, Basingstoke: Macmillan.

Ewan, E. (1990), *Townlife in Fourteenth-Century Scotland*, Edinburgh: Edinburgh University Press.

Falconer, P. (1996), 'Charterism and Consumerism', in R. Pyper (ed.), *Aspects of Accountability in the British System of Government*, Merseyside: Tudor.

Ferguson, K. (1984), *Introduction to Local Government in Scotland*, Glasgow: The Planning Exchange.

Flinders, M. V. and Smith, M. J. (eds) (1999), *Quangos, Accountability and Reform*, Basingstoke: Macmillan.

Friend, J. K. and Jessop, W. N. (1969), *Local Government and Strategic Choice*, London: Tavistock.

Glasgow City Council (2001), *Best Value Review: Museums, Heritage and Visual Arts (Part One)*, Glasgow: Glasgow City Council.

Glasgow City Council (2002), *Key Facts & Figures 2001/02*, Glasgow: Glasgow City Council.

Glasgow City Council (2003), *Key Facts & Figures 2003/04*, Glasgow: Glasgow City Council.

Goodlad, R., Flint, J., Kearns, A., Keoghan, M., Paddison, R. and Raco, M. (1999), *The Role and Effectiveness of Community Councils With Regard to Community Consultation*, Edinburgh: Scottish Executive Central Research Unit, http://www.scotland.gov.uk/cru/kd01/comm-01.htm

Greenwood, J. and Wilson, D. (1994), 'Towards the Contract State: CCT in Local Government', *Parliamentary Affairs*, vol. 47, no. 3, pp. 405–19.

Greenwood, J., Pyper, R. and Wilson, D. (2002), *New Public Administration in Britain*, 3rd edition, London: Routledge.

Gyford, J., Game, C. and Leach, S. (1989), *The Changing Politics of Local Government*, London: Unwin Hyman.

Hampton, W. (1991), *Local Government and Urban Politics*, 2nd edition, London: Longman.

Harding, A. (2000), 'Regime Formation in Manchester and Edinburgh', in G. Stoker (ed.), *The New Politics of British Local Governance*, Basingstoke: Macmillan.

Hassan, G. (2002), 'The Paradoxes of Scottish Labour: Devolution, Change and Conservatism', in G. Hassan and C. Warhurst (eds), *Tomorrow's Scotland*, London: Lawrence and Wishart.

Hassan, G. and Warhurst, C. (eds) (1999), *A Modernisers' Guide to Scotland: A Different Future*, Edinburgh and Glasgow: The Centre for Scottish Public Policy and the Big Issue in Scotland.

Hassan, G. and Warhurst, C. (eds) (2000), *The New Scottish Politics: The First Year of the Scottish Parliament and Beyond*, Norwich: The Stationery Office.

Hassan, G. and Warhurst, C. (eds) (2002a), *Tomorrow's Scotland*, London: Lawrence and Wishart.

Hassan, G. and Warhurst, C. (2002b), 'Future Scotland: The Making of the New Social Democracy', in Hassan and Warhurst (eds), *Tomorrow's Scotland*, London: Lawrence and Wishart.

Hay, C. (2002), 'Globalization, "EU-isation" and the Space for Social Democratic Alternatives: Pessimism of the Intellect: A Reply to Coates', *British Journal of Politics and International Relations*, vol. 4, no. 3, October, pp. 452–64.

Hayton, K. (1993), 'Two Into One Won't Go – An Analysis of the Proposals for the Reform of Scottish Local Government', *Local Government Policy Making*, vol. 19, no. 1, March, pp. 7–18.

HC 367 (2001), *Mapping the Quango State*, 5th Report, House of

Commons Select Committee on Public Administration, London: The Stationery Office, http://www.parliament.the-stationery-office.co.uk/pa/cm200001/cmselect/cmpubadm/367/36702.htm

Held, D., McGrew, A., Goldblatt, D. and Perraton, J. (1999), *Global Transformations*, Cambridge: Polity Press.

Held, D. and McGrew, A. (eds) (2000), *The Global Transformations Reader*, Cambridge: Polity Press.

Herbert, S. (2002), *Proportional Representation (Local Government Elections) (Scotland) Bill*, Edinburgh: Scottish Parliament Information Centre, http://www.scottish.parliament.uk/S1/whats_happening/ research/pdf_res_brief/sb02-124.pdf

Heseltine, M. (2000), *Life in the Jungle*, London: Hodder and Stoughton.

Himsworth, C. M. G. and Munro, C. R. (2000), *The Scotland Act 1998*, 2nd edition, Edinburgh: W. Green.

Hindess, B. (1997), 'Democracy and Disenchantment', *Australian Journal of Political Science*, vol. 32, no. 1, pp. 79–82.

Hunt, D. (1995), 'Worthwhile Bodies', in F. F. Ridley and D. Wilson, *The Quango Debate*, Oxford: Oxford University Press.

IDeA and EO (2001), *National Census of Local Authority Councillors in England and Wales 2001*, London: Improvement and Development Agency and Employers' Organisation, http://www.lg-employers.gov.uk/documents/performance_capacity/councillors/2001 census.pdf

John, P. (1989), *Introduction of the Community Charge in Scotland*, London: Policy Studies Institute.

John, P. (2001), *Local Governance in Western Europe*, London: Sage.

Judge, D. (1995), 'Pluralism', in D. Judge, G. Stoker and H. Wolman (eds), *Theories of Urban Politics*, London: Sage.

Judge, D. (1999), *Representation: Theory and Practice in Britain*, London: Routledge.

Kane, M. J. (1996), *The Management of Change in Scottish Local Authorities: The Experience of CCT*, unpublished Ph.D. thesis, Glasgow: Glasgow Caledonian University.

Kantor, P. (2000), 'Can Regionalism Save Poor Cities? Politics, Institutions and Interests in Glasgow', *Urban Affairs Review*, vol. 35, no. 6, July, pp. 794–820.

Keeling, D. (1972), *Management in Government*, London: George Allen and Unwin.

Kellas, J. G. (1984), *The Scottish Political System*, 3rd edition, Cambridge: Cambridge University Press.

Kellas, J. G. (1990), 'Scottish and Welsh Nationalist Parties Since 1945', in A. Seldon (ed.), *UK Political Parties Since 1945*, London: Philip Allan.

Kendrick, A. (1995), 'The Integration of Child Care Services in Scotland', *Children and Youth Services Review*, vol. 17, nos. 5–6, pp. 619–35.

Kerevan, G. (2002), 'City States and Local Governance', in G. Hassan and C. Warhurst (eds), *Anatomy of the New Scotland: Power, Influence and Change*, Edinburgh: Mainstream.

Kingdom, J. (1991), *Local Government and Politics in Britain*, London: Philip Allan.

Kingdon, J. W. (1984), *Agendas, Alternatives and Public Policies*, Boston and Toronto: Little, Brown and Co.

Laffin, M., Taylor, G. and Thomas, A. (2002), *A New Partnership? The National Assembly for Wales and Local Government*, York: Joseph Rowntree Foundation, http://www.jrf.org.uk/bookshop/publications.asp?quicksearch=local+government&I2.x=26&I2.y=1

Lang, I. (1994), 'Local Government Reform: Change for the Better', *Scottish Affairs*, no. 6, Winter, pp. 14–24.

LAMSAC (1980), *Corporate Management and Planning in Scottish District Councils*, London: Local Authorities' Management Services Advisory Committee.

Lavalette, M. and Mooney, G. (1989), 'The Struggle Against the Poll Tax in Scotland', *Critical Social Policy*, issue 26, Autumn, pp. 82–100.

Leach, R. and Percy-Smith, J. (2001), *Local Governance in Britain*, Basingstoke: Palgrave.

Leach, S. and Stewart, J. (1992), *Local Government: Its Role and Function*, York: Joseph Rowntree Foundation.

Leeke, M. (2003), *UK Election Statistics: 1945–2003*, House of Commons Research Paper HC 03/59, http://www.parliament.uk/commons/lib/research/rp2003/rp03-059.pdf

Levy, R. (1990), *Scottish Nationalism at the Crossroads*, Edinburgh: Scottish Academic Press.

Levy, R. (1992), 'The Scottish Constitutional Convention, Nationalism and the Union', *Government and Opposition*, vol. 27, no. 2, pp. 222–34.

Levy, R. (1995), 'Governing Scotland, Wales and Northern Ireland', in R. Pyper and L. Robins (eds), *Governing the UK in the 1990s*, Basingstoke: Macmillan.

Lindblom, C. E. (1959), 'The Science of Muddling Through', *Public Administration Review*, vol. 19, pp. 78–88.

Lindblom, C. E. (1977), *Politics and Markets*, New York: Basic Books.

Local Government Committee (2002), *Local Government Committee: Report of Inquiry into Local Government Finance, Vols 1–4*, Edinburgh: Scottish Parliament, http://www.scottish. parliament.uk/S1/official_report/cttee/local-02/lgr02-06-vol01-01.htm

Local Government Committee (2003a), *Local Government Committee: 3rd Report 2003, Report on Inquiry into Local Democracy, Volume 1, Committee Report*, Edinburgh: Scottish Parliament, http://www. scottish.parliament.uk/S1/official_report/cttee/local-03/lgr03-03-vol01-01.htm

Local Government Committee (2003b), *Local Government Committee:*

3rd Report 2003, Report on Inquiry Into Local Democracy, Volume 2, External Research Report, Edinburgh: Scottish Parliament, http://www.scottish.parliament.uk/S1/official_report/cttee/local-03/lgr03-03-vol02-01.htm

Local Government Committee (2003c), *Local Government Committee: 3rd Report 2003, Report on Inquiry Into Local Democracy, Volume 3, Report on Civic Participation Events*, Edinburgh: Scottish Parliament, http://www.scottish.parliament.uk/S1/official_report/cttee/local-03/lgr03-03-vol03-01.htm

Local Government Committee (2003d), *Legacy Paper*, Edinburgh: Scottish Parliament, http://www.scottish.parliament.uk/S1/official_report/cttee/local-03/lgr03-legacypaper-01.htm

Local Government Information Unit (2003), *New Research Traces Causes of Council Tax Crisis*, press release, 17 November, London: Local Government Information Unit.

Lowndes, V. (1999), 'Management Change in Local Governance', in G. Stoker (ed.), *The New Management of British Local Governance*, Basingstoke: Macmillan.

Lowndes, V., Pratchett, L. and Stoker, G. (2001), 'Trends in Public Participation: Part 1 – Local Government Perspectives', *Public Administration*, vol. 79, no. 1, pp. 205–22.

Lynch, M. (1992), *Scotland: A New History*, London: Pimlico.

Lynch, P. (2001), *Scottish Government and Politics*, Edinburgh: Edinburgh University Press.

Lynch, P. (2002a), *SNP: The History of the Scottish National Party*, Cardiff: Welsh Academic Press.

Lynch, P. (2002b), 'Partnership, Pluralism and Party Identity: The Liberal Democrats After Devolution', in G. Hassan and C. Warhurst (eds), *Tomorrow's Scotland*, London: Lawrence and Wishart.

Lynch, P. (2003), 'Increasing Electoral Turnout in British Elections: An Evaluation of Electoral Pilot Schemes, 2000–2', *Representation*, vol. 39, no. 4. pp. 236–44.

Mair, C. (2000), 'The Executive and Local Government', in G. Hassan and C. Warhurst (eds), *The New Scottish Politics: The First Year of the Scottish Parliament and Beyond*, Norwich: The Stationery Office.

Mackie, J. D. (1964), *A History of Scotland*, Middlesex: Penguin.

MacPherson, C. B. (1966), *The Real World of Democracy*, Oxford University Press: Oxford.

Mallabar, N. (1991), *Local Government Administration – In a Time of Change*, Sunderland: Business Education Publishers.

March, J. G. and Olsen, J. P. (1996), 'Institutional Perspectives on Political Institutions', *Governance*, vol. 9, no. 3, pp. 248–64.

Marsh, D., Richards, D. and Smith, M. (2003), 'Unequal Plurality: Towards an Asymmetric Power Model of British Politics', *Government and Opposition*, vol. 38, no. 3, July, pp. 306–32.

Martin, S. (2000), 'Implementing "Best Value": Local Public Services in Transition', *Public Administration*, vol. 78, no. 1, pp. 209–27.

Martlew, C. (1988), *Local Democracy in Practice: The Role and Working Environment of Councillors in Scotland*, Aldershot: Avebury.

Marwick, J. D. (1904), *The Municipal Institutions of Scotland: An Historical Survey*, reprinted from the *Scottish Historical Review*, January and April 1904, available from The Mitchell Library, Glasgow.

Maud, J. (1967), Committee on the *Management of Local Government: Volume 1: Report of the Committee*, London: HMSO.

McAteer, K. and Orr, K. (2003), 'The "Modernisation" of Political Management Arrangements in Post Devolution Scottish Local Government', *Public Policy and Administration*, vol. 18, no. 1, Spring, pp. 66–83.

McEwan, N. (2002), 'The Scottish National Party After Devolution', in G. Hassan and C. Warhurst (eds), *Tomorrow's Scotland*, London: Lawrence and Wishart.

McConnell, A. (1993), *Parliamentarism, Policy Networks and the Poll Tax*, Strathclyde Papers on Government and Politics, no. 91, Department of Government: University of Strathclyde.

McConnell, A. (1995), *State Policy Formation and the Origins of the Poll Tax*, Dartmouth: Aldershot.

McConnell, A. (1997), 'The Recurring Crisis of Local Taxation in Post-War Britain', *Contemporary British History*, vol. 3, no. 11, Autumn, pp. 39–62.

McConnell, A. (1998), 'Global Experiences of Local Taxation: Lessons for a New Scottish Parliament', Working Paper, no. 2, Faculty of Business: Glasgow Caledonian University.

McConnell, A. (1999), *The Politics and Policy of Local Taxation in Britain*, Wirral: Liverpool Academic Press.

McConnell, A. (2000a), 'Local Taxation, Policy Formation and Policy Change: A Reply to Peter John', *British Journal of Politics and International Relations*, vol. 2, no. 1, pp. 81–8.

McConnell, A. (2000b), 'Governance in Scotland, Wales and Northern Ireland', in R. Pyper and L. Robins (eds), *United Kingdom Governance*, Basingstoke: Macmillan.

McFadden, J. (1993), 'The Reorganisation of Scottish Local Government: A Councillor's Perspective', *Local Government Policy Making*, vol. 19, no. 4, March, pp. 23–9.

McGarvey, N. (2002), 'Intergovernmental in Scotland Post-Devolution', *Local Government Studies*, vol. 28, no. 3, pp. 29–48.

McNish, A. (Chair) (2001), *Scottish Local Government's Self-Review of its Political Management Structures: Report of the Leadership Advisory Panel*, Edinburgh: The Stationery Office, http://www.scotland.gov.uk/library3/localgov/rlap-00.asp

McTavish, D. (2002), *Case Studies in British Management, Public, and Business Sectors 1900–Present: An Analysis of Internal and External Management*, unpublished Ph.D. thesis, Glasgow: University of Glasgow.

McVicar, M., Jordan, G. and Boyne, G. (1994), 'Ships in the Night: Scottish Political Parties and Local Government Reform', *Scottish Affairs*, vol. 9, Autumn, pp. 80–96.

McVicar, M., Boyne, G. and Jordan, G. (1995), 'Recurring Issues in Scottish Local Government Reform', *Public Policy and Administration*, vol. 10, no. 3, Autumn, pp. 1–14.

Midwinter, A. F. (1978), 'The Implementation of the Paterson Report in Scottish Local Government, 1975–77', *Local Government Studies*, vol. 4, no. 1, January, pp. 23–8.

Midwinter, A. (1982), *Management Reform in Scottish Local Government*, Glasgow: University of Strathclyde.

Midwinter, A. (1984), *The Politics of Local Spending*, Edinburgh: Mainstream.

Midwinter, A. (1989), 'Economic Theory, the Poll Tax and Local Spending', *Politics*, vol. 9, no. 2, October, pp. 9–15.

Midwinter, A. (1990), 'A Return to Ratepayer Democracy? The Reform of Local Government Finance in a Historical Perspective', *Scottish Economic and Social History*, vol. 10, pp. 61–9.

Midwinter, A. (1992), 'The Review of Local Government in Scotland – A Critical Perspective', *Local Government Studies*, vol. 18, no. 2, Summer, pp. 44–54.

Midwinter, A. (1994), 'Developing Performance Indicators for Local Government: The Scottish Experience', *Public Money and Management*, vol. 14, no. 2, April–June, pp. 37–43.

Midwinter, A. (1995), *Local Government in Scotland: Reform or Decline?*, Basingstoke: Macmillan.

Midwinter, A. (1998), 'The Fiscal Crisis in Scottish Local Government', *Local Governance*, vol. 24, no. 1, pp. 57–65.

Midwinter, A. (2001), 'New Labour and the Modernisation of British Local Government: A Critique', *Financial Accountability and Management*, vol. 17, no. 4, pp. 311–20.

Midwinter, A. (2002), 'The New Politics of Local Spending: Central-Local Financial Relations Under Scottish Devolution', *Public Money and Management*, April–June, pp. 37–45.

Midwinter, A., Keating, M. and Mitchell, J. (1991), *Politics and Public Policy in Scotland*, Basingstoke: Macmillan.

Midwinter, A., Keating, M. and Taylor, D. (1984), '"Excessive and Unreasonable": The Politics of the Scottish Hit List', *Political Studies*, vol. xxxl, pp. 394–417.

Midwinter, A. and McGarvey, N. (1997), 'The Reformed System of Local Government Finance in Scotland', *Policy and Politics*, vol. 25, no. 2, pp. 143–52.

Midwinter, A. and McGarvey, N. (1999), 'Developing Best Value in Scotland: Concepts and Contradictions', *Local Government Studies*, vol. 25, no. 2, pp. 87–101.

Midwinter, A. and McGarvey, N. (2001), 'In Search of the Regulatory State: Evidence from Scotland', *Public Administration*, vol. 79, no. 4, pp. 825–49.

Midwinter, A. and Monaghan, C. (1993), *From Rates to the Poll Tax*, Edinburgh University Press: Edinburgh.

Midwinter, A. and Monaghan, C. (1995), 'The New Centralism: Local Government Finance in the 1990s', *Financial Accountability and Management*, vol. 11, no. 2, May, 141–51.

Miliband, R. (1969), *The State in Capitalist Society*, London: Weidenfeld and Nicolson.

Mill, J. S. [1861] (1972), *Utilitarianism, On Liberty, and Considerations on Representative Government*, London: J. M. Dent.

Miller, W. L. (1988), *Irrelevant Elections? The Quality of Local Democracy in Britain*, Oxford: Clarendon Press.

Mitchell, J. (1996), *Strategies for Self-Government: The Campaigns for a Scottish Parliament*, Edinburgh: Polygon.

Mitchell, J. (2003), *Governing Scotland: The Invention of Administrative Devolution*, Basingstoke: Palgrave Macmillan.

Mitchison, R. (1982), *A History of Scotland*, 2nd edition, London: Routledge.

Moore, C. (1991), 'Reflections on the New Political Economy: Resignation, Resistance and Reform', *Policy and Politics*, vol. 19, no. 2, pp. 73–85.

Morgan, B. (2001), *General Election Results, 7 June 2001*, House of Commons Research Paper 01/54, http://www.parliament. uk/commons/lib/research/rp2001/rp01-054.pdf

Morgan, B. and Connolly, J. (2001), *UK Election Statistics: 1945–2000*, House of Commons Research Paper 01/37, http://www. parliament.uk/commons/lib/research/rp2001/rp01-037.pdf

Morton, G. and Morris, R. J. (2001), 'Civil Society, Governance and the Nation, 1832–1914', in R. A. Houston and W. W. J. Knox (eds), *The New Penguin History of Scotland*, London: Allen Lane, The Penguin Press.

Murray, D. (1924), *Early Burgh Organization in Scotland, Volume 1: Glasgow*, Glasgow: Maclehose, Jackson and Co.

Newton, K. (1976), *Second City Politics*, Oxford: Oxford University Press.

Newton, K. (1982), 'Is Small Really So Beautiful? Is Big Really So Ugly? Size, Effectiveness, and Democracy in Local Government', *Political Studies*, vol. xxx, no. 2, pp. 190–206.

Niskanen, W. (1971), *Bureaucracy and Representative Government*, Chicago: Aldine-Atherton.

OECD (2001), *Engaging Citizens in Policy-Making: Information,*

Consultation and Public Participation, Paris: Organisation for Economic Co-operation and Development, http://www.oecd.org/dataoecd/24/34/2384040.pdf

Office for National Statistics (2003), *Regional Trends*, no. 37, online edition, http://www.statistics.gov.uk/downloads/theme_compendia/Regional_Trends_37/Regional_Trends_37_contents_revised.pdf

Ogden, S. (1994), *The Impact of Compulsory Competitive Tendering on the Management of Local Government Industrial Relations: A Qualitative Investigation into Strategic Choices and Constraints*, unpublished Ph.D. thesis, Glasgow: Glasgow Caledonian University.

Ohmae, K. (1995), *The End of the Nation State?*, London: HarperCollins.

Osborne, D. (1988), *Laboratories of Democracy*, Boston: Harvard Business School Press.

Page, E. C. and Midwinter, A. F. (1979), *Remote Bureaucracy or Administrative Efficiency: Scotland's New Local Government System*, Glasgow: Centre for the Study of Public Policy, University of Strathclyde.

Pahl, R. E. (1970), *Whose City? And Other Essays on Sociology and Planning*, London: Longman.

Painter, C. (1999), 'Public Service Reform from Thatcher to Blair: A Third Way', *Parliamentary Affairs*, vol. 52, issue 1, pp. 94–112.

Painter, J. and Goodwin, M. (2000), 'Local Government After Fordism: A Regulationist Perspective', in G. Stoker (ed.), *The New Politics of British Local Governance*, Basingstoke: Macmillan.

Pateman, C. (1970), *Participation and Democratic Theory*, London: Cambridge University Press.

Paterson Report (1973), *The New Scottish Local Authorities: Organisation and Management Structures*, Edinburgh: HMSO.

Payne, J. (2002), *The Dog Fouling (Scotland) Bill*, Edinburgh: Scottish Parliament Information Centre, http://www.scottish.parliament.uk/S1/whats_happening/research/pdf_res_brief/sb02-120.pdf

Pimlott, B. and Rao, N. (2002), *Governing London*, Oxford: Oxford University Press.

Pollard, S. (1983), *The Development of the British Economy*, 3rd edition, London: Edward Arnold.

Pratchett, L. (2002), 'Local Government: From Modernisation to Consolidation', *Parliamentary Affairs*, vol. 55, no. 2, pp. 331–46.

Pryde, G. S. (1965), *The Burghs of Scotland: A Critical List*, Oxford: Oxford University Press.

Public Works Loan Board (2002), *127th Annual Report 2001–02*, London: The Stationery Office, http://www.pwlb.gov.uk/annrep0102.pdf

Public Works Loan Board (2003), *128th Annual Report 2002–03*, London: The Stationery Office, http://www.pwlb.gov.uk/annrep0203.pdf

Pyper, R. (ed.) (1996), *Aspects of Accountability in the British System of Government*, Wirral: Tudor Business Publishing.

Rallings, C. and Thrasher, M. (1997), *Local Elections in Britain*, London: Routledge.

Rao, N. (1994), *The Making and Unmaking of Local Self-Government*, Aldershot: Dartmouth.

Report of the Renewing Local Democracy Working Group (2000), Chair: Richard Kerley, http://www.scotland.gov.uk/library2/doc16/rldw.pdf

Rex, J. and Moore, R. (1967), *Race, Community and Conflict: A Study of Sparkbrook*, Oxford: Oxford University Press.

Rhodes, R. A. W. (1981), *Control and Power in Central–Local Relations*, Farnborough: Gower.

Rhodes, R. A. W. (1986), *The National World of Local Government*, London: Allen and Unwin.

Rhodes, R. A. W. (1988), *Beyond Westminster and Whitehall*, London: Unwin Hyman.

Rhodes, R. A. W. (1996) 'The New Governance: Governing Without Government', *Political Studies*, vol. 44, pp. 652–7.

Rhodes, R. A. W. (1997), *Understanding Governance: Policy Networks, Governance, Reflexivity and Accountability*, Buckingham: Open University Press.

Rhodes, R. A. W. (1999), *Control and Power in Central–Local Relations*, 2nd edition, Aldershot: Ashgate.

Rhodes, R. A. W. and Midwinter, A. F. (1980), *Corporate Management: The New Conventional Wisdom in British Local Government*, Glasgow: Centre for the Study of Public Policy, University of Strathclyde.

Ridley, F. F. and Wilson, D. (eds) (1995), *The Quango Debate*, Oxford: Oxford University Press.

Rodger, R. G. (1983), 'The Evolution of Scottish Town Planning', in G. Gordon and B. Dicks (eds), *Scottish Urban History*, Aberdeen: Aberdeen University Press.

Rose, R. (1990), 'Inheritance Before Choice in Public Policy', *Journal of Theoretical Politics*, vol. 2, no. 3, pp. 263–91.

Rose, R. and McAllister, I. (1990), *The Loyalties of Voters: A Lifetime Learning Model*, London: Sage.

Rosie, G. (2002), 'Network Scotland: The Power of the Quango State', in G. Hassan and C. Warhurst (eds), *Anatomy of the New Scotland: Power, Influence and Change*, Edinburgh: Mainstream.

Schattschneider, E. E. (1960), *The Semi-Sovereign People*, New York: Holt, Rinehart and Winston.

Schumpeter, J. A. [1943] (1976), *Capitalism, Socialism and Democracy*, 5th edition, London: Allen and Unwin.

Scottish Conservatives (2003), *Time to Do Something About It*, Scottish Parliament Manifesto, http://www.scottishtories.org.uk/manifesto/scpmanifesto.pdf

Scottish Executive (1999), *Report of the Commission on Local Government and the Scottish Parliament: The Scottish Executive's Response*, Edinburgh: Scottish Executive, http://www.scotland.gov.uk/library2/doc04/ser-00.htm

Scottish Executive (2001), *Council Tax in Scotland: A Guide to the New Tax for Local Government in Scotland*, Edinburgh: Scottish Executive, http://www.scotland.gov.uk/library3/localgov/ctlg-00.asp

Scottish Executive (2002a), *Scottish Local Government Financial Statistics 1998–99*, http://www.scotland.gov.uk/library3/localgov/ lgfs-00.asp

Scottish Executive (2002b), *Scottish Public Finance Manual*, http://www.scotland.gov.uk/library5/finance/spfm/spf-00.asp

Scottish Executive (2002c), *Scottish Economic Statistics*, http://www.scotland.gov.uk/stats/ses2002/ses2-00m.asp

Scottish Executive (2002d), *Code of Conduct for Councillors*, Edinburgh: The Stationery Office, http://www.scotland.gov.uk/library5/localgov/cocc.pdf

Scottish Executive (2002e), *Local Government in Scotland Bill: Policy Memorandum*, Edinburgh: The Stationery Office, http://www.scottish.parliament.uk/parl_bus/bills/b53s1pm.pdf

Scottish Executive (2002f), *Joint Staffing Watch: December 2001*, Edinburgh: Scottish Executive and the Convention of Scottish Local Authorities, http://www.scotland.gov.uk/library5/government/jswd02.pdf

Scottish Executive (2003a), *Building Better Cities: Delivering Growth and Opportunities*, Edinburgh: The Stationery Office, http://www.scotland.gov.uk/library5/finance/bbcs.pdf

Scottish Executive (2003b), *Review of Scotland's Cities – The Analysis*, Edinburgh: The Stationery Office, http://www.scotland.gov.uk/library5/society/rsca.pdf

Scottish Executive (2003c), *Scottish Local Government Financial Statistics 2000–2001*, Edinburgh: Scottish Executive, http://www.scotland.gov.uk/stats/bulletins/00223.pdf

Scottish Executive (2003d), *Scottish Economic Statistics 2003*, Edinburgh: Scottish Executive, http://www.scotland.gov.uk/stats/ses2003/ses03.pdf

Scottish Executive (2003e), *A Partnership for a Better Scotland*, Edinburgh: Scottish Executive, http://www.scotland.gov.uk/library5/government/pfbs.pdf

Scottish Executive (2003f), *Scotland's People: Results from the 2001/2002 Scottish Household Survey*, Edinburgh: Scottish Executive National Statistics, http://www.scotland.gov.uk/library5/finance/spv7.pdf

Scottish Executive (2003g), *Scottish Local Government Financial Statistics 2001–02*, Edinburgh: Scottish Executive, http://www.scotland.gov.uk/stats/bulletins/00283.pdf

Scottish Executive (2003h), *Statistical Bulletin Housing Series*, Edinburgh: Scottish Executive National Statistics, http://www.scotland.gov.uk/stats/bulletins/00274.pdf

Scottish Executive (2003i), *Joint Staffing Watch: June 2002*, Edinburgh: Scottish Executive and the Convention of Scottish Local Authorities, http://www.scotland.gov.uk/library5/government/jswj.pdf

Scottish Executive Central Research Unit (1999), *Perceptions of Local Government: A Report of Focus Group Research*, Edinburgh: The Stationery Office, http://www.scotland.gov.uk/cru/kd01/local-gov-01.htm

Scottish Executive EU Office (2002), *Scotland and the European Union*, http://www.scotland.gov.uk/euoffice/scot_eu1.asp#1

Scottish Executive Finance and Central Services Department (2003), *Consultation on Business Improvement Districts (BIDS) in Scotland*, Edinburgh: Scottish Executive Finance and Central Services Department, http://www.scotland.gov.uk/consultations/finance/consultbids.pdf

Scottish Executive Private Finance Unit (2001), *Public Private Partnerships/Private Finance Initiative In The Local Authority Sector*, Submission to Inquiry by Local Government Committee of the Scottish Parliament in Local Government Finance in Scotland, reproduced in Local Government Committee: Report of Inquiry into Local Government Finance, vol. 3, Edinburgh: Scottish Parliament, 2002, http://www.scottish.parliament.uk/official_report/cttee/local-02/lgr02-06-vol03-06.htm#50

Scottish Executive Private Finance Unit (2003), *Project Facts and Figures*, http://www.scotland.gov.uk/pfi/facts-02.asp

Scottish Executive Social Research Unit (2003), *National Survey of Local Government Candidates*, Edinburgh: The Stationery Office, http://www.scotland.gov.uk/library5/localgov/nslg.pdf

Scottish Green Party (2003), *Reach for the Future*, Scottish Parliament Manifesto, http://web.viewport.co.uk/sgpmirror/SGP2003.pdf

Scottish Labour Party (2003), *On Your Side: Scottish Labour's Manifesto 2003*, http://www.scottishlabour.org.uk/getdataattached.php?fileid=13

Scottish Liberal Democrats (2003), *Make the Difference*, Scottish Parliament Manifesto, http://www.scotlibdems.org.uk/

Scottish Local Government Information Unit (1989), *Scottish Guide to the Local Government and Housing Act*, Glasgow: Scottish Local Government Information Unit.

Scottish Local Government Information Unit (1990), *Bulletin*, no. 33, October, Glasgow: Scottish Local Government Information Unit.

Scottish Local Government Information Unit (1991), *Bulletin*, no. 42, September, Glasgow: Scottish Local Government Information Unit.

Scottish Local Government Information Unit (1994), *Bulletin*, no. 64, February, Glasgow: Scottish Local Government Information Unit.

Scottish Local Government Information Unit (1995), *Bulletin*, no. 75, August, Glasgow: Scottish Local Government Information Unit.

Scottish Local Government Information Unit (1996), *Bulletin*, no. 82, April/May, Glasgow: Scottish Local Government Information Unit.

Scottish Local Government Information Unit (2000), *Bulletin*, no. 119, January/February, Glasgow: Scottish Local Government Information Unit.

Scottish Local Government Information Unit (2002), *Bulletin*, no. 144, July/August, Glasgow: Scottish Local Government Information Unit.

Scottish Office (1958), *Local Government in Scotland*, Edinburgh: HMSO.

Scottish Office (1991), *The Structure of Local Government in Scotland: The Case for Change – Principles of the New System*, Edinburgh: HMSO.

Scottish Office (1992), *The Structure of Local Government in Scotland: Shaping the New Councils*, Edinburgh: HMSO.

Scottish Office (1993), *The Internal Management of Local Authorities in Scotland: A Consultation Paper*, Edinburgh: The Scottish Office.

Scottish Office (1999a), *Report of the Commission on Local Government and the Scottish Parliament*, McIntosh Report, Edinburgh: Scottish Office, http://www.scotland.gov.uk/library/documents-w10/clg-00.htm

Scottish Office (1999b), *Scottish Local Government Financial Statistics 1996–1997*, Edinburgh: Scottish Office, http://www.scotland.gov.uk/library/documents-w8/lgfs-00.htm

Scottish Office Central Research Unit (1995), *Baseline Study of Public Knowledge and Perceptions of Local Government in Scotland*, Edinburgh: HMSO.

Scottish Office Central Research Unit (1997), *Local Authority Organisation and Management in Scotland*, Edinburgh: The Stationery Office.

Scottish Parliament European Committee (2002), *An Inquiry into Scotland's Representation in the European Union*, 5th report, http://www.scottish.parliament.uk/S1/official_report/cttee/europe-02/eur02-05-01.htm

Scottish Parliament Information Centre (1999), *Local Government*, http://www.scottish.parliament.uk/S1/whats_happening/research/pdf_subj_maps/smda-02.pdf

Scottish Parliament Information Centre (2001), *EU Structural Funds*, http://www.scottish.parliament.uk/S1/whats_happening/research/pdf_subj_maps/smda01-03.pdf

Scottish Parliament Information Centre (2002a), *An Introduction to Local Government Finance*, http://www.scottish.parliament.uk/S1/whats_happening/research/pdf_subj_maps/smda-03.pdf

Scottish Parliament Information Centre (2002b), *Councillor Remuneration*, http://www.scottish.parliament.uk/S1/whats_happening/research/pdf_res_brief/sb02-56.pdf

Scottish Parliament Information Centre (2002c), *Local Government in*

Scotland – Best Value, http://www.scottish.parliament.uk/S1/whats_happening/research/pdf_res_brief/sb02-66.pdf

Scottish Parliament Information Centre (2003), *Local Government – Subject Profile*, http://www.scottish.parliament.uk/research/briefings-03/sb03-49.pdf

Scottish Socialist Party (2003), *Holyrood Election Manifesto 2003*, http://www.scottishsocialistparty.info/resources/SSPmanifesto2003.pdf

Seawright, D. (2002), 'The Scottish Conservative and Unionist Party', in G. Hassan and C. Warhurst (eds), *Tomorrow's Scotland*, London: Lawrence and Wishart.

Shaw, J. E. (1942), *Local Government in Scotland*, Edinburgh: Oliver and Boyd.

Simon, H. A. (1958), *Administrative Behaviour*, 2nd edition, Basingstoke: Macmillan.

Simon, H. A. (1976), *Administrative Behaviour*, 3rd edition, New York: Free Press.

Skelcher, C. (1998), *The Appointed State: Quasi Governmental Organizations and Democracy*, Buckingham: Open University Press.

Sloat, A. (2002), *Scotland in Europe*, Bern: Peter Lang.

Smith, J. (2001), *The Europeanisation of the Scottish Office 1973–1997*, unpublished Ph.D. thesis, Glasgow: Glasgow Caledonian University.

Smith, M. (1995), 'Pluralism', in D. Marsh and G. Stoker (eds), *Theories and Methods in Political Science*, Basingstoke: Macmillan.

SNP (2003), *Release Our Potential*, Scottish Parliament Manifesto, http://www.releaseourpotential.com/manifesto/pdfs/snp_english.pdf

Stanyer, J. (2002), *Understanding Local Government*, Glasgow: Fontana.

Stewart, J. (1993), *The Rebuilding of Public Accountability*, unpublished paper.

Stewart, J. (1995), 'The Internal Management of Local Authorities', in J. Stewart and G. Stoker, *Local Government in the 1990s*, Basingstoke: Macmillan.

Stewart, J. (1996), 'Reforming the New Magistracy', in L. Pratchett and D. Wilson (eds), *Local Democracy and Local Government*, Basingstoke: Macmillan.

Stewart, J. (2003), *Modernising British Local Government: An Assessment of Labour's Reform Programme*, Basingstoke: Palgrave Macmillan.

Stewart, J. D. (1971), *Management in Local Government: A Viewpoint*, London: Charles Knight and Co.

Stewart, J. D. (1974), *The Responsive Local Authority*, London: Charles Knight and Co.

Stoker, G. (1991), *The Politics of Local Government*, 2nd edition, Basingstoke: Macmillan.

Stoker, G. (1993), 'Introduction: Local Government Reorganisation as a

Garbage Can Process', *Local Government Policy Making*, vol. 19, no. 1, March, pp. 3–5.

Stoker, G. (1994), *The Role and Purpose of Local Government*, London: Commission for Local Democracy.

Stoker, G. (1998), 'The Leadership Issue in Local Government', *Scottish Affairs*, no. 25, Autumn, pp. 119–28.

Stoker, G. (1999), 'Introduction: The Unintended Costs and Benefits of New Management Reform for British Local Government', in G. Stoker (ed.), *The New Management of British Local Governance*, Basingstoke: Macmillan.

Sutcliffe, J. B. (1997), 'Local Government in Scotland: Reorganization and the European Union', *Regional and Federal Studies*, vol. 7, no. 2, Summer, pp. 42–69.

Thain, C. and Wright, M. (1995), *The Treasury and Whitehall: The Planning and Control of Public Expenditure, 1976–1993*, Oxford: Clarendon Press.

Thatcher, M. (1977), *Let Our Children Grow Tall*, London: Centre for Policy Studies.

Travers, T. (2004), *The Politics of London: Governing an Ungovernable City*, Basingstoke: Palgrave Macmillan.

Turner, S. H. (1908), *The History of Local Taxation in Scotland*, Edinburgh: William Blackwood and Sons.

Twigger, R. (1998), *The Barnett Formula*, House of Commons Research Paper 98/8, http://www.parliament.uk/commons/lib/research/rp98/rp98-008.pdf

Vestri, P. and Fitzpatrick, S. (2000), 'Scotland's Councillors', *Scottish Affairs*, no. 33, Autumn, pp. 62–81.

Webb, P. (2000), *The Modern British Party System*, London: Sage.

Weir, S. and Hall, W. (eds) (1994), *Ego Trip: Extra-Governmental Organisations in the United Kingdom and their Accountability*, London: Charter 88 Trust.

Wildavsky, A. (1984), *The Politics of the Budgetary Process*, 4th edition, Boston and Toronto: Little, Brown and Co.

Wilson, D. (1995), 'Quangos in the Skeletal State', in F. F. Ridley and D. Wilson (eds), *The Quango Debate*, Oxford: Oxford University Press.

Wilson, D. (2003), 'Unravelling Control Freakery: Redefining Central–Local Relations', *British Journal of Politics and International Relations*, vol. 5, no. 3, August, pp. 317–46.

Wilson, D. and Game, C. (1998), *Local Government in the United Kingdom*, 2nd edition, Basingstoke: Macmillan.

Wilson, D. and Game, C. (2002), *Local Government in the United Kingdom*, 3rd edition, Basingstoke: Palgrave Macmillan.

Woods, M., Edwards, B., Anderson, J., Gardner, G. and Hughes, R. (2002), *Research Study into the Role, Functions and Future Potential of Town and Community Councils in Wales*, Aberystwyth: University of Wales, http://www.aber.ac.uk/communitygovernance/report1.pdf

Yates, K. (2003), 'View From the Top – Time for a Change', *Local Government Chronicle*, 9 September, http://www.lgc.net.com

Young, R. (1977), *The Search for Democracy: A Guide to Scottish Local Government*, Milngavie: Heatherbank Press.

Index

Aberdeen District Council, 54
Aberdeenshire Council, 34, 54,
    111, 126, 139, 144, 194
Abolition of Feudal Tenure etc.
    (Scotland) Act 2002, 9
Abolition of Poindings and
    Warrant Sales Act 2000, 9
access to power, 122
accountability and Scottish
    local government, 43, 58–9,
    84, 87, 110, 118, 124,
    172–4; principles of, 111,
    116, 174–6; reconstruction
    of, 174–5, 184; traditional
    view of, 110, 174
Accounts Commission 2, 9, 29,
    31, 32, 61, 80, 98, 155, 156,
    161, 163, 165, 170, 173,
    176, 195–6, 206–7, 208,
    214, 226
Adam Smith Institute, 80, 156
ADES see Association of
    Directors of Education in
    Scotland
administrative devolution, 87–9
Adonis, A., 208
Adoption and Children Bill, 10
Advisory Committee on Sites of
    Special Scientific Interest, 131
AEF see Aggregate External
    Finance
age bias in profile of
    councillors, 94
Aggregate External Finance
    (AEF), 180, 183, 184, 213
Aims of Industry, 156
ALACHO see Association of
    Local Authority Chief
    Housing Officers
Allen, G., 202, 208

Angus Council, 34, 54, 86,
    125, 141
Angus District Council, 54
Angus Youth Congress, 125
appointments, ministerial, 132
Argyll and Bute Council, 1, 34,
    54, 148, 185
Argyll and Bute District
    Council, 54
Arnstein, S., 127
Arshad, R., 96
Arthur Andersen and Enterprise
    LSF, 204
arts and tourism, 15
Asenova, D. and Beck, M., 204
Association of Direct Labour
    Organisations, 204
Association of Directors of
    Education in Scotland
    (ADES), 226
Association of Liberal
    Democrat Councillors, 100
Association of Local Authority
    Chief Housing Officers
    (ALACHO), 226
Association of Scottish
    Chambers of Commerce, 188
Atkinson, H., 69, 227
Atlantic Arc, 226
Attendance Allowance, 103
Audit Commission, 155, 176
Audit Scotland, 3, 29, 31, 32,
    40, 98–9, 156, 170, 173,
    176, 204, 206–7, 208, 214,
    226, 229
Auditor General for Scotland,
    9, 171, 173

Bachrach, P., 90, 230
Bailey, S. J., 196

Bains Report 1972, 76, 79
Balanced Scorecard, 98–9, 163
Baldovie Waste to Energy Plant,
    203
Banff and Buchan District
    Council, 54
Baratz, M. S., 90, 230
Barber, B., 122–3
Barnett Formula, 182, 226, 229
Bearsden and Milngavie District
    Council, 54
Beer, S. H., 148
Beetham, D., 93, 117–19
Bell, J., 45
Benefits Agency, 125
Bennett, M., 33, 37, 135, 231
Bennie, L., 140, 146
Bentham, J., 94
Berwick, 44
Best Value in England and
    Wales, 85, 152, 161, 176,
    236; in Scotland, 3, 15, 87,
    98, 124, 140, 176, 206,
    213–4, 215, 219, 236;
    nature and principles of,
    108, 118, 161–2, 165–6;
    origins, 8, 155, 161;
    strengths, 163; weaknesses,
    165; workings of, 10, 15,
    33, 85, 121, 161, 165, 225
Better Neighbourhood Services
    Fund, 184
Birch, A. H., 148
Bishop, P., 133–4, 230
Black, R., 61
Blair Government's attitude to
    devolution, 27
Block Grant, 225–6
Board of Supervision for Poor
    Relief, 129

Bochel, C., 99, 101, 138
Bochel, H. M., 99–100, 101, 111, 138–9, 153
Borders Council, 148, 155, 192
Borders Regional Council, 54
Brown, A., 140, 148
Bruce, A., 174
Buchanan, J. M., 80, 157
Building (Scotland) Act 2003, 10
burgh councils, 8, 46–7
Burgh Reform Act, 46
burials, 197
Burnham, J., 19
Burnside, R., 102
Business Excellence Model, 98, 163
Business Improvement Districts, 189
business rates *see* non-domestic rates
Butcher, H., 81
Butler, D., 190, 208
bye-laws, 11, 15, 39, 108, 223–4
Byrne, T., 24, 100

Campaign to Welcome Refugees, 122
capital income and expenditure borrowing, 198; consents, 198, 214; formula, 198, 200; general, 180–1, 197–9
capitalism, general, 21; local government and early stages of, 45; local government as part of a capitalist system, 21–2, 223; Scottish local government in a capitalist system, 45–6, 66
capping, 217, 235
Carmichael, P., 7, 64, 234
Castells, M., 21
cause groups, 122
CBI *see* Confederation of British Industry
CCT *see* Compulsory Competitive Tendering
CEMR *see* Council of European Municipalities and Regions
central–local relations agency model of, 218–19; and multi-level governance, 134, 175, 211–12, 216, 222, 223–7, 230, 236; COSLA view of, 188, 216–17; dual state thesis, 218, 222 in Scotland, 30, 66, 69, 81, 85, 89–90, 118–19, 215, 233–5; in England and Wales, 90,

217, 234; in UK, 143, 183; marxist view of, 117, 218; models of, 3, 218–23; national legislation, 8, 212–13, 220; partnership model, 18–19, 218–19; power-dependence model, 109, 176, 179, 218–20; revenue raising, 2, 30, 137, 188–9, 192; Scottish Executive view of, 89, 140, 142, 174–5, 188, 189, 206–7, 215–16; theories of, 4, 18, 48, 168, 218–20, 222–3, 236; uneven development model, 75, 218–19
Centre for Education and Racial Equality, 96
Centre for Public Services, 160, 204
Chancellor of the Exchequer, 59, 183, 215
Chandler, J. A., 196
Changing Children's Services Fund, 184
characteristics of Scottish local government, 6
charging for local services, 197, 212
Chartered Institute of Public Finance and Accountancy (CIPFA), 28–9, 172, 188
chief executives, 38, 74, 77, 78
Chisholm, M., 61
CIPFA *see* Chartered Institute of Public Finance and Accountancy
Cities Review 2000–3, 31, 184
Citizen's Charter, 167, 168, 175
citizens' juries, 3, 16, 100, 121, 124, 125
citizens' panels, 126, 166, 219
City of Aberdeen Council, 54, 139, 144, 226
City of Dundee Council, 6, 14, 38, 39, 55, 139, 192, 203
City of Dundee District Council, 54
City of Edinburgh Council, 1, 54, 86, 87, 88, 104, 105, 122, 126, 139, 189, 194, 196, 217, 222, 224, 226
City of Edinburgh District Council, 54
City of Glasgow Council *see* Glasgow City Council
City of Glasgow District Council *see* Glasgow District Council

Civic Government (Scotland) Act 1982, 224
civil marriages, 15
Clackmannan District Council, 54
Clackmannanshire Community Access Volunteers, 122
Clackmannanshire Council, 37, 54, 141
Clancy, T. O., 44
Client Group approach, 182, 184
Clydebank District Council, 55
Clydesdale District Council, 55
Cochrane, A., 67
Cockburn, C., 21, 74, 76, 123, 231
code of conduct for councillors, 13, 82
Code of Practice on Access to Government Information, 59
Cohen, M., 57
Comhairle nan Eilean Siar *see* Western Isles Council
Commission for Local Democracy, 18
Commissioner for Local Administration, 118, 155, 174
Commissioner for Public Appointments, 132–3,
committee system, 6, 48, 63, 70–3, 74, 80, 84–6, 102
Communities Scotland, 226
Community Care, 6, 8
Community Care and Health (Scotland) Act 2002, 9
Community Charge *see* Poll Tax
community consultation, 33, 86, 87, 121, 141, 165
community councils in Scotland, 49, 52, 63, 234; in Wales, 63
community forums, 16, 89, 125, 126, 166, 172
Community Planning, 8, 10, 15, 16, 33, 87, 121, 124–5, 219
Compulsory Competitive Tendering (CCT) client–contractor split, 80–1, 158, 159–60; impact of, 49, 82, 158, 234; in England and Wales, 158–9, 160, 234; in Scotland, 3, 53, 80, 81, 137, 140, 160, 214, 234–5; origins of, 8, 156; workings of, 156–7, 160, 166, 189
concordats, 11

Confederation of British Industry (CBI) (Scotland), 122, 188

Connolly, J., 150

Conservative Party see Scottish Conservative and Unionist Party

Conservative Political Centre, 156

consultation between Scottish local authorities and local communities, 16, 33, 85, 87, 123, 127–8, 164, 172; between Scottish local authorities and the Scottish Executive, 28–9, 125; general, 56

consumerism in Scottish local government, 51, 157

contract arrangements, 58, 157–8

Controller of Audit to the Accounts Commission, 174

Convention of Scottish Local Authorities (COSLA) attitude to proportional representation, 19, 112, 116; general, 15, 34; links beyond the UK, 35, 202; lobbying at Westminster and EU levels, 35, 183, 202, 226; membership difficulties, 37, 80; relations with the Scottish Office/Scottish Executive, 14–15, 28, 34, 37, 82, 105, 125, 167, 182, 188, 196, 199, 217, 220; roles and purpose, 35–6, 163, 184

coordination in councils in practice, 9, 58, 59, 158, 166; lack of, 31, 53, 73, 74

Copus, C., 34–5, 85, 89, 99, 101, 120, 137, 153

corporate management adoption of in England, 74–5; adoption of in Scotland, 3, 75–9, 167–70, 234–5; links with other forms of local authority management, 6, 78, 90, 167; origins of, 1, 66, 75–6; principles of, 74–6, 79, 168, 172

corruption, 20, 21

COSLA see Convention of Scottish Local Authorities

Council of Ministers (EU), 11

Council of European Municipalities and Regions

(CEMR), 226

Council Tax arguments against, 194; banding, 191–3; collection of rates, 61, 188–9; in England and Wales, 7, 152, 194; in Scotland, 3, 6, 144, 192–3, 195; levels in England, 195; levels in Scotland, 104, 137, 181, 188, 191, 192, 193, 225–6; origins of, 8, 190–1; workings of, 30, 191–2, 216

Council Tax Benefit Subsidy, 191, 192

councillors access to, 20, 32; and constituents, 20, 96–7, 114; and officers, 71, 97, 98, 219; and party groups, 34, 97, 101; and political parties, 34, 72, 88–90, 97, 99–102, 139; and Standards Commission for Scotland, 9, 13, 22, 98; as a microcosm of society, 94; attitudes to public participation, 96, 128; autonomy, 99, 152, 218–19; career structure, 102, 105; code of conduct, 10, 13, 172; expectations of, 93, 128; in England and Wales, 64–6, 103; independent councillors, 3, 72, 147–8, 222; influences on, 198; lack of autonomy of, 30, 58, 71, 102; legislative control of, 97; management role of, 93; numbers in Scotland, 93, 104; party politician role of, 93, 96–8; personal interpretation of role, 93, 96; power of, 20, 78, 90, 98; priorities, 97; profile of, 94–5, 103, 119; remuneration of, 2, 82, 103–6; representative role of, 16, 32, 34–5, 84, 93–9, 117–19, 122, 127–8, 144–5, 214; roles of, 16–17, 95–6, 98, 102; sanctions against, 13, 97–8; variability in attitudes, 17, 96; workload of, 95, 103–4

Councillors Remuneration Progress Group, 105

county councils, 45, 47

Crawford, B. E., 44

crematoriums, 2, 197

Criminal Justice (Scotland) Act 2003, 10

Crofters' Commission, 115

culture and sport, 62, 167, 169

Cumbernauld and Kilsyth District Council, 55

Cumnock and Doon Valley District Council, 54

Cunninghame District Council, 55

customers' panels, 59

Dahl, R. A., 18, 109

Danson, M., 195

Davis, G., 133–4, 230

DCMS see Department for Culture, Media and Sport

Dearlove, J., 65, 71, 74, 75, 96

Debt Arrangement and Attachment (Scotland) Act 2002, 10

decision making in local government Conservative reforms in 1980s and 1990s, 65–6, 79, 82, 84, 199; corporate approach to, 78–9, 80; differences in Scotland vs England and Wales, 62–6, 89–90; executive structures and, 69, 84, 88; general, 3, 6, 64, 69, 82, 88, 237; models of, 75–6, 218–20; modernisation under the Scottish Executive, 3, 70; principle of collective decision-making, 70; traditional approach to in early post-war period, 3, 69, 70–2;

Dehousse, R., 11

democracy and local government, 3, 19, 43, 58, 93, 106, 109, 119, 132–3, 174–5, 214, 223, 235, 237; and non-elected local governance, 58, 121, 131, 133; elitist view of at local level, 117, 165; general, 84, 116, 118, 212–13, 229–30; health of local democracy, 109, 119, 133–4, 165, 230; limitations of local democracy, 4, 212, 214; marxist view of at local level, 116; pluralist view of at local level, 117–18;

Demos, 126, 162, 226

Denver, D., 100, 111, 113, 138–9, 147, 153

Department for Culture, Media and Sport (DCMS), 164

Department for Work and Pensions, 183

Department of the
 Environment, 160, 161
Department of Transport, Local
 Government and the
 Regions, 28
depoliticisation, 3, 81, 90
DERL *see* Dundee Energy
 Recycling Ltd
devolution and Scottish local
 government, 31, 50, 87,
 89–90, 125, 142, 215, 233,
 235, 237; difference made to
 local government in
 Scotland, 34, 37, 90, 214,
 218; general, 27, 149, 236
Dewar, D., 161
Dialogue Youth Initiative, 126
Direct Labour Organisations
 (DLOs), 158
Direct Service Organisations
 (DSOs), 81, 158
distinctiveness of Scottish
 elements, 4, 59
dispersal of power, 18–19
district councils (general), 47, 48
DLOs *see* Direct Labour
 Organisations
dog fouling, 224
Dog Fouling (Scotland) Act
 2003, 10, 197, 224
Downs, A., 80, 157
Drinking Water Quality
 Regulator, 59
DSOs *see* Direct Service
 Organisations
Dumfries and Galloway
 Council, 1, 3, 54, 86, 87,
 141, 148, 192
Dumfries and Galloway
 Regional Council, 54
Duncan, A. A. M., 44
Duncan, S. and Goodwin, M.,
 21–2, 63, 65, 67, 81, 129,
 221–3, 231
Dundee Council *see* City of
 Dundee Council
Dundee Energy Recycling Ltd
 (DERL), 203
Dunleavy, P., 19, 80

East Ayrshire Council, 54, 139
East Dunbartonshire Council,
 54, 86, 144, 192
East Kilbride District Council, 55
East Lothian Council, 55, 86,
 87, 139
East Lothian District Council, 55
East of Scotland European
 Consortium, 58, 202
East Renfrewshire Council, 55, 87

Eastern Scotland European
 Partnership, 202
Eastwood District Council, 55
ECHR *see* European
 Convention of Human
 Rights
economic development, 28, 202
Economic and Social Research
 Council (ESRC), 18
Edinburgh Chamber of
 Commerce, 122
education, 2, 8, 15, 22, 45, 46,
 47, 62, 72, 167, 169, 197,
 205, 212, 219, 223
education authorities, 46
Education (Disability Strategies
 and Pupils' Educational
 Records) (Scotland) Act
 2002, 9
e-government, 126
ELAN *see* European Local
 Authority Network
Elcock, H., 74, 180, 217
elected mayors in England and
 Wales, 63, 84, 90; Scottish
 attitudes to, 71, 83, 84, 86,
 90, 105–6
elections and independent
 councillors, 137, 147–8; and
 Scottish Conservative and
 Unionist Party, 142–3; and
 Scottish Green Party, 146;
 and Scottish Labour Party,
 137–8; and Scottish Liberal
 Democrats, 144; and
 Scottish National Party, 145;
 and Scottish Socialist Party,
 144; constitutional view of,
 174, 212; differences north
 and south of the border,
 109–10, 150; early reform
 acts, 46; electorate in
 Scotland, 94, 107–8; elitist
 theory and, 114; first past
 the post system, 106,
 111–16, 117, 145, 146;
 format of voting, 109–10;
 local election results in
 England, Wales and
 Northern Ireland, 108, 150;
 local election results in
 Scotland, 149–50; Marxist
 view of, 21 methods of
 improving turnout, 109–10;
 national issues, 110–11;
 proportional representation,
 114–16, 143–4, 212;
 similarities north and south
 of the border, 107, 151–2;
 Single Transferable Vote

Working Group, 115;
 turnout, 3, 106, 107–10;
 voting in accordance with
 national preferences,
 110–11, 140; voting on local
 issues, 109, 110–11
elective principle, 18
Electoral Reform Society, 120
elites customer, 7, 59; political,
 7, 20, 21, 59, 165
elitism, general, 20; view of
 local government, 19–21
ELLD *see* Scottish Executive
 Enterprise and Lifelong
 Learning Department
Ellwood, S., 63
Employers' Organisation (EO),
 95, 103, 226
employment tribunals, 38, 39
enabling role of local
 government, 126
England and Wales, general, 4,
 22, 156; local government
 in, 7, 27–8, 62–5, 84, 115,
 150, 158, 186, 199, 221,
 233, 237
environment, 144, 189, 225
Environmental Impact
 Assessments, 214
Environmental Protection Act
 1990, 224
environmental services, 6, 197,
 206
EO *see* Employers'
 Organisation
ERDF *see* European Regional
 Development Fund
Escott, K., 160
ESF *see* European Social Fund
ESRC *see* Economic and Social
 Research Council
Ethical Standards in Public Life
 etc. (Scotland) Act 2000, 9, 13
ethnic bias in profile of
 councillors, 94–5
EU *see* European Union
Eurocities, 226
European Charter of Local
 Self-Government (1985), 12
European Convention of
 Human Rights (ECHR) and
 local government, 10, 225;
 general, 225
European Foundation for
 Quality Management, 163
European Investment Bank, 53,
 198
European Local Authority
 Network (ELAN), 226
European Parliament, 101

European Regional Development Fund (ERDF), 53, 201, 202, 226
European Social Fund (ESF), 53
European Union (EU) and environment, 225; impact on local government (general), 10, 223–5, 228; impact on local government (Scotland), 11, 201–2, 223–4, 225; primacy of EU law, 11, 224
European Union funding of local government, 126, 197, 201–2
European Union Landfill Directive 1999, 225
European Union members, 201
European Union Structural Funds, 201–2
Evans, M., 19
Ewan, E., 44, 68
Excellence Fund, 184
executive structures in local government in Scotland, 6, 56, 69, 77, 85, 86–7; in local government in England and Wales, 6, 84

Fabians, 18
Fair Rewards Model of councillor remuneration, 104
Fairley, J., 231
Falconer, P., 167
Falkirk Council, 37, 54, 86, 87, 141, 172, 192, 205
Falkirk District Council, 54
FCSD see Scottish Executive Finance and Central Services Department
Federation of Scottish Ratepayers, 156
Federation of Small Businesses, 188
fees and charges see charging for local services
Ferguson, K., 79
feudalism, general, 43; and origins of Scottish local government, 44–5
Fife Council, 1, 30, 54, 57, 124, 172, 192
Fife Institute of Directors, 122
Fife Regional Council, 57
finance of local government in Scotland capital income and expenditure, 1, 198–9; Council Tax, 188; EU funding, 198; general, 3, 207; non-domestic rates, 188; revenue income and

expenditure, 62, 140, 179, 198–9, 228–9; Revenue Support Grant, 229; ring-fenced grants see Value for Money
fire boards, 3, 16, 118, 131, 173, 198; fire service, 3, 15, 16, 30, 48, 58, 167, 205–6
Fire Brigades Union, 122
Fire Services Act 1947, 30
First Past the Post system (FPTP) and political parties, 114, 139, 144, 146, 150; basis of, 106; case in favour of, 112; criticisms of, 112–13, 117
fiscal crisis, 65
Fitzpatrick, S., 17, 94, 102, 120
Flinders, M. V., 129
Forsyth, M., 60, 156
Forum of Private Business in Scotland, 188
franchise, 46
Freedom of Information (Scotland) Act 2002, 10
Friend, J. K., 72
Friends of the Earth Scotland, 122
further education colleges, 3, 121, 129, 121, 129

GAE see Grant Aided Expenditure
Game, C., 24, 60, 63, 64, 68, 84, 91, 125, 212
gender bias in profile of councillors importance of, 95; in England and Wales, 95; in Scotland, 94–5; reasons for, 95
General Board of Commissioners in Lunacy for Scotland, 129
general competence powers, 221
General Teaching Council for Scotland, 225
GLA see Greater London Authority
Glasgow Campaign Against Housing Stock Transfer, 122
Glasgow City Council, 1, 6, 11, 21, 34, 35, 37, 55, 56, 62, 86, 104, 105, 122, 126, 139, 163, 166, 184, 189–90, 192, 194, 219, 226
Glasgow Corporation, 72
Glasgow District Council, 54
GLC see Greater London Council

globalisation, general, 227–8; and Scottish local government, 67, 228–30, 237; and local government in the UK, 228, 230
Goodlad, R., 52
Gordon District Council, 54
Gould, B., 21
governance, general, 4, 62, 66, 71, 228, 235; multi-level, 4, 225–6
Grant Aided Expenditure (GAE), 182, 184
Greater London Authority (GLA), 63, 150
Greater London Council (GLC), 63, 65, 76, 115
Green, D., 115
Greenwood, J., 159
Group for Large Local Authority Museums, 164
Guild Socialists, 18
Gyford, J., 72, 91, 96

Hall, W., 130
Hamilton District Council, 55
Hampton, W., 110
Harding, A., 122
Hassan, G., 148–9, 151, 152, 236
Hay, C., 228
Hayton, K., 58, 60
HBOS, 1
Head of Paid Service, 69
health boards, 129, 131, 165
Heath government, 77
Heclo, H., 217
Held, D., 22 7–8
Herbert, S., 120
Heseltine, M., 83
hierarchical organisational model, 167
Highland Council, 6, 55, 148, 166
Highland Regional Council, 55
Highlands and Islands Council, 148, 201
Highlands and Islands Development Board, 129
Highlands and Islands Partnership Programme, 202, 226
Highland Sports Development Association, 122
Himsworth, C. M. G., 10
Historic Scotland, 175
history of local government in Scotland, 43–9
HM Customs and Excise, 225
HM Fire Inspectorate for

Scotland, 29, 32
HM Inspectorate of Education, 29, 31, 32
HM Inspectors of Schools, 225
'hollowing out of the state' thesis, 228–9
homogeneity/union model of party trends, 148–9
hospitals, 129
House of Commons Select Committee on Public Administration, 131
Housing (Scotland) Act 2001, 9
housing associations, 123, 129, 145; council house sales, 138, 200, 214; finance of, 199; general, 15, 22, 47, 212, 223
Housing Action Trusts, 130
Housing Revenue Account, 200
Hughes Report 1967, 73
Human Rights see European Convention of Human Rights
Human Rights Act 1998, 10, 225
Hunt, D., 132

IDeA see Improvement and Development Agency
IMF see International Monetary Fund
Improvement and Development Agency (IDeA), 95, 103
incrementalism, 76, 166
independent councillors in Scotland, 138, 147–8
industrialisation and local government in Scotland, 45, 46; general, 228
industrial development, 28, 46
Institute of Economic Affairs, 80
interest groups, 121–2, 146
International Monetary Fund (IMF), 174, 182, 227–8, 229
Inverclyde Council, 55, 144
Inverclyde District Council, 55
Investors in People, 36

Jamieson, C., 220
Jessop, W. N., 72
John, P., 31, 67, 80, 227, 231
Joint Area Housing Committees, 123
joint arrangements, 47, 58
joint boards, 58, 63
joint committees, 58
Joint Futures initiatives, 214
Jordan, G., 19

Judge, D., 17, 32, 35, 94, 122

Kane, M. J., 81
Kantor, P., 122
Kellas, J. G., 148–9, 234
Kendrick, A., 60
Kerevan, G., 20,
Kerley, R., 82, 85, 105, 114, 120
Kerr, A., 186, 222
Keynesian ideas and local government, 47
Kilmarnock and Loudoun District Council, 54
Kincardine and Deeside District Council, 54
Kingdom, J., 98
Kingdon, J. W., 57
Knox, C., 7, 64
knowledge of local government, 56, 108
Kyle and Carrick District Council, 54

Labour–Liberal Partnership Agreement, 37, 105, 199, 215
Labour Party and local government in Scotland, 34, 77, 138–41; general, 83, 100, 140; in Scotland, 87
Labour Research Department, 159
Laffin, M., 7
Lambeth (London Borough of), 75
LAMSAC see Local Authorities' Management Services Advisory Committee
Land Reform (Scotland) Act 2003, 10
land tenure, 44
Landfill Tax, 225
Lang, I., 51, 57
LAP see Leadership Advisory Panel
Lavalette, M., 190
Law and Hairmyres Hospital, 203
Layfield Committee, 208
Leach, R., 67, 91
Leach, S., 16
Leadership Advisory Panel (LAP), 85–6
Learning and Teaching Scotland, 225
LECs see Local Enterprise Companies
Leeke, M., 150
legal basis of local government

in England and Wales, 7, 28; in Northern Ireland, 28; in Scotland, 7, 38, 84–5, 218
legal services departments in local authorities, 9–10, 38
leisure facilities, 48, 88, 158
Lehmbruch, G., 19
Levy, R., 50, 141
libraries, 48, 62
licences for taxis, 2, 16, 197
Lindblom, C. E., 76, 122, 217
LIT see Local Income Tax
Litter (Animal Droppings) Order 1991, 224
Lloyds TSB, 1
LOAs see Local Outcome Agreements
Local Authorities' Management Services Advisory Committee (LAMSAC), 78
Local Authority Business Growth Scheme, 189
local communities, 29, 32–3
Local Development Committees, 126
Local Enterprise Companies (LECs), 53, 131, 202
local governance, general, 4, 128, 130, 131, 143, 211, 223–7, 229; multi-level, 236
Local Governance (Scotland) Bill 2003, 105, 115
Local Government and democracy, 117–19; and spread of power, 18; in Demark, 12; in EU countries, 126, 227; in France, 5–6, 12; in India, 6, 12; in Norway, 12; in Sweden, 12; in UK, 7, 62–6; political science view of, 17–18, 21, 222
Local Government Act 1988, 158, 171
Local Government Act 1992, 158, 167, 213
Local Government Act 2000, 84, 106
Local Government Act 2003, 197
Local Government and Housing Act 1989, 82
Local Government Association, 226
Local Government Boundary Commission for Scotland, 13
Local Government Commission, 56, 64
Local Government Committee (Scottish Parliament), 9, 19, 34, 96, 127–8, 179, 185,

196, 199, 205, 208, 213
Local Government etc.
(Scotland) Act 1994, 8, 52, 55
Local Government Finance Act 1992, 8
Local Government Finance (Scotland) Order, 213
Local Government in Scotland and community planning, 16; and ECHR rights, 225; and globalisation, 227–8; and multi-level governance, 118, 137, 171, 224–7, 236; and Scottish Parliament, 18, 29, 56–7, 118, 175, 191, 195, 199–200, 217–9; aims of, 15; as client, 80, 159, 235; as contractor, 80, 155, 157, 159, 167, 235; as employer, 1, 59–60, 169; attempted depoliticisation by Conservatives 1980s and 1990s, 2, 12, 56–7, 81–3, 157; autonomy of, 3, 11–12, 152, 179, 197, 205–6, 207, 214–15, 219, 236–7; Best Value, 32, 118, 163–5; budgets, 30, 81; bye-laws, 15, 223; characteristics of, 2, 5, 6, 59–60, 117–19; complexity of, 23, 59; committee structures, 6, 80, 81, 86; Compulsory Competitive Tendering, 156–7; conflicts in, 59–60; consultation, 3, 33, 118; continuous service improvement, 86–7, 124; corporate management, 3, 76–8, 167, 195–6; councillors, 80, 93–106; 'creature of statute', 218–19, 223–4; democracy in, 3, 19, 43, 58, 93, 106, 109, 119, 132–3, 174–5, 214, 223, 235, 237; democratic legitimacy of, 2, 94–9; departments in, 80, 98; differences compared to local government elsewhere in UK, 43, 62–6, 170–6, 180, 235–6; discretionary powers, 23; elections, 32, 106–10, 139–40; elitist view of, 2, 5, 17, 19–21, 23; employment in, 1; expenditure of, 1, 12, 13, 15, 48, 53, 75, 138, 157, 159, 180, 183, 188, 198–200, 206–7, 235;

finance of, 1, 7–8, 57–8, 60–2, 137, 140, 167, 179–81; functions of, 5, 48; historical development of, 2, 44–7; implementer of legislation, 5, 16–17; international management of, 225, 227–8; joint boards, 59; leadership, 83–4; legal basis, 2, 7, 27, 52, 75, 118; legislation affecting, 11, 16, 51–3, 85–6, 124; licence awards, 48, 225; links with MSPs, 34, 175; mandatory powers, 15, 18; marxist view of, 2, 5, 17, 21–3; meetings, 85–6, 125; miscellaneous fees and charges, 195, 225–6; non-elected aspects of, 3, 59, 121; officers in, 2, 20, 71, 73, 80, 82, 89–90, 118, 219; party groups, 81, 82, 83, 237; performance management, 32, 86, 118, 170–1, 207; performance reporting, 166, 175; pluralist view of, 2, 5, 17–19, 23, 223; political science view of, 17; powers of, 2, 6–7, 18, 78, 80, 89–90, 98, 137; relations with Scottish Executive, 27–30, 48, 144, 212–13; relations with Scottish Office, 33, 57, 60–1, 64, 82, 214–15, 233; relations with Scottish Parliament, 2, 23, 29, 33–5, 48, 118, 137, 143, 211–16; revenue income, 3, 9, 12, 28, 45, 65, 89, 137, 160, 179, 181, 190–1, 195, 197, 198–9, 203, 205, 207, 214, 216, 220; roles of, 2, 6, 20, 22; services, 1–2, 5, 6, 15–16, 22, 32, 38, 43, 53, 80, 89, 117–18, 128–9, 155, 156, 158, 166, 182, 205–6, 224; similarities compared to local government elsewhere in UK, 156; standardisation to charges, 196; structures, 6, 7, 43, 48, 62, 76, 137, 229; under Conservatives 1979–97, 2, 7, 57, 129–30, 215, 217, 233; under Labour 1974–9, 47–50; under Scottish Executive 1999 onwards, 58–9, 191–2, 211–13, 224–5
Local Government in Scotland

Act 2003, 8, 10, 12, 33, 87, 124, 161, 207, 213, 214, 215, 225
Local Government Information Unit, 195
Local Government Management Board, 158
Local Government (Northern Ireland) Act 1972, 64
Local Government Planning and Land Act 1980, 158
Local Government (Scotland) Act 1929, 129
Local Government (Scotland) Act 1973, 8, 49, 52, 198
Local Income Tax (LIT), 142, 144, 194–5, 207
Local Outcome Agreements (LOAs), 207
Local Sales Tax (LST), 194
London local government, 63
Lowndes, V., 80, 123
LST *see* Local Sales Tax
Lynch, M., 45, 108–9, 141, 147
Lynch, P., 110, 124, 145, 148, 151, 152

Maastricht criteria, 183
McAllister, I., 149
McAteer, M., 88–9, 91, 231
McConnell, A., 12, 46, 50, 77, 137, 140, 145, 157, 174, 186, 191, 194, 205, 208, 235
McCrone agreement on teachers' pay, 183, 220
McCrory Review, 65, 220
McFadden, J., 56
McGarvey, N., 31, 40, 99, 161, 176, 191, 204, 217, 231, 235
McGrew, A., 227–8
McIntosh Commission outcome of recommendations, 235; recommendations for local government, 12, 18, 85, 106, 114; Report of, 114
Mackie, J. D., 45
McNish, A., 86
McNish Report, 86
MacPherson, C. B., 116
McTavish, D., 72–3
McVicar, M., 49, 50
Mair, C., 236
Major, J., 57, 167, 199
Mallabar, N., 80
Mallaby Report 1976, 73
Management by Objectives, 76
Management Team, 77, 78
Marriage (Scotland) Act 2002, 9

Marsh, D., 219, 228, 230, 231
Martin, S., 166
Marwick, J. D., 44, 45
Maud Report 1967, 73, 76, 90
mayors see elected mayors
Members of Parliament (MPs),
  36
Members of the European
  Parliament (MEPs), 36
Members of the Scottish
  Parliament (MSPs), 36
MEPs see Members of the
  European Parliament
Michels, R., 19
middle-class bias in profile of
  councillors, 94–5
Midlothian Council, 55, 81, 86,
  139
Midlothian District Council, 55
Midwinter, A., 14, 24, 31, 34,
  40, 49, 53, 60, 61, 68, 71,
  74, 76, 77–8, 79, 85, 89, 91,
  99, 148, 157, 161, 167, 171,
  176, 180, 182, 190, 191,
  208, 215, 217, 231, 233,
  234–5
Miliband, R., 122, 222
Mill, J., 94
Mill, J. S., 17, 94
Miller, W. L., 108, 109, 111
Mitchell, J., 7, 34, 66, 233
Mitchison, R., 44, 45
mobilisation of bias, 228–9,
  230
modernisation and impact on
  local government, 70, 102,
  110, 133; New Labour
  principles, 83, 112, 123–4,
  141, 215, 221
Monaghan, C., 167, 171, 176,
  182, 190
Monklands District Council,
  21, 55
Montgomery Report 1983, 49
Mooney, G., 190
Moore, C., 217
Moray Council, 55, 141, 148,
  224
Moray District Council, 55
Morgan, B., 108, 150
Mosca, G., 19
Motherwell District Council, 54
MPs see Members of
  Parliament
MSPs see Members of the
  Scottish Parliament
Multi-level governance, 67
Munro, C. R., 10
Murray, D., 45
MVA Consultancy, 56

nation states, 228–9
National Assembly for Wales,
  115
National Association of
  Ratepayers' Action Groups,
  157
National Census of Councillors,
  95
National Gallery of Scotland,
  164
National Health Service (NHS),
  1, 130, 173
National Lottery, 197
National Museums of Scotland,
  164
national parties and local
  government, 34–5, 141–5
NDPBs see Non-Departmental
  Public Bodies
NDRI see Non-Domestic Rate
  Income
neighbourhood councils, 123
neo-marxist view of local
  government, 21, 221–2
neo-Weberian view of local
  government, 19
New Labour, 35, 83, 107,
  150–1
New Public Management
  (NPM), general principles of,
  80; impact on local
  government, 80–1, 233
Newton, K., 58, 96
NHS see National Health
  Service
Niskanen, W., 19, 80, 157
Non-Departmental Public
  Bodies (NDPBs), 30–1, 129,
  173; advisory role, 131; and
  local government in
  Scotland, 30–1, 58–9, 129,
  173; and Scottish Executive,
  131, 224–5; forming
  policies, 31; general, 30–1,
  129, 173 in UK, 130
Non-Domestic Rate Income
  (NDRI), 181, 188, 230,
  233–4
non-domestic rates case for
  reform of, 189, 215
  differences north and south
  of the border, 188, 189, 234
  distribution, 189; general,
  29, 30, 138, 140, 144, 212,
  225–6; workings of, 108,
  186–8, 214
non-housing allocation, 198
North Ayrshire Council, 54,
  139
North Lanarkshire Council, 54,

  126, 163
Northern Ireland and local
  government, 4, 7, 43, 62, 64;
  general, 4
Northern Ireland Assembly, 7
Northern Ireland Office, 64
Not For Profit Trusts, 205

ODPM see Office of the
  Deputy Prime Minister
OECD see Organisation for
  Economic Cooperation and
  Development
Office of the Deputy Prime
  Minister (ODPM), 28 106,
  115, 186, 189, 194
officers in local government and
  Best Value, 99; Conservative
  attempts to depoliticise, 70;
  general, 32, 76, 123; power
  of, 71, 97–8, 101; restraints
  on, 125
Ogden, S., 81
Ohmae, K., 228
O'Leary, B., 19
Olson, M., 19
ombudsman, 9, 22, 39, 174
opinion polls attitudes to
  councillors, 20, 104, 108;
  attitudes to local services,
  20, 56, 62, 108–9; attitudes
  to the power of central
  government, 109;
  deliberative, 125; knowledge
  of local services, 56, 108
Organisation for Economic
  Cooperation and
  Development (OECD)
Orkney Islands Council, 1, 6,
  49, 55, 148, 192, 222
Orkney Islands District
  Council, 55
Orr, K., 88–9, 91

P&R Committees see Policy
  and Resources Committees
Page, E. C., 49
Pahl, R. E., 20
Painter, C., 67
Pareto, V., 19
parish councils, 40, 46, 62, 63,
  234
participation at local level and
  political parties, 102; case
  for, 84–6; councillor
  attitudes to, 96; development
  of, 124–6; drawbacks of, 99,
  127–8; forms of, 93, 99,
  127–8; New Labour
  encouragement of, 124–5;

non-electoral, 3, 128–30;
problems with, 127–8;
public attitudes to, 123;
Scottish Executive
encouragement of, 122,
124–6; world-wide trend
towards in liberal
democracies, 108–9, 227–9
Partnership Agreement, 36, 179
party groups roles of, 99–102;
power of, 71, 81, 85, 87, 89,
98, 237
party politics, 101, 109, 114,
134, 137
Passport Agency, 128
Pateman, C., 122–3
Paterson Report 1973, 76,
77–8, 79
Paton, J., 45
Pay as You Earn (PAYE), 160
PAYE see Pay as You Earn
Payne, J., 224
Peacock, P., 132, 170
People's Panels, 3, 16, 121
Percy-Smith, J., 67
Performance Indicators,
general, 175; origins of, 155,
166; strengths, 168;
weaknesses, 168–70
performance management,
general, 3, 31, 98, 155;
policing of, 163, 167, 170–1
Performance Management and
Planning (PMP), 171–2
Perth and Kinross Council, 55,
81, 141, 163, 172
Perth and Kinross District
Council, 55
Percy, I., 168
PESC see Public Expenditure
Survey Committee
PFI see Private Finance
Initiative
PI see Performance Indicators
Pimlott, B., 63
Planning, Programming,
Budgeting (PPB), 76
PMP see Performance
Management and Planning
police, 3, 16, 22, 30, 48, 58,
108, 129, 167, 205–6
Police and Fire Services
(Finance) (Scotland) Act
2001, 9
police boards, 3, 121, 131, 173,
198
Police (Scotland) Act 1967, 30
Policy and Resources
Committees, 76–8, 79
political parties in Scottish local

government, general, 3, 35,
72, 82, 88–9,137, 152;
homogeneity model, 87,
148–9; party groups, 70,
88–9; politics of semi-
autonomy model, 149;
national standing orders,
34–5; Scottish Conservative
and Unionist Party, 3, 81,
143; Scottish distinctiveness
model, 149; Scottish Green
Party, 3, 146; Scottish
Labour Party, 3, 106, 144–5;
Scottish Liberal Democrats,
3, 106, 144–5, 194; Scottish
National Party, 3, 194;
Scottish Socialist Party, 3,
149, 195
political science view of Scottish
local government, 2, 5, 17
politically restricted posts, 82
politics of semi-autonomy
model in party trends, 149,
152
Poll Tax, 8, 50, 137, 181,
190–1, 192, 208, 235
Pollard, S., 47
Polsby, N., 18
Poor Law, 45–6
power-dependence model of
central–local relations
applied to local government
in Scotland, 11, 12; general,
9, 228
PPB see Planning,
Programming, Budgeting
PPPs see Public Private
Partnerships
PR see Proportional
Representation
pre-school provision for 3- and
4-year-olds, 183, 184, 206
pressure groups see interest
groups
prisons, 129
Private Finance Initiative (PFI)
case for, 203–4; criticisms of,
132, 203, 204; examples of,
118, 166, 197–8, 203–4,
219; principles, 132
Private Finance Unit, 202–3
Procurator Fiscal, 29, 38
Programme Area Committees,
77
property taxation Council Tax,
190–1; for non-domestic
properties, 186–9; general,
191, 207; rates, 188, 191;
revaluation, 194
Proportional Representation

(PR), 30, 37, 106, 114–15,
141–2, 143–4, 146, 217, 220
Protection of Children
(Scotland) Act 2003, 10
Pryde, G. S., 44
Public Appointments and Public
Bodies Bill 2002, 132
public choice theory, general,
157; applied to local
government, 20
public expenditure cutbacks,
53–4, 60–1; constrained by
global pressures, 198;
constraints on local
government, 30, 157; review
process at Westminster, 182
Public Expenditure Survey
Committee (PESC), 76
Public Finance and
Accountability Act 2000, 9
public participation see
participation at local level
Public Performance Reporting,
98
Public Private Partnerships
(PPPs), 3, 66, 130, 131, 145,
197–8, 202–3
Public Service Model of
councillor remuneration, 104
Public Spending Review, 229
Public Transport Fund, 184
Public Works Loan Board
(PWLB), 198
PWLB see Public Works Loan
Board
Pyper, R., 174

QUANGOs see Quasi
Autonomous Non-
Governmental Organisations
Quasi Autonomous Non-
Governmental Organisations
(QUANGOs), 2, 8, 29–30,
38, 58, 129, 130, 131, 223,
224

Rallings, C., 95, 120, 139, 149,
151, 153
rate-capping, 81, 137
rate poundage, 186–8
Rate Support Grant, 14, 181
rational approach to decision-
making, 76, 86, 117
Raynsford, N., 195
recycling, 11, 16
Redcliffe Maud Report 1969,
74, 76
Reform Acts, 46
refuse collection, 158, 171
regional assemblies in

England, 7
regional councils in Scotland,
    63; in Wales, 64
Regulation of Care (Scotland)
    Act 2001, 9
Renewing Local Democracy
    Working Group, 85, 120
Renfrew District Council, 55
Renfrewshire Council, 55, 192,
    224
reorganisation of Scottish local
    government 1975 aftermath
    of, 49, 60–1; background to,
    47–50, 156–7; criticisms of,
    49, 52–7, 159–60; political
    context of, 155; rationale
    for, 48, 155–6
reorganisation of Scottish local
    government 1996 and
    democratic deficit, 82;
    Conservative rationale for,
    60; costs of, 60–1; criticisms
    of, 31, 60–2, 79–80, 82–3;
    impact on accountability, 61;
    impact on services, 30–1,
    59–60; origins of, 50–3
Report of the Commission on
    Local Democracy 1995, 12
Report of the Renewing Local
    Democracy Working Group,
    103, 114
representation and local
    government, 32, 47, 85,
    95–6, 212–13; general,
    112–15
Representation of the People
    Act 1918, 47
repression, 22
reserve powers, 14, 157
residents' surveys, 126
resistance to central control,
    217
revenue income and
    expenditure, 45, 74, 180,
    195, 197–8
Revenue Support Grant (RSG),
    7–8, 29, 180, 181–2, 192,
    212, 214, 225–6, 229, 230
Rex, J., 20
Rhodes, R. A. W., 47, 65, 74,
    76, 79, 91, 219–20, 227,
    228, 231
Richardson, J. J., 19
Ridley, F. F., 129
ring-fencing see VFM
Robertson, G., 130
Rodger, R. G., 44, 45
roles of local government,
    general, 16, 83–4, 233; in
    Scotland, 6, 28, 199; in UK,

6, 62–6
Rose, R., 15, 149
Rosie, G., 133
Rough Sleepers Initiative, 184,
    207
Royal Infirmary, 203
RSG see Revenue Support
    Grant

Safeway, 1
sanctions against councillors,
    13
Schattschneider, E. E., 228
Schmitter, P., 19
school boards, 123
School Education Amendment)
    (Scotland) Act 2002, 9
Schumpeter, J. A., 19, 122
Scotland Act 1998, 7, 8, 10
Scotland Europa, 202, 226
Scottish Assembly, 49, 50
Scottish Assessors' Association,
    187
Scottish Borders Council, 86,
    148, 174
Scottish Campaign for Nuclear
    Disarmament, 122
Scottish Chambers of
    Commerce see Association of
    Scottish Chambers of
    Commerce
Scottish Children's Reporter
    Administration (SCRA),
    30–1, 58
Scottish Civic Forum, 124
Scottish Coalition for Justice
    Not War, 122
Scottish Confederation of
    British Industry, 188
Scottish Conservative and
    Unionist and Party, general,
    138, 142–4; policies for local
    government, 2, 34, 50, 58,
    62, 77, 81, 82, 100, 130,
    143, 214; relations with
    national party, 35, 53; voting
    patterns for, 111, 142–3, 145
Scottish Consumer Council,
    167
Scottish Development Board,
    129
Scottish distinctiveness model
    of party trends, 149–50
Scottish District Councils
    Working Party, 78
Scottish Enterprise, 51, 122,
    173, 202, 226
Scottish Environment
    Protection Agency (SEPA), 8,
    58, 59, 225, 226, 229

Scottish ESF Objective 3, 202
Scottish European Structural
    Funds Forum, 202, 226
Scottish Examination Board,
    129
Scottish Executive departmental
    responsibilities for local
    government, 105, 114,
    133–4, 167, 175, 184;
    mandatory powers, 11, 175,
    214; ministers in, 28, 132,
    173, 205–6, 213–14,
    217–18; relations with local
    government, 2, 3, 4, 12, 14,
    19, 20, 28–9, 31, 37, 70, 95,
    104, 124, 1, 149–50, 198,
    205–6, 212, 214, 218, 221;
    relations with business, 188,
    204–5, 216
Scottish Executive Central
    Research Unit, 59, 127–8,
    208
Scottish Executive Development
    Department (SEDD), 28
Scottish Executive Education
    Department (SEED), 28
Scottish Executive Enterprise
    and Lifelong Learning
    Department (ELLD), 28
Scottish Executive Environment
    and Rural Affairs
    Department (SEERAD), 28,
    225
Scottish Executive European
    Union Office, 226
Scottish Executive Finance and
    Central Services Department
    (FCSD), 28
Scottish Executive Health
    Department (SEHD), 28
Scottish Executive Private
    Finance Unit, 202–3
Scottish Executive Social
    Research Unit, 104, 108,
    120
Scottish Green Party, 3, 112,
    138, 146–7, 146
Scottish Homes, 51
Scottish Household Survey, 107
Scottish Labour Party
    allegations of corruption in,
    35; general, 3, 34–5,
    138–41; policies for local
    government, 50, 62, 130,
    139; relations with national
    party, 34–5, 140, 150, 215;
    voting patterns for, 111, 113,
    139, 149–50
Scottish Liberal Democrats,
    general, 138, 144–6; model

standing orders, 100; policies for local government, 144–5; voting patterns for, 111

Scottish Local Authorities Remuneration Committee, 105

Scottish Local Authority Economic Development Group (SLAED), 226

Scottish Local Government (Elections) Act 2002, 9, 106, 110

Scottish Local Government Information Unit (SLGIU), 29, 37, 59, 176, 203

Scottish National Party (SNP), general, 3, 138, 141–2, 204; model standing orders, 100; policies for local government, 34, 49, 50, 141–2; relations between national party and local branches, 141–2; voting patterns for, 141

Scottish Office and central–local relations, 48, 122, 157, 235; and local government, 20, 35, 57, 60–1, 64, 82, 214–15, 233; constitutional position of, 7, 35, 129, 233; in post-war period, 157–9, 233

Scottish Office Central Research Unit, 20, 56, 68, 82

Scottish Parliament and European Union, 11; and the Westminster Parliament, 66, 213, 235; elections, 115; legislation produced affecting local government, 2, 7, 9–10, 19, 57, 62, 66, 173, 199, 211–13, 214, 218, 225, 236–7

Scottish Parliament European Committee, 223

Scottish Parliament Information Centre, 120

Scottish Public Services Ombudsman, 22, 132, 229

Scottish Public Services Ombudsman Act 2002, 9, 118

Scottish Qualifications Authority (SQA), 225

Scottish Ratepayers Forum, 187

Scottish Rating and Valuation Council, 187

Scottish revaluation crisis, 190

Scottish Service Tax, 146, 195

Scottish Socialist Party (SSP), 3, 138, 146–7

Scottish Special Housing Association, 129

Scottish Statutory Instruments, 213

Scottish Trades Union Congress (STUC), 188

Scottish Waste Strategy Advisory Group, 225

Scottish Water, 3, 8, 29–31, 58, 59, 121, 192, 229

SCRA see Scottish Children's Reporter Administration

Seawright, D., 151

SEDD see Scottish Executive Development Department

SEED see Scottish Executive Education Department

SEERAD see Scottish Executive Environment and Rural Affairs Department

SEHD see Scottish Executive Health Department

Select Committee of the House of Lords, 12

SEPA see Scottish Environment Protection Agency

separation of functions, 85–6

services provision cuts, 61–2, 205; general, 2, 89, 118, 128, 130–1, 145, 166, 170, 172; grant-aided expenditure, 182, 205–8; traditional system, 71, 155

Sewel Convention, 8–10, 149

Shaw, J. E., 45, 68

Sheridan, T., 146

Sheriff Officers, 29

Shetland Islands Council, 49, 55, 104, 148

Simon, H. A., 76

single tier councils and political parties, 50, 62, 141; and rates, 191; arguments in support of in Scotland, 50–1, 57, 130; criticisms of in Scotland, 56–7, 59–60; in England, 7, 63, 234; in Scotland, 60–2, 234; in Wales, 7, 63–4; origins of in Scotland, 8, 43, 49, 50

Single Transferable Vote (STV) see proportional representation

Single Transferable Vote Working Group, 115

Skelcher, C., 129

Skye Bridge, 203

SLAED see Scottish Local Authority Economic Development Group

SLGIU see Scottish Local Government Information Unit

Sloat, A., 223, 227, 231

Smith, J., 7, 233

Smith, M., 17, 129

SNP see Scottish National Party

social inclusion, 124

Social Inclusion Partnership Fund, 184, 206

social services, 15, 22, 47, 59–60, 62, 128–9, 181–2, 223

social work, 15, 22, 48, 128–9, 182, 205–6, 219

Society of Local Authority Chief Executives and Senior Managers (SOLACE), 38, 172, 226

SOLACE see Society of Local Authority Chief Executives and Senior Managers

South Ayrshire Council, 55, 86, 142

South Lanarkshire Council, 55, 124

South of Scotland European Partnership, 202

Special Responsibility Allowances (SRAs), 103

SPTA see Strathclyde Passenger Transport Authority

SPTE see Strathclyde Passenger Transport Executive

SQA see Scottish Qualifications Authority

SRAs see Special Responsibility Allowances

SSP see Scottish Socialist Party

Standards Commission for Scotland, 9, 13, 22, 229

Standards in Scotland's Schools etc. Act 2000, 9

standing orders for council decision-making general, 82, 190; local government as local state, 221, 223; marxist view of, 221; party models of, 34–5, 82, 100–1; Scottish local government as local state, 66, 143

statutory instruments, 173, 205–6, 213

Stewart, J., 16, 83, 85, 91, 106, 130, 165, 174

Stirling Assembly, 124, 219

Stirling Council, 55, 86, 124, 217

Stirling District Council, 14, 55
Stodart Report 1981, 49
Stoker, G., 18, 57, 79–80, 81,
    85, 122, 129–30, 217
Strategic Waste Fund, 184, 206
Strathclyde Passenger Transport
    Authority (SPTA)
Strathclyde Passenger Transport
    Executive (SPTE)
Strathclyde Regional Council,
    50, 53, 56, 57, 123, 199
street lighting, 16
structural funds see EU Funding
    and European Regional
    Development Fund
STUC see Scottish Trades
    Union Congress
survey panels, 125
Sutcliffe, J. B., 53, 231
System Three Scotland, 109

Tayside, 57
Tayside Region, 81
Tenant Led Inspection, 126
Tesco, 1
Thain, C., 76
Thatcher, M., 215, 221, 234
Thatcher Government 1979–97,
    50, 63, 65, 142–3, 166, 170,
    174, 218
Thrasher, M., 95, 120, 139,
    149, 151, 153
Three Es, 155, 167
three tier system of local
    authorities in England, 62–5,
    234
Title Conditions (Scotland) Act
    2003, 10
Touche Ross, 60
tourism, 28, 202
town councils, 62–3
trade unions, 29, 32, 85, 122,
    156, 157, 169
training and enterprise councils,
    130
transport and early local
    authorities, 46; general, 28,
    212; under Scottish
    Parliament, 58, 224
Transport for London, 63
Transport (Scotland) Act 2001, 9
Travel and Subsistence
    Allowance, 103
Travers, T., 63, 115, 208
Tullock, G., 80, 157
Turner, R., 196
Turner, S. H., 45
Twigger, R., 182, 229
two tier system of local

authorities advantages of,
    48–9, 59–60; disadvantages
    of, 50–1, 59; in England,
    62–3, 65, 234; in London,
    63, 65; in Scotland, 8, 47,
    48, 58, 233

UBR see non-domestic rates
uneven development model of
    local government, general,
    22, 67, 218, 221–2; applied
    to Scottish local government,
    22, 221–3
union state, general, 6, 66,
    235–6; and local
    government, 151–2
Unison, 122
Unison Scotland, 204
unitary authorities see single
    tier councils
United Nations, 227
United States of America (USA),
    18, 75, 109
Urban Development
    Corporations, 130
urban gatekeeper approach, 20

valuation boards, 187, 192;
    history of, 186; of non-
    domestic properties, 186–7
Value for Money (VFM), 3, 51,
    138, 155–6, 159, 166, 167,
    170–1, 175–6, 181, 184–5,
    195, 206, 207, 215, 236
Vestri, P., 17, 94, 102, 120
VFM see Value for Money
Victim Support Scotland, 122
voting see elections
voluntary sector groups, 32,
    122, 202

Wales and community councils,
    64, 234; general, 63; local
    government in, 7, 62, 150
Warhurst, C., 148–9, 152, 236
waste management and
    recycling, 198, 225
water Drinking Water Quality
    Regulator for Scotland, 59;
    early local government
    provision of, 46; services
    removed from local
    government, 58, 129;
    Strathclyde Region
    referendum in 1994, 58, 123
Water Consultation Customer
    Panels, 59
Water Industry Commissioner
    for Scotland, 132

Webb, P., 150, 153
Weber, M., 19
Weir, S., 130
well-being (power to promote)
    in England and Wales, 236;
    in Scotland, 12, 14, 16–17,
    33, 38, 140, 212–13, 214,
    215, 221, 236
Welsh Local Government
    Association, 226
Welsh Office, 64
West Dunbartonshire Council,
    55, 86, 141, 192, 205, 219
West Lothian Council, 34, 55,
    86, 126, 139, 166
West Lothian District Council,
    55
West of Scotland European
    Consortium, 202, 226
Western Isles Council
    (Comhairle nan Eilean Siar),
    54, 148
Western Isles Islands Council,
    55, 222
Western Scotland European
    Partnership, 202
Westminster Parliament, 7, 22,
    33–4, 48, 65–6, 82, 101,
    213, 215, 218, 223–4, 226,
    229, 235
Wheatley Report (1969), 11,
    18, 43, 47–9, 65, 68, 74, 76,
    123, 144, 148–9, 157, 183
Whitfield, D., 160
Whittam, G., 195
Widdecombe Report 1986, 18,
    56, 70, 81–2, 110, 233
Widening Access to Council
    Membership Progress Group,
    95
Wildavsky, A., 76, 217
Wilks-Heeg, S., 69, 227
Wilson, D., 24, 60, 63, 64, 68,
    84, 125, 129, 210, 219, 221,
    230, 231
Wilson Government, 48, 73
Wolfinger, R., 18
Woods, M., 64
World Bank, 227–8, 229
World Trade Organisation, 227
Wright, M., 76
Wright Mills, C., 19

Yates, K., 165
Young Persons Housing Forum,
    125
Young Persons Website, 126
Young, R., 74, 78, 123
Younger, G., 217